Favorite Counseling
and Therapy
Homework Assignments

Second Edition

Favorite Counseling
and Therapy
Homework Assignments

Second Edition

Edited by Howard G. Rosenthal

With Contributions by
Albert Ellis, William Glasser, Samuel Gladding,
Lorna Hecker, Jon Carlson, Patricia Arredondo,
Luciano L'Abate, Nikolaos Kazantzis, and others

Routledge
Taylor & Francis Group
New York   London

Routledge
Taylor & Francis Group
711 Third Avenue
New York, NY 10017

Routledge
Taylor & Francis Group
2 Park Sqaure, Milton Park,
Abingdon, Oxon, OX12 4RN

© 2011 by Taylor and Francis Group, LLC
Routledge is an imprint of Taylor & Francis Group, an Informa business

International Standard Book Number: 978-0-415-87105-1 (Paperback)

Library of Congress Cataloging-in-Publication Data

Favorite counseling and therapy homework assignments / [compiled by] Howard
G. Rosenthal. -- 2nd ed.
    p. cm.
    Includes bibliographical references (p.   ).
    ISBN 978-0-415-87105-1 (pbk. : alk. paper)
    1. Counseling--Study and teaching. 2. Psychotherapy--Study and teaching.
3. Counselors--Training of. 4. Psychotherapists--Training of. I. Rosenthal,
Howard, 1952- II. Title.

BF637.C6F356 2010
158'.3--dc22
                                         2010026032

Visit the Taylor & Francis Web site at
http://www.taylorandfrancis.com

and the Routledge Web site at
http://www.routledgementalhealth.com

Contents

Acknowledgments

This, my dear reader, is a landmark book: It includes more accomplished, eminent therapists sharing their psychotherapeutic homework strategies than any previous work ever published, including the original edition of this book! The text even contains (dare I say it) a few legends. Our dream team of experts includes Albert Ellis, William Glasser, Allen E. Ivey, Richard N. Bolles, Judith S. Beck, Patricia Arredondo, Maxie C. Maultsby Jr., Peter R. Breggin, Claudia Black, Jon Carlson, Luciano L'Abate, Nikolaos Kazantzis, Walter Kempler, Windy Dryden, Robert W. Firestone, Arthur Freeman, Muriel James, Jeffrey A. Kottler, Samuel T. Gladding, Edwin S. Shneidman, Gerald Corey, Marianne Schneider Corey, Lorna L. Hecker, Lia Nower, Connirae Andreas, Steve Andreas, Dorothy S. Becvar, Raphael J. Becvar, Alvin R. Mahrer, Gary Schultheis, Bob Bertolino, Jesper Juul, Robert A. Neimeyer, Len Sperry, Raymond J. Corsini, Paul A. Hauck, Nancy K. Schlossberg, William J. Weikel, Robert E. Wubbolding, and many others.

My only claim to fame is that I created the vehicle to make this happen. The real stars here are our cast of creative counselors and therapists. Each of these folks possesses a very special, rare gift. Each has been blessed with the know-how to help others who are experiencing distress and is kind enough to share it with others. A 15-minute long-distance chat with Muriel James, for example, is probably more emotionally profitable than a year of catharsis on the couch and leaves one with the impression that we truly are *Born to Win*. Let's pause to give all of our contributors a well-deserved round of applause. Without their spirit of intellectual and artistic generosity, this text would not have been possible. These contributors took the task of writing their homework assignments very seriously. I know. Many of them contacted me repeatedly for feedback. Others contributed despite the fact that they were working on numerous projects of their own or were experiencing extreme personal hardships. Special thanks to contributors Ed Beck, Nikolaos Kazantzis, and Walter Kempler, who suggested other contributors, thus making the arduous task of compiling this book a little easier.

Next, accolades go to Professor Joanne Galanis of the St. Louis Community College at Florissant Valley Library for her extraordinary research assistance. I am also grateful to my editor Dana Bliss. Dana is hands-down the finest book editor I have ever worked with.

My wife, Patricia, a consummate scholar of social work intervention strategies, made a host of invaluable suggestions, not to mention that she and my sons, Paul and Patrick, were forced to endure my near pathological codependent relationship with my manuscript.

And last, thanks to two very special gentlemen—my late father Merle Lewis Rosenthal, the best writer I ever knew, and contributor Dr. Joseph Hollis, also deceased, who believed in my ideas and my novel writing style and generously gave me my start writing books. Many people live their entire lives and never have the good fortune to meet an individual with the vision and integrity that were radiated by Dr. Joseph Hollis. Therefore, I consider myself to be a very lucky person.

Remember, don't make any plans for tonight because ... you've got homework!

About the Editor

Howard G. Rosenthal, EdD, received his master's degree from the University of Missouri, St. Louis, and his doctorate from St. Louis University. He is the author of the best-selling comprehensive counseling exam prep book and audio program of all time, *Encyclopedia of Counseling: Master Review and Tutorial for the National Counselor Examination, State Counseling Exams, and the Counselor Preparation Comprehensive Examination* (special 15th anniversary edition) and *Vital Information and Review Questions for the NCE, CPCE, and State Counseling Exams* (special 15th anniversary edition). He also authored the first ever *Human Services Dictionary,* unique in that the definitions help the reader answer typical or prototype exam questions. Counselors from coast to coast have used his lively materials to secure state licensing and certification or to pass their comps.

Dr. Rosenthal's humorous, reader-friendly writing style landed him an interview—along with other influential authors such as Barry Sears of *Zone Diet* books and Mark Victor Hansen, coauthor of the *Chicken Soup for the Soul* series—for Jeff Herman's book, *You Can Make It Big Writing Books: A Top Agent Shows You How to Develop a Million-Dollar Bestseller.*

Some of his other popular books include the companion to this book, *Favorite Counseling and Therapy Techniques* (2nd edition); *Not With My Life I Don't: Preventing Your Suicide and That of Others; Before You See Your First Client: 55 Things Counselors, Therapists, and Human Service Workers Need to Know; Help Yourself to Positive Mental Health* (coauthored with Joseph W. Hollis); and *Therapy's Best: Practical Advice and Gems of Wisdom From Twenty Accomplished Counselors and Therapists.* More than 100,000 people have now heard his lively, humorous presentations, making him one of the most popular speakers in the Midwest.

He holds the national record for winning the most "teaching tips of the year awards" given by the publication *Teaching for Success.* He has been inducted into the St. Louis Community College Hall of Fame, is an Emerson Excellence in Teaching Award Recipient, and is included in *Who's Who in America.* He has written over 20 articles for *Counselor: The Magazine for Addictions Professionals* and has penned a number of mental health columns.

He currently serves as professor and program coordinator of Human Services and Addictions Study at St. Louis Community College at Florissant Valley and teaches graduate courses for Webster University in Webster Groves, Missouri. His Web site is www.howardrosenthal.com.

Chapter 1

Crime Scenes and Crazy Cola Cures
An Introduction to the Wonderful World of Psychotherapeutic Homework

Howard G. Rosenthal

Psychotherapy can begin in the office, but it must be lived outside of the office. Homework while therapy is going on is a good way to get this process started.

—**Dr. William Glasser, Father of Reality Therapy,**
Personal correspondence to Dr. Howard Rosenthal,
July 28, 1999

Sarah prided herself on the fact that the men who patronized her retail establishment referred to her as the "Merchant of Venom" when they thought she wasn't listening. Like so many other therapists, I had spent countless hours counseling abusive men, but this client was the exception: Sarah—by her own admission—was a male batterer, and proud of it. Her psychiatrist referred her to my aftercare group after discharging her from the local stress unit. Sarah had been admitted after she brutally beat her husband Don with a wrought iron lamp. Don was treated at the local emergency room for some nasty cuts, scrapes, bruises, and abrasions. This was not the first time Don was the recipient of a vicious assault.

When I asked Sarah why she had attacked her husband with a wrought iron living room lamp, she glared at me and barked back, "Look, he stupidly came home with an ice cream treat and didn't purchase one for me, okay?"

Had the couple tried marriage counseling? "Many times," Don replied when I saw him for an individual session, "but I always paid for it after the sessions."

"Paid for it," I asked, "How so?"

Sarah would nitpick at every statement Don uttered during the session that was even remotely critical of her and then often would physically assault him. Pots and pans often were cited as the weapons of choice in addition to the aforementioned living room lamp.

"I love her," he sheepishly confessed. "Nevertheless, I may need to leave her soon. To be frank, Dr. Rosenthal, I'm afraid for my life."

Her intense hatred toward males was evident in all of her transactions in our therapy group. Let me assure the reader that my therapist status did not render me exempt from her caustic wrath.

Therapeutic dialogue with this bright, well-educated, attractive 34-year-old revealed that she behaved in a similar fashion outside of the confines of her marriage. No inappropriate hostility, I might add, was ever shown toward females either in or out of the group therapy setting.

On a number of occasions Sarah would "hit the sleazy local bars" as she so eloquently put it, for the sole purpose of picking a fight with the meanest-looking fellow in the establishment. Sarah went in "packed" with a concealed knife or an ice pick just in case she needed a little extra firepower. This behavior hardly could be considered commensurate with her status as an upper-middle-class businesswoman who refrained from drinking alcohol.

Interestingly enough, the fact that Sarah physically and verbally abused men was clearly an ego syntonic disorder. That is to say, she didn't really feel her behavior was abnormal nor did I ever hear her express a desire to make changes in this respect.

Sarah did want therapy, nevertheless, and she wanted it in the worst way. Her panic attacks were predictable and unrelenting. Every night she would wake up at almost precisely 3:50 a.m. She would then hyperventilate, sweat profusely, and experience profound cardiac awareness. A sense of intense terror would invade her entire being, and this woman who was so mean, tough, and arrogant during her waking hours would be overcome by panic and a fear that she was dying. Night after night this horrifying scenario manifested itself.

Sarah had been treated by myriad highly creative inpatient and outpatient therapists to no avail. Helpers of every persuasion sporting MDs, PhDs, MSWs, DSWs, MEds, EdDs, and PsyDs after their names graced the pages of her record. Although I marveled at many of their insights and interventions, the end result was that the anxiety monster always was ready to flash its ugly fangs as the hands of the clock slowly made their sojourn toward the 4 a.m. mark.

A host of psychiatric medicinals and natural remedies failed to ameliorate this horrendous condition.

Had she seen a female therapist? "Yes, I've seen a number of them. They were very nice, but nothing changed." So much for that hypothesis.

Was she ever hypnotized? "Yes, many times."

Biofeedback? "Get serious, of course."

I must confide in the reader that despite a wealth of experience and training, I did not have the foggiest notion of how I was going to help this woman.

When I implemented cognitive strategies, they were generally met with, "Don't tell me how to think," whereas my empathy responses usually yielded something like, "Don't tell me how I feel."

I whipped out the miracle question and was told by my client, "Save your brief strategic solution oriented stuff for someone who also believes in Santa Claus, Rosenthal. Been there, done that, and it didn't do squat."

Then it happened. Like a scene from a Freudian epic, it was just the therapeutic break we needed, or so I thought. After a session in which we spent an inordinate amount of time dwelling on the specifics of the client's childhood, she went home and vividly relived a repressed memory that I was convinced had monumental therapeutic value.

Sarah recalled that when she was approximately 6 years of age she and her father lived in a small apartment located upstairs from a tavern. (Sarah's mother died from unknown medical complications when Sarah was just an infant.) Sarah remembered that she was sitting in the stairwell that went from their apartment to the sidewalk in front of the bar. One night as she was sitting on the steps playing with her doll, an inebriated man who was leaving the bar charged up the stairs and announced that he was going to rape her. Sarah didn't truly comprehend what the man meant, but she knew it wasn't going to be a positive experience. As the man raped her, Sarah repeated again and again in her mind: "Where is my daddy? Where is my daddy? He's downstairs in the bar getting drunk. He should be here to protect me. He should be here to protect me."

If this were a Hollywood movie, Sarah—armed with this insight—would have mounted her horse and ridden off into a picture-perfect sunset to live happily ever after. Real life, nevertheless, dealt her a hand that was far cry from the psychodynamic Tinseltown version.

In reality, Sarah's nightly panic attacks continued with a vengeance, while her hostility toward men, including her husband, exacerbated until it had reached a new zenith. Several of the men in the group confided in me that—like Sarah's husband Don—they, too, were afraid for their own physical safety.

I knew my time was running out. I could not ethically keep Sarah Crown (not her real name) in my group much longer. Although my psychotherapeutic style typically is biased in the direction of cognitive-behavioral strategies (or cognitive-behavioral after an initial period of person-centered counseling to build a relationship with the client), I decided to stick with the possibility that her repressed memory was indeed significant and that, like the proverbial iceberg that sunk the *Titanic*, only the tip of the tragedy was evident.

I asked Sarah if the apartment she lived in growing up and the adjacent tavern were located in our general geographical location. Sarah stated that it was less than a 40-mile drive and that she had not been back to the "scene of the crime" since she moved out of the area. She was approximately 8 years of age at the time.

"Sarah," I said, "I want you to return to the 'scene of the crime' as you put it. I want you to carry a notebook with you and write down any thoughts, feelings, and memories you experience. I don't care how silly or outlandish the memories seem at the time. I also want you to ride around the neighborhood, scope out the school you attended as a child, and visit any other points of interest where you spent time growing up. Furthermore, I want you to keep the notebook with you after the visit at all times until you return to this group. It is especially imperative that you keep it next to your bedside in case you have a significant dream. Just make sure you stay out of physical danger and promise me that no matter what happens you won't go into the bar for the purpose of starting a fight with one of the male patrons!"

"Frankly, Dr. Rosenthal, your 'returning to the scene of the crime' homework assignment strikes me as incredibly stupid; nevertheless, since I've tried almost everything else in the world—including a few other homework assignments from my previous therapists that were almost as dumb as yours—I imagine it won't kill me to try one more thing."

I had to admit that Sarah certainly had a way of keeping her therapists humble.

Sarah returned to her next group therapy session with her notebook in hand. Somehow she even looked different. Something had changed. What she told the group next held us spellbound. She had returned to the scene of the crime and jotted down a few seemingly insignificant notes. That night, however, when she woke up for her nightly panic attack, she relived the final chapter of her repressed memory. My clinical hunch was correct. Sarah had observed merely the tip of the iceberg. What lurked beneath the surface held the morbid secret to the final piece of this enigmatic psychic puzzle.

Sarah's new memory began where the initial saga left off. Yes, the man from the bar had raped her. Afterward, the poor child curled up in a fetal position, clutching her doll for comfort, as tears streamed down her face. Simply put, she was in a state of psychological shock. Finally, after what seemed like eternity, she saw her father walking up the stairs. Her father represented security—somebody who would hold her, hug her, and comfort her in her time of need.

The two entered the apartment. Sarah told her father what had ensued. Her father did not console her but rather burst into a fit of laughter. The smell of alcohol on his breath was overpowering. "I too am going to rape you," he announced, still laughing uncontrollably.

Rape her he did, but Sarah's mind and body could not endure another hellish assault. Her mind needed to go away: to disassociate, to detach, to flee from the anguish. Since Sarah was learning to tell time, she looked up at the clock and began chanting to herself: "It's 10 minutes to four. It's 10 minutes to four."

Sarah looked up. The other group members were mesmerized. She had finally come face-to-face with the devilish secret that her mind had kept locked away for nearly three decades. She now had the insight to begin the cognitive restructuring process. Her symptoms made sense. She was normal for what had happened to her. For the first time in her adult life, the lights were on and she could deal with the grim truth that reality often brings. Slowly but surely her panic attacks began to subside so she could sleep past the ominous 4:00 hour. Like a vapor trail left by a high-powered military jet that slowly begins to evaporate, her anger began to dissipate. It was going to take some time, but at least Sarah was traveling on the road to recovery.

This therapeutic saga does not in any way, shape, or form prove the superiority of a psychodynamic approach. It is, however, a glowing testimonial to the power of psychotherapeutic homework, which I firmly believe can be utilized with virtually any form of ethical intervention.

Simplicity and the Art of the Therapeutic Homework Deal

Some therapists I have spoken with believe that effective homework assignments are by nature very complex, complicated, esoteric, or abstruse. Not so. Quite to the contrary, often the simplest ploy can produce outstanding results.

I recall a woman who came to see me because she felt that her husband was uncommunicative. When she suggested they see a marriage counselor, her husband stated that he didn't feel their communication was a problem and refused. I remembered that one of my former professors in graduate school, Raphael J. Becvar (also a contributor to this book and a recognized expert in marriage, family, and couple's counseling), used to say that in many cases any change—even an infinitesimal change—could initiate a significant change in the family system.

Working under the aforementioned assumption, I asked the client how her day began. She told me that for the last 23 years she brought her husband his favorite brand of cola in bed. I advised the woman to bring her hubby a different brand of cola and to let me know what transpired. The woman had some trepidation as she feared her husband would be downright furious. Nevertheless, my client agreed to give it a try. It turned out that her prediction was correct: Indeed her husband was furious; an argument ensued over her inept behavior, and the couple talked more that day than they had in years. (It reminded me of the statement some politicians make that they would rather have people dislike them than not have any opinion about them.) Although the couple's situation was certainly not transformed into an ideal one, the argument, spawned via the wrong cola, set a precedent, and their rate of conversation escalated to a level my client felt was acceptable.

Some homework assignments—unlike the two previously mentioned—can consist of a periodic, as needed, or ongoing activity. Permit me to share just one more, somewhat remarkable cola cure. A male client of mine recently told me that he was rushed to an urgent care center for severe anxiety, depression, and an overwhelming desire to mutilate himself, which he had done numerous times in the past. The attending physicians tried to use drugs to calm him down. As the physicians were hooking up his IV, he began yelling that he wanted a certain brand of cola. "I would have killed for the cola at that moment," he told me. After he received his drink of choice, his panic, depression, and desire to harm himself were ameliorated almost instantaneously.

The urgent care staff members were amazed. Frankly, so was I! In fact, in over 20 years of doing therapy I had never come across anything quite like it. "Why do you think that particular brand of soda pop was so effective?" I asked.

"Oh it's really very simple," he replied, "My mother and father were terribly cruel. They were physically and emotionally abusive to me. But several times as a child, when I was sick they would bring me this brand of soda pop. I believe it was the only time in my whole life that they were kind and comforting to me."

I thus gave my client the simple assignment that he should always have a bottle or can of this particular soda at home as well as in his vehicle. If and only if he felt panicky, self-destructive, or severely depressed, he was instructed to take several sips of the beverage. To avoid a habituation response, the client was instructed never to drink the beverage at meals, social events, or for recreational purposes. It was intended specifically as an emergency medicinal. As of this date, the technique has been effective. Long live the cola cure!

It is also noteworthy that covert homework assignments (or covert assignments combined with overt assignments) often can have an enormous impact.

Katie, a brilliant 27-year-old advertising executive, sought treatment after she discovered that her boyfriend Bob was having an affair with another woman who worked in the office.

"Tell me about the other woman."

Katie said that everybody—including Katie up to this point in time—liked her. Not only was the "other woman" perhaps the most popular employee, but she also was a rising star in the ad agency, had a terrific personality, and had worked as a former swimsuit model to boot.

I suspect that the protective side of me secretly wanted the "other woman" to be inferior to my client in one or more important ways. If that was indeed the case, then I could merely explain to Katie that water seeks its own level and that Bob had consciously or unconsciously picked a partner to whom he could feel superior. (Countertransference, anyone?) Unfortunately reality, or at least Katie's perception of reality, threw a monkey wrench into my therapeutic strategy. I thus opted for a homework assignment that championed both covert as well as overt behaviors.

I looked Katie squarely in the eye. "How would you have behaved if *you* had decided to have an affair on Bob?" I inquired.

Katie seemed shocked. Perhaps "offended" would be a more accurate description. "I would never, never in a million years have had an affair on Bob!"

"Yes, I know that. But that's not what I asked you. Let's just suppose for a moment that you were going to have an affair with another man. How would your thoughts, actions, feelings, and behavior be different? I would like you to dwell on this hypothetical situation and share your conclusions with me during our next session."

Katie protested again that such behavior was almost unthinkable and she could not give me an honest answer. She told me she would give the issue some serious thought and would, at the very least, attempt to complete her homework.

Katie returned and, much to my chagrin, had completed her covert homework. Amazingly enough, my client revealed that this covert activity took the edge off her severe depression. Perhaps the mere act of focusing her attention on something other than the breakup had a mild curative effect.

Here were some of the things Katie decided she would *hypothetically* do:

1. Act in a more effervescent, bubbly manner.
2. Talk, laugh, and joke more with colleagues.
3. Try a slightly different hairstyle and color.
4. Wear clothing and makeup that she felt others would perceive as sexier.
5. Eat a little better and exercise to lose a minimal amount of weight.
6. Secure a professional manicure.

I then suggested to Katie that nothing she contemplated was the least bit immoral or risqué and therefore part two of her homework assignment was to actually engage in the six aforementioned strategies. Katie began to behave *as if she were having an affair.* In an exceedingly short period of time, her mood began to lift markedly. Although the client was hardly thrilled about the situation, her incessant obsessive thoughts about Bob began to subside.

After several weeks, Bob approached her about the possibility of getting back together and Katie turned him down. My client had befriended another gentleman in the office and could imagine herself dating him in the near future.

Another Rosenthal Effect? When Less Is Clearly More

Not only can psychotherapeutic homework be simple, but assuming the client is not harboring suicidal or homicidal feelings, I have discovered the paradox—just call it the other Rosenthal Effect, if you will—that less is often more. Telling a client to make numerous changes outside the session is often not as efficacious as instructing the client to make minor, barely noticeable, almost nonexistent, alterations in their behavior.

Take a client who decides to begin an exercise program on her stationary bicycle. Unfortunately, she readily admits she has tried many times in the past but could never stick with the activity for more than a few days. The prevailing advice is generally that the client should initially work out the first day for approximately 20 minutes or some such nonsense. My advice to this client would be: Don't even think about it! This client has already tried to throw herself into an exercise program and it has failed. Why? Most likely because exercising was an aversive experience.

Instead, instruct the client to ride the bike for just 15 seconds the first day. You should even go the extra mile (pun intended) and warn her that she is not to go beyond the figure of 15 seconds. Day 2 is identical to Day 1; with no progress being good progress. On Day 3 she can ride the bike for perhaps 20 or 30 seconds. On Day 4 she can really pump up the volume … um, I mean the pedals … and go for a record-breaking figure of 45 seconds. And so on until she reaches a desirable time.

Advice to Therapists Who Advocate Behavior Change at Warp Speed

Rather than trying to make changes at warp speed, progress using this paradigm will unfold with the velocity, power, and acceleration of a turtle strapped with ankle weights. Fifteen seconds of exercise on the first day will most likely not cause this client to be out of breath, nor will she be too sore to walk the next day. Since she will have plenty of time to become acclimated, riding the exercise bike then becomes a pleasurable experience rather than a dismal failure or a trigger to binge on over-the-counter anti-inflammatory pain medications. The activity has become a success (albeit a small one at first) rather than a defeat.

A man came to see me who claimed that procrastination was ruining his life. He had been putting off writing his dissertation (which had to be "perfect") for so long that his doctoral committee was toying with the idea of not giving him another extension. Several sessions with a cognitive therapist and a behavior modification expert who recommended a positive reinforcement schedule had not altered the situation. I gave the man the assignment to write three mediocre sentences for his paper (and not one sentence more!) and bring them to the next session. The client returned with nearly 20 pages that seemed to be in excellent order.

Mind Games: What to Do When "Just Do It" Homework Just Isn't Working

A homework assignment can boil down to little more than a mind game. Chris was living in a rather plush neighborhood. He came to see me after the fire department paid a visit to his house. His "nosy neighbors," as he put it, had reported him because his garage was filled with hundreds of boxes stacked to the ceiling. The fire marshal explained that his garage was considered a fire hazard and that he would receive a citation if the situation was not rectified within a short period of time.

Chris was angry about the situation and rapidly hired an attorney. He was ready to take on City Hall, so to speak, until his newly hired attorney rode past his property and got a quick glimpse of his garage that just happened to be open. The attorney called him and said he agreed with the fire marshal's assessment and subsequently refused to take the case!

Chris perceived the task of cleaning his garage as monumental and, from the description he gave me, his perception was deadly accurate. I prescribed a homework assignment that basically revolved around a mind game.

"I want you to play a mind game with yourself," I explained. "Go home and take a long hard look at the mess in your garage. Then convince yourself that there is absolutely no way you could actually clean the garage because the job is bigger than life. This should be easy since you have basically felt this way for a long time. Make sure you reinforce in your mind the notion that the place is a total pit. Just terrible.

"Next, tell yourself that you will break down one box (and only one box) and place it in your recycling bin. Also, firmly use self-talk to insist that no matter how determined you are to continue the job and remove more boxes, you just won't do it."

Chris protested. "Well I know I'm an ace procrastinator, but one box isn't a whole heck of a lot. What if—even with my extreme lazy streak—I decide I could tear down a second or a third box?"

"If that happens—and it probably won't—once again convince yourself that you will cap the job at two boxes and no more."

I'd like to say that Chris's homework assignment earned his garage a place in *House Beautiful,* but that would be a downright lie. He did, however, go well beyond the one, two, or three box mark and removed enough so that one of his vehicles could actually have a roof over its head.

Homework interventions such as the ones described thus far in this chapter (and hundreds of others) have convinced me that in many instances homework assignments can and do improve the client's situation.

The Evolution of This Book: Now and Then

In 1998 I edited an innovative book, titled *Favorite Counseling and Therapy Techniques: Fifty-one Therapists Share Their Most Creative Strategies,* for Accelerated Development publishers, a member of the Taylor & Francis Group. Based on sales (it became an academic best seller for the publisher in less than a year) and feedback I received from numerous individuals who read the book, I was convinced that the text was providing a valuable service. I therefore felt that a sequel—dealing specifically with psychotherapeutic homework, which merely is a specific type of therapy technique—could be extremely helpful to counselors and educators, as well as to neophyte and experienced clinicians. I've made an uncanny discovery that when you have a real-life client sitting in front of you, you can never have too many creative therapeutic ideas!

Because the process of selecting the original cast of therapists is well depicted in my earlier work (Rosenthal, 1998), I shall not explicate the specifics here except to say that I stipulated that all contributors needed to be book authors or editors, or both, in the field. This was done intentionally to keep me from packing the book with my friends and colleagues. To be sure, I was cognizant of the fact that there were thousands of therapists who have never written or edited a book who were eminently qualified to contribute to this book.

I began the process of creating the original work by asking all 51 therapists who had previously contributed to my techniques book to contribute once again to the homework text. Unfortunately, several had retired from academia or practice. Others had too much going on in their lives and thus reluctantly had to turn down the project. Others I was unable to contact, despite my best efforts.

I therefore gave myself poetic license to fill these open slots with some of the most creative therapists in the world: pioneers in the field who were not included in the initial work. Fortunately, a number of these individuals were enthused about the project and agreed to contribute. No attempt was made to favor one profession over another. Therefore, you will find psychiatrists, psychologists, counselors, social workers, marriage and family therapists, a nurse, and, yes, even a playwright and theater director who provides psychotherapy. All contributors received a reasonable facsimile of the letter included in Figure 1.1 as well as the format sheet included in Figure 1.2.

In 2008 the decision was made to update the book into an updated edition. Perhaps the most important decision was to leave all the original homework techniques contained in the original edition in the new work. Why? The answer is easy.

Legends Share Their Favorite Homework Assignment

Many contributors to the first edition were master therapists and their contributions were extremely valuable to neophytes as well

Dear Dr. Jones:

I am writing to invite you to contribute to a new book I am editing entitled *Favorite Counseling and Therapy Homework Assignments, Classic Anniversary Edition.* The book is an updated version of my book *Favorite Counseling and Therapy Homework Assignments* published in 2001.

Because you are a recognized expert in psychoanalysis I would be honored if you could find time to contribute, since I know you are extremely busy. The *contributions are generally very short; a couple of pages would be typical, although longer entries are certainly permissible.* I believe the book will be very strong. Like the previous book, I am packing the book with persons of notoriety in mental health, psychiatry, and counseling such as yourself.

I have enclosed a format sheet as well as an actual sample contribution that will be used in the book. Thank you for taking the time to read this letter. *Please let me know immediately if you cannot send an entry.* Best wishes in your future endeavors and I hope you will be able to send a contribution.

Sincerely,

Howard Rosenthal, Ed.D., CCMHC, LPC, NCC, MAC

FIGURE 1.1 Letter mailed to all therapists.

as seasoned professionals. Why replace excellent ideas? Another dilemma was that several of our luminaries, such as Albert Ellis, Raymond J. Corsini, Joseph W. Hollis, and Edwin S. Shneidman, had passed away and thus could not contribute to the new anniversary edition. How do you replace an Ellis, or a Corsini, a Hollis, or a Shneidman? To put it bluntly: You simply cannot. (Just for the record, without the assistance of Dr. Joseph W. Hollis, who wholeheartedly believed in my ideas, this series would most likely never have made it into print.) Therefore, the unaltered homework assignments from all the distinguished therapists from the first edition remain in this new edition for your edification and reading pleasure. Their legacy lives on in these pages.

This Book Includes a Bevy of Some of the Finest Therapists in the World

One goal of mine in writing this original text was to include more famous therapists within these covers than any other book regarding psychotherapeutic homework in print—and to this end

---

BRIEF FORMAT FOR WRITING YOUR FAVORITE COUNSELING
OR THERAPY HOMEWORK ASSIGNMENT

Please do not submit a document that has appeared in another book or journal.

1. Your name and highest degree as you would like it to appear in the book (e.g., Joe Smith, Ph.D.).
2. Your profession (e.g., licensed counselor, psychologist, board-certified psychiatrist, licensed clinical social worker, etc.).
3. Primary affiliations. No more than two (e.g., University of Missouri, Columbia, and private practice).
4. Major works. You may list up to three books using APA style. If you have other works, simply say something such as "and 14 other books."
5. Give your homework assignment a name (e.g., Family Role-Playing for Children of Divorce).
6. Stipulate the population for whom the technique is appropriate (e.g., Adult Children of Alcoholics in couples counseling sessions).
7. Give any cautionary notes (e.g., "This technique is not suitable for suicidal clients and children less than 18 years of age.")
8. *Describe your technique in approximately two or three double-spaced pages. If your idea is a little longer, that won't be a problem.* Use step-by-step procedures when appropriate. Try to use easy-to-understand language, avoiding technical jargon whenever possible. If you need to reference or document your idea, please do so using APA manuscript style. If your idea is novel, references may be inappropriate.
9. As soon as I can, I will contact you and let you know when the book will be published. Please give me your address, phone number, and e-mail in case clarification is needed regarding your strategy.

THANK YOU FOR YOUR TIME, KNOWLEDGE,
ASSISTANCE, AND EXPERTISE!
THIS BOOK WILL BE EXTREMELY BENEFICIAL TO
EDUCATORS AND THERAPISTS.

FIGURE 1.2   Format of technique contribution.

I succeeded. In this new edition my goal was to raise the bar and add more talented clinicians, and here again I can only say: mission accomplished.

You Won't Find Sigmund Freud as a Contributor but …

Please indulge me as I share a humorous little anecdote. As I searched somewhat obsessively both near and far to snag the top therapists as contributors for the new edition, my colleagues chided me: "Well, Rosenthal, do you have Sigmund Freud in the book yet?"

Now obviously Sigmund Freud was not a viable option since he left us in 1939. Nevertheless, as a former child abuse treatment worker I'm a pretty good amateur private investigator. I discovered that Sophie Freud (Sigmund's granddaughter!) was still alive. Even more remarkable was the fact that she had taught social work and practiced psychotherapy. The most amazing point, however, was that she was very critical of her grandfather's theory of psychoanalysis! Because I believe in swinging for the fence, I contacted Sophie and asked her to contribute. Sophie did indeed respond.

> Dear Dr. Rosenthal,
>
> I am honored by your invitation to contribute to your book but I retired some time ago and have not kept up with the program in the field. I regret that I will not be able to contribute to your books. Thank you.
>
> Sincerely,
> Sophie Freud

Are There Any Therapists Who Don't Use Homework Assignments?

I cannot forgo mentioning that during the composition of this work I was asked repeatedly: "What type of therapist uses homework assignments?"

Based on the contributors in this work, a better question might be, "What type of therapist does not prescribe homework?" Consider the notoriety and expertise, as well as the variation in terms of psychotherapeutic modalities, of some of the contributors.

- **Albert Ellis** was the founder of rational emotive behavior therapy (REBT) and the author of 75 books and monographs as well as over 1,200 articles. Ellis received APA *and* ACA Living Legend status prior to his death. In 1982 U.S. and Canadian psychologists rated him the second most influential psychologist in history, right behind Carl

Rogers, beating out Sigmund Freud, who placed third! Sadly, Dr. Ellis died July 24, 2007.

- **William Glasser** is the founder of reality therapy with choice theory and is considered one of the most influential psychiatrists of all time. Glasser received ACA's Living Legend Award and was also given the Life Achievement Award by the Center for the Study of Psychiatry and Psychology.
- **Robert E. Wubbolding** is the director for the Center for Reality Therapy and the recipient of numerous accolades.
- **Allen E. Ivey** is a pioneer in microcounseling and attending skills, and his training materials are used in numerous institutions who train counselors, social workers, and therapists.
- **Maxie C. Maultsby, Jr.** created rational behavior therapy and rational self-counseling.
- **Edwin Shneidman** was the founding father of the American Association of Suicidology. He literally changed the face of mental health forever in 1958 when he helped found the Los Angeles Suicide Prevention Center. He gained national attention when he investigated the death of Marilyn Monroe. In my humble opinion, Shneidman was one of the brightest and most insightful clinicians in history. Try reading one of his books or articles without a dictionary or thesaurus in hand. Go ahead, I dare you! Dr. Shneidman passed away on May 15, 2009.
- **Walter Kempler** is considered a pioneer in Gestalt therapy as well as family therapy.
- **Peter R. Breggin** is the former director of the International Center for the Study of Psychiatry and Psychology and is well known for his books *Talking Back to Prozac* and *Talking Back to Ritalin*. He is often a guest on national television shows.
- **Robert W. Firestone** is the creator of voice therapy and has expertise in numerous areas, including child abuse, suicide prevention, and relationships, to name a few.
- **Judith S. Beck** is the director of the Beck Institute for Cognitive Therapy and Research.

- **Arthur Freeman** is one of the most influential figures in the cognitive-behavior therapy (CBT) movement.
- **Richard Bolles** is the author of *What Color Is Your Parachute?*, the best-selling job-hunting book of all time.
- **Gerald Corey and Marianne Schneider Corey** are authors of some of the most popular textbooks and reference tomes used by psychology, counseling, and human services programs.
- **Raymond J. Corsini** has been cited as one of the most influential psychologists in the past 150 years. He authored some of the premier textbooks and reference books in psychology and psychotherapy. Dr. Corsini passed away on November 8, 2008.
- **Samuel Gladding** is a former ACA president, a past president of the Association for Specialists in Group Work, and served as president of the Association of Counselor Education and Supervision. Like the Coreys and Dr. Corsini, his textbooks are considered staples in the field.
- **Connirae Andreas and Steve Andreas** are noted experts in the field of Neuro-Linguistic Programming.
- **Windy Dryden, Paul A. Hauck,** and **John D. Boyd** are recognized as leaders in REBT.
- **Bea Wehrly** is an expert in multicultural and interracial issues in counseling.
- **Nancy Schlossberg** is regarded as an eminent developmentalist.
- **Dorothy S. Becvar** and **Raphael J. Becvar** are acknowledged scholars and textbook authors in family therapy.
- **Lorna L. Hecker** and **Catherine Ford Sori** are the editors of the well-known *Therapist's Notebook* series devoted to therapeutic activities and homework.
- **Gary Schultheis** is the coauthor of several texts on homework as it relates to brief therapy.
- **Bob Bertolino** has written extensively about brief solution-oriented therapy as well as methods for treating adolescents.
- **Robert E. Alberti** coauthored the classic assertiveness training text, *Your Perfect Right.*

- **Muriel James** coauthored *Born to Win,* a Gestalt/transactional analysis book that has been selling strong since 1971 and has been published in 22 languages.
- **Al Mahrer** is a recipient of APA's Living Legend in Psychotherapy Award. He also created experiential therapy.
- **Luciano L'Abate** and **Nikolaos Kazantzis** recently edited their own book on using homework assignments in psychotherapy and are both noted experts in CBT. Dr. L'Abate has authored, coauthored, or edited over 35 books and has penned over 250 papers in scientific and professional journals. In my opinion, his contribution in this book is so scholarly it is more of a philosophical piece on the current state and future of psychotherapy than merely another homework assignment.
- **Jon Carlson** is yet another ACA Living Legend. In addition to holding two doctorates, he created over 200 DVDs and videos showcasing the work of top therapists.
- **Patricia Arredondo** also snared an ACA Living Legend Award and is considered a leading expert in multicultural diversity studies.
- **Claudia Black** is recognized as a leader in addiction studies, codependency, and the recovery movement.
- **Lia Nower**, a psychotherapist, an attorney, and a social worker, is a leading figure in the treatment of gambling addiction.

Thus, our therapists more than adequately represent assertiveness training, REBT, CBT, Gestalt therapy, transactional analysis, marriage and family therapy, Neuro-Linguistic Programming, multicultural counseling, voice therapy, suicidology, addictions, career and vocational counseling, brief strategic solution-oriented therapy, a developmentalist perspective, and rational self-counseling. If we add therapies not mentioned in this chapter but featured in this text, we could add logotherapy, grief counseling, and nucleus therapy, to name a few.

Although homework is not used as frequently in psychodynamic or person-centered/client-centered counseling, *it is used on some occasions.* My opening saga, in which my client was instructed to "return to the scene of the crime" to help unearth a repressed memory, is a perfect illustration of a psychodynamic homework assignment. Corey and Corey's contribution to this book, as well as the one included by Allen E. Ivey, demonstrates how a therapist who is basically nondirective (i.e., person-centered) can use homework to enhance the treatment process. The bottom line is that a therapist practicing nearly any legitimate psychotherapeutic paradigm can employ efficacious homework tactics. Several of our contributors wisely point out that because the word *homework* often conjures up negative connotations (you can thank the high school teacher you disliked the most later), a synonym such as *task* or *exercise* may be more appropriate to use when giving directives to your client.

Herein you will discover homework intervention strategies for adults, children, and adolescents, in individual, group, couples, or marriage and family counseling. To keep the material fresh and lively, I insisted that every therapist's contribution was specifically written for this text.

Global Learning Personified

This is a world-class book in the literal sense of the term. That is to say, our experts come from near and far. Although most are housed in the United States, we have a number of experts from afar. For example, REBT expert **Windy Dryden,** who has authored or edited more than 115 books, is at Goldsmiths College at the University of London. **Jesper Juul** is the executive director of the Kempler Institute of Scandinavia and the author of an international best seller (eight countries) on children. **Alvin R. Mahrer** is a well-known therapist from the University of Ottawa School of Psychology in Canada, while social worker **Christine Byriel** is a member of the Danish Association for Psychotherapists as well as a member of the European Association for Psychotherapy. CBT homework specialist and award-winning therapist **Nikolaos Kazantzis** maintains a part-time practice in Auckland, New Zealand. **Susan Paxton**, who has expertise in eating disorders and body image issues, comes to us from the School of Psychological Science, La Trobe University, Australia. Canadian **Keith Dobson** is president of the Academy of Cognitive Therapy and the president for the International Association of Cognitive Therapy.

Last, although this book is decidedly prohomework, even I must admit that all techniques (yes, even homework assignments) have their pitfalls: plenty of them. Remember the old medical adage: First do no harm. Indeed homework assignments have their dark side. I would be remiss if I did not mention it. The eminent therapist Jeffrey Kottler and I will spill the psychotherapeutic beans in the next chapter.

Here's to your successful homework assignments.

Dr. Howard Rosenthal
St. Louis, Missouri
September 2010

Reference

Rosenthal, H. G. (Ed.). (1998). *Favorite counseling and therapy techniques: Fifty-one therapists share their most creative strategies.* Philadelphia: Accelerated Development/Taylor & Francis.

Chapter 2

Fright Night
Exploring the Dark Side of Therapeutic Homework Assignments

Howard G. Rosenthal and Jeffrey A. Kottler

The best laid schemes o' mice and men
Gang aft a-gley [often fail]
And leave us naught but grief and pain
For promised joy.*

—Robert Burns,
To a Mouse

I just don't know how to thank you, they keep saying and writing, for having written that wonderful book! I keep rereading it all the time and have found it the greatest of help. But when we keep talking to them we find that they often have done little to follow our 'wonderful book'—or that they are actually doing almost the opposite of what we advocated.

—Albert Ellis, PhD, and Robert Harper, PhD,
A New Guide to Rational Living (1997, 3rd ed., p. 1)

---

* Language updated.

When I was writing the original 2001 version of Chapter 2 of this book, my son Patrick was just 2½ years old. As I geared up to write the current chapter of this book, Patrick walked up to me and tugged very forcefully on my right shirt sleeve. I looked up from my computer. "Make me a shake," he demanded. His tone of voice and nonverbal behavior clearly signified intense anger.

"Say 'please,'" I said.

His face contorted to an even greater extent and his anger had now escalated to near rage.

"Clease" (yes, I know you won't find Patrick's enunciation in the dictionary, but I'm trying to keep this account of our transaction as accurate as possible), he barked back in a very nasty tone of voice.

I remained totally calm. "Say it nicely," I admonished.

Patrick summoned up his meanest possible look, gave me a riveting eyeball-to-eyeball stare, and yelled at the top of his lungs, "Nicely!"

Such is the fate of many homework assignments. The best-laid plans often result in inaction or, worse yet, disaster.

I'll never forget one of my first experiences with psychotherapeutic homework. I was seeing a youngster named Kelly who was about 10 years of age. The child was missing such an excessive amount of school that the family court informed me in no uncertain terms that her absenteeism was so extreme that placement in a foster care home seriously was being considered.

There was no time for long drawn-out psychotherapeutic ploys. This youngster needed to start attending school immediately. The little girl and her mother were petrified at the prospect of foster care, and, thus, the young lady agreed to follow my directives to ward off this highly undesirable situation.

I was in graduate school at the time and our professor had just completed a lecture on the merits of combining therapeutic homework with behavioral contracting that utilized positive reinforcement. I was convinced that by serving up an eclectic psychotherapeutic cocktail, by mixing a healthy dose of homework, and just a pinch of Skinnerian operant conditioning, I could ward off placement.

My next move was to meet with Kelly and rapidly ascertain what would be a suitable positive reinforcer for this child.

Kelly suggested that "fright night" was just days away and she had nothing to wear. When I pleaded ignorance regarding "fright night," Kelly rolled her eyes and said, "Hello, what planet are you living on? It's Halloween, but everybody at school calls it fright night you know, and I don't even have a mask."

Actually, I didn't know, but now I knew what would be a perfect reinforcer for this child. We discussed the precise mask she wanted, and I was ready to prescribe the perfect homework assignment. I told Kelly that if she went to school the following day, I would give her the mask she needed to go trick or treating on fright night. To say that Kelly was excited would be putting it mildly. She was ecstatic. She was so overzealous that she suggested that her best friend who lived next door would even witness her actions. (Hey, great idea, why didn't I think of that?)

I was excited, first because I was convinced I had just pulled off a world-class psychotherapeutic homework coup, and second because this young lady was taking the first step to steer clear of the state foster care system.

When I arrived at the office the next morning, I had a note saying that the school social worker called. Of course she called. Why wouldn't she? I was certain she was calling to tell me that Kelly was in class and to discover what psychotherapeutic gems of wisdom I utilized to motivate her to attend.

Much to my chagrin the school social worker was calling to say that Kelly was *not* present. I was in disbelief and even asked the social worker to personally check the classroom once more. The school social worker honored my request only to report that Kelly was still nowhere to be found.

I was dumbfounded and quite frankly disappointed. On my way home from work I drove to Kelly's house. Before I could even knock on the front door, Kelly enthusiastically ran out to see me.

"Where's my mask … my mask … do you have it … do you have it? I'm gonna look so cool."

She was bubbly and excited. I, on the other hand, was very serious and solemn. "Kelly," I reminded her, "we made a deal. … We had a contract. Remember? I said that you had to go to school to get the mask."

Now she was in tears. "But I did go. I went to school. Honest, I swear I did."

"No, I'm afraid you didn't."

Kelly wiped her tears and broke into a smile. "Tammy, my neighbor. Remember, I told you I would have a witness? Well, I do."

Before I could confront Kelly with the school social worker's observation, or, more aptly, her lack of it, Kelly was dragging Tammy over to see me.

"She's telling the truth, mister," Tammy said.

"Okay, Tammy," I conceded, "then you tell me what happened."

"Well, mister. Kelly went to school this morning. I went with her. I even made her touch the building."

"Then why did the school social worker tell me that Kelly wasn't in class today?" I wanted to know.

Both girls smiled. "Well, that's easy enough to answer," Kelly declared. "Remember you just said I had to go to school? Well, I did. I even touched the building. You didn't say anything about going inside."

I believe there are two morals associated with this story: (1) Be *specific* when giving homework assignments to make certain the client understands your directives, and (2) consider the notion that in many cases homework assignments will prove futile, if not downright counterproductive.

At times homework assignments fail precisely because they work too well! As an example, I have often given couples who know each other well the assignment of reversing roles during an argument. That is to say, the couple agrees to stop the traditional argument they are engaged in and then to resume the quarrel with each party acting as if he or she is the other party (e.g., a husband argues as if he is his wife, while the wife argues as if she is the husband). Often—if the couple is willing to engage in this practice— the assignment abets empathy for the other person's position and can be quite effective. Nevertheless, on one occasion when I prescribed this exercise between sessions, the husband played the role of his wife for several minutes and exclaimed, "Hey, no fair! Now I know exactly how you feel. I'm not going to do *this* anymore."

A somewhat analogous position was taken by a woman who sought my help to quit smoking. I gave her a homework assignment that required her to carry a lipgloss stick with her at all times. The lipgloss stick is a posthypnotic article of sorts that wards off the desire to smoke. (Note: For a more in-depth explanation, see my contribution titled, "Olfactory Conditioning: The Sweet Aroma of Post-Hypnotics" in *Favorite Counseling and Therapy Techniques* [Rosenthal, 2011, pp. 261] for specific details). "Your technique failed," she chided. "I threw my lipgloss out the window of my car. It made me detest cigarettes and I actually began to dislike smoking."

Paradoxical as it may seem—and much as helpers hate to admit it—there are indeed clients who are comfortable with their dysfunctional behaviors. These clients feel safe in the sense that they are familiar with the behavior and, more importantly, receive a sense of satisfaction from such conduct. In cases such as this (where the client explicitly or implicitly argues for his or her misery) the therapist must help the client replace these inappropriate behaviors with appropriate ones that yield a healthy payoff, lest the most elegant homework assignment will prove to be a discouraging failure.

When I edited the favorite techniques text (Rosenthal, 2010) I contacted Jeffrey Kottler, who is now the author of over 75 books, to contribute. Dr. Kottler wrote me a letter depicting why he was not a fervent proponent of techniques. The piece was so insightful that I decided to print it, in its entirety, in a chapter that delineated the pitfalls of techniques.

Inasmuch as this format was extremely successful, I wrote Dr. Kottler a letter stating that I assumed that he did not relish psychotherapeutic homework, and thus would he be willing to write an entry supporting his position. What follows is the unaltered response of noted expert, Dr. Jeffrey Kottler.

Why I Don't Believe in Favorite Homework Assignments

Jeffrey A. Kottler

Howard asked me to say something on this subject because he knew that I would be rebellious and provocative. "I am making the assumption," Howard told me in his invitational letter, "that you are also not extremely fond of homework assignments since they are, after all, a form of technique." This was a reasonable prediction considering that in my contribution to his companion book, *Favorite Counseling and Therapy Techniques* (Rosenthal, 2011, Chapter 2), I wrote about why I thought a focus on techniques gets in the way of the process of therapy. I like techniques as much as the next person; I just don't think they are all that important compared with the relationships we develop, the atmosphere we create to foster trust and risk taking, the modeling we do, the attributes we demonstrate, and the spirit of growth that we engender.

If I'm not too keen on techniques, it would make sense that I also don't care too much for homework assignments. This is actually not the case. I believe that talking without action is *almost* a waste of time. I have seen far too many people who talk and talk but who don't *do* anything constructive to change anything in their lives. They come to session week after week, talk about their problems, complain about their misery, enjoy a wonderful therapeutic relationship, but they continue to do the same crazy, dysfunctional things. That's why I believe that homework assignments are *essential* to lasting change.

My objection (and certainly you knew that one was coming) is not with homework but with *favorite* homework assignments. "Favorite" implies that I already know what is best for my clients before I even hear their stories. "Favorite" means that I am doing what I like, what pleases me, rather than what a given client may need.

If I am completely honest, *of course* I have favorite things I like to do in therapy. Like most practitioners, I believe I know what is best for people. I even have a short list of proven, time-tested recipes for success that do work most of the time. The problem for me is that the longer I practice, the less sure I am that I really do know what is best for others. The best work that I do transcends technique. The most successful, lasting changes that I have been privileged to be part of did not come from my efforts to structure and prescribe homework; rather they emerged from our collaborative partnership in which we invented something altogether brand new. These homework assignments could not possibly have been my favorites because, prior to this collaboration, they never existed. Furthermore, they will not be useful for anyone else.

I notice so often with beginners that they often introduce homework (or techniques) not because it is what the client needs but because it addresses their own sense of helplessness and powerlessness. I want to help. I believe I don't have much to offer, so I give the client something to do so I can feel better about my efforts, as if now I am really doing something therapeutic.

One case in point: I was supervising a new therapist this week who was relating her frustration because her client was not complying with the homework assignment that the therapist had *assigned*. When I asked the therapist to say more about what happened, she mentioned that she'd asked her client to complete some task that worked quite well with several other clients. With her limited experience, she had already developed a favorite between-session technique that she intended to use with most of her other clients. The problem, however, is that she hadn't bothered to adapt, customize, and personalize the homework for this particular client, nor had she negotiated the task in such a way that the client felt committed to doing it.

I also don't believe that everyone *needs* homework or that it is appropriate for every case. I recall a business fellow who came to see me about some family problems. He was some high-powered executive, fully equipped with several phones, a laptop, plus a clipboard in which he would constantly write notes to himself. I hoped that he was at least taking notes on our session, but I couldn't be sure; for all I know he was writing down plans for his next takeover bid.

"So Doc," he'd say to me as if I was one of his accounting consultants, "what do I need to do to take care of this problem? Whatever it takes, I'm ready." He would sit there, stone still, with his pen poised to write down whatever I told him to.

I felt this uncontrollable urge to cackle out loud, so exhilarated I felt with power. If I told this guy to jump off the Empire State Building, I wondered if he really would.

This businessman, so ordered and goal driven in his world, wanted to direct our sessions by having me give him my favorite homework assignments that would cure him. I even deluded myself that I had such an antidote, but out of spite, I was not going to give it to him. It then occurred to me that homework was the *last* thing in the world this guy needed. It is novelty that often promotes significant change, and for him, more structured goal setting was just too familiar.

I asked him to put his clipboard aside, a request that he was very reluctant to do. I made him pack up his phones, all his stuff, and put it away. Then I made him look at me and talk to me.

"About what?" he pleaded, very uncomfortable with this strange request.

"About anything," I prompted.

The session went fine, even though it was very difficult to keep him from reaching into his briefcase to make notes. When it came time to leave, he asked, no, he *begged* for something he could work on between sessions. I opened my mouth and started to tell him what I thought he might do, when I stopped, looked him right in the eyes, and smiled.

"Best not to do anything for now," I cautioned him. "Just let this stuff sit a while."

The businessman shook his head in frustration and walked out, clearly unsatisfied with this state of affairs but unwilling just yet to fire me.

Now the reader, I'm sure, could easily conclude that I did structure a favorite homework assignment for this gentleman, a paradoxical directive of sorts. Indeed, I did think that what this person most needed was not more structure in his life, more goals and assignments, but *less* of them. In a sense, I deliberately restrained from having him create any homework for himself, which was a kind of homework in itself. I would plead guilty to this charge.

What I would vehemently deny, however, is that this particular assignment would work for anyone else. What I try to do with my clients is not get too comfortable with favorite techniques or homework assignments, but to apply some general principles to create unique ones for each person in each situation.

I see a lot of value in a book such as this one, which presents experienced practitioners talking about their most creative and favorite methods for promoting change. Such a presentation only encourages me—not to imitate or even use these techniques—but to create my own in collaboration with my clients. Alas I have few favorites that I think would work well for anyone else.

Okay, so homework assignments aren't perfect. What technique or therapeutic strategy can you name that is *always* effective? At times clients simply will not do the assignment. On other occasions they perform it incorrectly. An assignment that worked so eloquently with your 10:00 a.m. client is often a dismal failure with the person you are counseling at 11:00. And worse yet, the homework assignment that worked so well with your client this week may indeed prove futile if the same client tries it next week, even if it is used for the same problem.

To prescribe homework or not to prescribe homework; that is the question. Kick back, relax, and let over 70 of the world's most creative and accomplished therapists transport you into the confines of their respective offices to take you on an incredible therapeutic journey that you're unlikely ever to forget. So grab your case notes, some managed care panel applications, and hold onto your empathy scales. You have my personal guarantee, it's one heck of a ride.

References

Ellis, A., & Harper, R. A. (1997). *A new guide to rational living* (3rd ed.). Hollywood, CA: Wilshire Book Company.

Rosenthal, H. G. (Ed.). (2011). *Favorite counseling and therapy techniques* (2nd ed.). New York: Routledge.

Chapter **3**

Homework Assignments

Helping Others Deal With the "New Assertive You"

Therapist: Robert E. Alberti, PhD

Affiliation: Retired (formerly private practice in therapy and organizational consulting; University Counselor/ Professor/Dean; Book Editor and Publisher); Licensed Psychologist (California); Licensed MFT (California)

Major works:

Alberti, R. E. (Ed.). (1977). *Assertiveness: Innovations, applications, issues.* Atascadero, CA: Impact Publishers.

Alberti, R. E., & Emmons, M. L. (2008). *Your perfect right: Assertiveness and equality in your life and relationships* (9th ed.). Atascadero, CA: Impact Publishers. (Original work published 1970)

Fisher, B., & Alberti, R. E. (2000). *Rebuilding: When your relationship ends* (3rd ed.). Atascadero, CA: Impact Publishers.

Dr. Alberti, a pioneer in assertiveness training, is a fellow (psychotherapy and media psychology) of the American Psychological Association. His work has received international recognition as the "gold standard" for psychological self-help.

Population for whom the technique is appropriate: Adults, college students, adolescents

Cautionary notes: Individuals with social phobias, high levels of anxiety, or both are contraindicated.

Over the past 4 decades, assertiveness and social skills training have been such commonplace components of the preparation of psychotherapists and other human service professionals that there exist few dimensions of the process that are not widely known to those of us who endeavor to help clients grow and change. Indeed, the procedures have been so integrated into other therapies that you may be asking, "Why are we still talking about assertiveness training? Isn't that one of those cognitive-behavioral procedures that has been relegated to the history books?"

Well, perhaps it's worth another look. The social movements of the 1970s that helped popularize assertiveness as a tool for empowerment and, to a lesser degree, even social change, have indeed faded with the political times. In contrast, however, the number of people who need help with interpersonal effectiveness is arguably greater than it was 30 years ago. Women who have advanced into roles of increasing career responsibility, young people who face increased demands to conform and pressure to rebel, consumers who are bombarded with pushy salespeople, workers who are "downsized" into job seeking after 20 years with the same employer, clients whose social phobia is exacerbated by skill deficits … Is there anyone who doesn't face demands to act more assertively these days?

Overcoming obstacles to change is a routine topic in assertiveness training and therapy groups. Often neglected, however, are strategies for dealing with the most formidable obstacles of all: the significant other people in the client's or trainee's life. To help budding asserters to deal head-on with that obstacle, the assignment, "Helping Others Deal With the 'New Assertive You'" was developed.

As you have grown in your own assertiveness, you have noticed changes in those around you. Your family, friends, coworkers, and others may have found it strange to notice that you have changed, and they may not be altogether happy about it: "What's going on with Harold recently? He's been acting very strangely. I asked him if I could borrow his car, and he actually said no!"

People will notice. They'll wonder why you are a grump or no longer a pushover. Some will applaud the changes; others will decry them—but they'll notice. It's common for students of assertiveness to overdo it at first. That makes the changes even more noticeable. Others may see you as suddenly aggressive, and you may be. If you are saying no for the first time in your life, you may get a kick out of really belting it out. "NO—and don't ask me again!"

If you overreact like that and flaunt your newfound self-expression, others will resent it. Not only are you no longer predictable, you are a royal pain in the neck! From the point of view of your friends and family, you may appear to be a pushy so-and-so—someone they just as soon would have go away. If, instead, you're too tentative about your assertions, others may notice that something has changed but not realize what you are trying to do.

It may be a good idea to let those closest to you know what you are trying to do—at least those you can trust—and perhaps even to ask them for help. Becoming assertive will involve your friends eventually if you are successful—there is no reason to hide it from those who could help you along the way.

You will need to develop some sensitivity to the reactions of others to your assertiveness. You can teach yourself to observe the effects and to watch for the subtle clues others will give to their reactions. The same nonverbal behaviors we have stressed in your assertive expression are involved. You've learned to pay attention to your own eye contact, posture, gestures, facial expression, voice, and distance. Tune in to the same characteristics in your listeners to help you know how you are coming across and to gauge how they are responding.

Consider involving your most trusted friend(s) in your work on assertiveness. Try these steps:

How a Friend Can Help

Someone has trusted you enough to ask for your help.

A friend, relative, roommate, coworker, lover, or significant other has asked you to read this brief statement because he or she has decided to make some changes. The process your friend is pursuing is called assertiveness training (AT), and its purpose is to help folks become more capable in expressing themselves.

Assertiveness often is confused with aggressiveness, so let's clear that up right now. Learning to be more assertive does not mean learning to push other folks around to get your way. It does mean standing up for yourself, expressing feelings directly and firmly, and establishing equal relationships that take the needs of both people into account.

Your friend may be reading a book, taking a class, working with a counselor, or practicing alone or in a group—there are lots of ways AT can be effective. It may take a few weeks, or even a few months, but you'll begin to notice some changes. Your friend may be expressing opinions about where to go out to eat, what's wrong with the government, how you clean up your half of the apartment, maybe saying no when you ask a favor, taking more initiative in conversation, giving more compliments than before, or even showing anger once in a while. Not to worry. If these new actions were intended to threaten you, your friend would not have asked you to read this!

Most people find that increased assertiveness makes folks even more pleasant to be around. They're more spontaneous, less inhibited, more honest and direct, and feel better about themselves, maybe even feel healthier!

So, how do you figure into this? Well, your friend has asked you to read this so you'll know a little about what's going on in her or his life right now and better understand the changes you may be seeing in the coming weeks and months.

You are evidently a trusted person in your friend's life, because it can be risky to let someone know about changes one plans to make: sort of like telling people about your dreams or your New Year's resolutions. If things don't work out, the person is vulnerable to some real hurt. Please honor the trust that has been extended to you.

Here are some ways you can help:

- Find out something about how your friend hopes to change, so you'll know what to look for.
- When you see the desired changes—however small—give him a pat on the back.
- Be honest in your own dealings with your friend, including pointing out when she goes overboard trying to be assertive.
- Read up on assertiveness yourself.
- Actively coach your friend in specific behavior changes, such as improved eye contact or voice tone.
- Be a good model of assertiveness yourself.
- Help your friend rehearse special situations, such as job interviews or confrontations.

You'll likely find your thoughtfulness repaid manyfold. And you may find yourself learning a thing or two in the process!

FIGURE 3.1   How a friend can help. (Adapted from Alberti, R. E., & Emmons, M. L. 1995. *Your perfect right: A guide to assertive living* (7th ed.). Atascadero, CA: Impact Publishers. Reprinted with permission of publisher.)

- Tell your closest friend—be sure this is someone you can trust—that you are learning to be more assertive.
- Keep in mind that you will need to be careful when telling certain people about your attempts to become assertive. Those who have your best interests at heart will be supportive. Others—even some close friends and intimates—actually may undermine your efforts. Choose carefully.
- Tell your friend something about what it means to you to be assertive and the differences between assertion and aggression.
- Ask your friend if she will help you.
- If she agrees, decide together on some specific behaviors she can watch for, and ask her to give you periodic feedback on how you are doing in those specifics—particularly the nonverbal components of behavior.
- Recognize that sometimes your assertiveness will lead you to say no to your friend, or otherwise say or do something against her preferences. Discuss that with her in advance and as it occurs.
- Avoid announcing, "I'm going to be assertive now!"—as if that excuses rudeness or other inappropriate behavior or allows you to avoid responsibility for your actions.
- If you are developing your assertiveness as a part of some form of therapy, you need not disclose that to anyone. Simply talk about your goals, and point out that you are learning new skills.
- If you are working with a therapist or other trainer, you may wish to bring your friend in for an orientation/training session.
- If you decide to go ahead and let a friend in on your plans, you may find the following statement (Figure 3.1) useful in orienting that person to the assertiveness training process. Feel free to copy it, so long as you include the credit line at the bottom.

Gaining Additional Perspectives in Relationships

Therapists: Steve Andreas, MA, and Connirae Andreas, PhD

Affiliation: Neuro-Linguistic Programming Trainers and Consultants

Major works:

Andreas, S. (2006). *Six blind elephants: Understanding ourselves and each other: Vol. 1. Fundamental principles of scope and category.* Moab, UT: Real People Press.
Andreas, S., & Andreas, C. (1987). *Change your mind and keep the change.* Moab, UT: Real People Press.
Andreas, S., & Andreas, C. (1989). *Heart of the mind.* Moab, UT: Real People Press.

Population for whom the technique is appropriate: All adults; children above the age of 10 or 12
Cautionary notes: The process can be used with some children ages 6 to 10 if it is made into a game. Children may need some direction and assistance in carrying out homework. Only use with children if it goes easily, as the type of mental processing required does not mature at the same time for every child.

Over 200 years ago, Robert Burns wrote the following (in modern English):

> Oh, would some power the gift to give us,
> To see ourselves as others see us!
> It would from many a blunder free us,
> And foolish notion.

The ability to experience ourselves as someone else does is an essential part of any good relationship. Without some understanding of how others experience events differently than we do, the responses of others would be forever a puzzle to us, as it is to an autistic person. The basic idea of the importance of learning how to "walk in someone else's shoes" is a very old one and has been widely recognized in the field of psychology, as well as by many spiritual traditions.

However, few people have this ability, because it is a skill that is seldom taught in explicit detail. Fortunately, it is possible to help clients learn this key relationship ability through a simple exercise, which can then become a homework assignment. Although simple to understand and easy to do, it often has profound and far-reaching effects. Clients often are surprised that when they become naturally able to understand others' points of view better, their relationships improve, and they feel more resourceful in dealing with family, friends, and coworkers.

The homework assignment involves teaching the client three fundamental perceptual positions. Each offers a unique kind of wisdom, and together they provide a surprisingly complete range of information for finding our own solutions to the inevitable conflicts and challenges that occur as we relate with others.

Three Perceptual Positions

1. **Self Position.** When I think of an interaction with another person, I experience it from my own point of view, looking out of my eyes, and seeing the other person. This is the position that most of us assume that we are in all the time.

    When I use this position, I am in touch with my own needs and can pursue my own interests and goals.

    If I only use self position, I am like a small child, egocentric and selfish, and others' needs and desires mean nothing to me.

2. **Observer Position.** I can observe the same interaction between myself and someone else from the outside, as if I were an observer watching two strangers on a television set. From this position, I can dispassionately observe the interaction between us—the sequence of words, gestures, and expressions that occur in the communication. When I use this position, I am able to see my own behavior more clearly, as if I were watching someone else, and also see how each of us is responding to the other—free of evaluation and judgment. If I only use the observer position, I become detached and distant, and life becomes

meaningless, similar to a character in an existentialist novel.

3. **Other Position.** I experience the interaction between us from the perspective of the other person. I become the other and experience what it is like to be this person in this situation, looking out at me. When I do this well, I take on the other person's beliefs, attitudes, values, knowledge, and personal history to the best of my knowledge and ability. When I use this position, I am able to gain a deep, rich, and detailed experiential understanding of what someone else is experiencing. If I only use other position, I live for someone else rather than for myself, a life of self-sacrifice in which others' needs and desires always take precedence over my own.

Discussion

Each of these positions has unique advantages and limitations. The ability to fully utilize all three gives us all the advantages and leaves the limitations behind. Similar to many skills, at first this may be a mostly conscious process, but with practice it becomes predominantly unconscious and natural. Here are some examples of how this exercise has helped people spontaneously become more resourceful:

One woman (Pearson, 1997) wanted to pleasure her husband during lovemaking, but she had been disgusted by one aspect of it that her husband liked. When she took his position and discovered how much he enjoyed it, she said, "Wow, I didn't know he liked it this much!" When she moved to observer position, she saw herself being kind to her husband, giving him an experience that was very special to him. When she returned to self position, all the disgust was gone, replaced with happiness at being able to please him so much.

One man, while exploring a difficult quarrel with his wife, discovered how she felt shocked and attacked by some of the things that he had said, when from his own perspective he had seen it as simply fully expressing his frustration and confusion. This led him to take a much gentler and more compassionate approach in talking with her. And when he told her what he had experienced in taking her position, she was moved to tears that he finally understood how she felt.

Perceptual Positions Exercise

These directions are designed to provide an example of a general path; different people will need more instruction on different aspects, have different questions or concerns requiring explanation, and so on. After at least one (and preferably two or three) guided experience of the process, the client is asked to find a quiet place and do the same process daily with one or two incidents from each day.

1. **Choose Event.** "Fred, I want you to think of a minor difficulty that you have had with your wife Ann. When first learning this method, it is very important to use a small difficulty. Later, when you are more experienced and fluent with the steps of the process, it will be much easier and more useful to process major issues."

2. **Self Position.** "Relive this experience from your own point of view. You are seeing out of your own eyes, hearing with your own ears, and having the feelings you had in response to those events."

3. **Observer Position.** "Now I want you to allow yourself to move out to the side to a comfortable position from which you can see yourself and Ann equally well (or allow the scene to move around until you are in a comfortable position to observe them).

   From this position, run the exact same videotape that you just saw, but from this new perspective, seeing and hearing all those events again, this time simply with an attitude of curiosity about what you can learn about this interaction between Fred and Ann over there.

   If you have any feelings other than curiosity or a gentle compassion for them, those feelings probably belong to either Fred or Ann, and you can let those feelings move over there to where they belong.

Now take a little while to allow your whole being to memorize what this observer position is like, so that it will be easy to return to it in the future whenever you might find it useful."

4. **Other Position.** "Now look over at Ann and notice how her way of being in the world is expressed nonverbally in her voice tone, her tempo, her postures, movements, and gestures, and so on. Temporarily leaving behind your own beliefs, values, and assumptions, gently move toward her and step into her, so that you can experience this situation as she does.

As Ann, run that same video of that event, as you discover what it is like to be her in this interaction. Take some time to do this, again with a sense of curiosity about what you can learn from this. You may want to repeat the video once or twice to be sure that you experience it all thoroughly from this perspective."

5. **Observer Position.** "Now return to the observer position. Keeping all the learnings of the other position, you can completely let go of that position, and again run the video, noticing any changes in how you experience these events from this observer position after having experienced Ann's perspective."

6. **Self Position.** "Now return to your own self position, and again run the video, noticing any changes in how you experience these events from this position after having experienced Ann's perspective and the observer position."

Summary

A person can continue to move from one position to another as long as it continues to provide useful information. Usually we end in self position, because this is the way we can most resourcefully live most of our lives. (However, if an experience is very intense, the client may feel more comfortable and resourceful ending in the observer position.)

Using this process on a situation always clarifies it, sometimes profoundly. The learnings that are made in each position carry over and enrich the others. Usually this exercise results in the client's accomplishing the following:

1. Becoming clearer about wants, needs, and goals
2. Feeling more personally resourceful
3. Becoming more intuitively accurate about others' experiencing
4. Being more compassionate toward others
5. Having more access to creative solutions
6. Experiencing greater wisdom in relationships

Similar to any other skill, learning how to enter each position and experience it, and learning how to spontaneously shift quickly and easily from one position to another, improves with practice. Using this process as homework hones the skill at the same time that it clarifies and enriches situations that have been difficult and troublesome. These new learnings are felt understandings, not mental ones, and they carry over into the daily interactions with the other person, changing how the other person is perceived, understood, and responded to.

Aligning Perceptual Positions

Once the client has learned the basic exercise presented in the previous paragraphs, the benefits can be increased dramatically through additional exercises in which each position becomes carefully aligned. Everyone that we have worked with so far has had misalignments, in which some aspects of the positions are out of place. For instance, a feeling belonging to the other person may be located in the self position, a self voice may be located in the observer position, or the eyes in the self position may be looking from a point 3 inches to the left of the actual eyes, and so on. These misalignments prevent us from gaining everything we can from the positions. Learning to align the positions increases the purity of our access to each position and the resulting benefits.

Ideally, the observer position is at the same eye level as the two people in the interaction. If the observer eye level is higher, it is likely that the observations will become criticisms. Moving the position down to eye level will change criticism to neutral observation. This simple move, when practiced over time, has helped people become less judgmental.

If the observer is not equidistant from the two people being observed, there is usually a tendency to take the side of the person who is closer. Moving the observer position to be the same distance from the two people will eliminate this bias.

One client had been tested and diagnosed as biologically depressed and needing antidepressants. Through aligning his relationship with his mother, he discovered that "his" voice was actually his mother's voice stuck in his throat. After allowing his mother's voice to return to her, making room for his own voice, his depression spontaneously cleared up over the next 2 weeks. For more information about how to do these alignment exercises, the many other alignment criteria, and how to deal with objections, see Andreas (1991, 1992) and Andreas and Andreas (1991).

The basic perceptual positions exercise comes from the field of Neuro-Linguistic Programming. The alignment criteria and exercises were developed by Connirae Andreas.

References

Andreas, C. (1991). *Aligning perceptual positions* [Videotape]. Lakewood, CO: NLP Comprehensive.

Andreas, C. (1992). *The aligned* self [Audiotape set]. Lakewood, CO: NLP Comprehensive.

Andreas, C., & Andreas, T. (1991). Aligning perceptual positions: A new distinction in NLP. *Anchor Point, 5*(2), 1–6.

Burns, Robert. (1994). *Selected poems.* NY: Penguin Classics.

Pearson, J. (1997). Aligning perceptual positions in sex therapy. *Anchor Point, 11*(1), 13–18.

"Talking Back" to Distorted Thinking

Therapist: Patricia Arredondo, EdD

Affiliation: Associate Vice Chancellor of Academic Affairs and Professor of Counseling Psychology, University of Wisconsin–Milwaukee; National Certified Counselor and Licensed Psychologist; APA Fellow of Divisions 17 & 45; American Counseling Association Living Legend; Owner and President, Empowerment Workshops, Inc., Boston

Major works:

Arredondo, P., Toporek, R., Brown, S. P., Jones, J., Locke, D.C., Sanchez, J., et al. (1996). Operationalization of the multicultural counseling competencies. *Journal of Multicultural Counseling and Development, 24,* 42–78.

Santiago-Rivera, A., Arredondo, P., & Gallardo-Cooper, G. (2002). *Counseling Latinos y la familia.* Thousand Oaks, CA: Sage.

Population for whom the technique is appropriate: Primarily adult populations but can be used with older adolescents

Cautionary notes: Therapists and counselors using this technique should be familiar with David Burns's *Feeling Good* (1980) and Aaron Beck's cognitive-behavioral therapy (CBT).

The "talking back" technique is based on the principles of cognitive-behavioral therapy (CBT) and aims to disrupt what Burns (1980) describes as automatic thoughts associated with a cognitive distortion. This technique was used in conjunction with certain chapters from *Feeling Good.* A worksheet, based on the "triple column technique" exercise in the book, was given to clients as a homework assignment. At times, they were prompted to write down the automatic thoughts when in session but generally they prepared everything outside of the clinical session.

I decided to apply the technique with the adult women and men who presented with issues of poor self-worth and self-efficacy. They were constantly being self-critical, some were adult children of alcoholics, and others manifested behaviors symptomatic of adult children. Clients' automatic thoughts and self-assessments were highly influenced by old tapes from authority figures, like their parents. In other words, the client's self-appraisal was primarily informed by others' assessments in spite of their accomplishments and station in life (all were professionals). As adults, these women and men gave away their power to authority figures and continued to minimize their capabilities and self-worth. I would point out their erroneous thinking and they would recognize the automatic distortion about what someone said or what they perceived the other was thinking, but they were very conditioned to assume there was something wrong about them, something negative was going to befall them, and/or that they were powerless to stand up for their ideas. In spite of their ability to comprehend the irrationality of their automatic thought processing, my clients could not readily shake the long-standing negative thought processes.

The self-depreciating thoughts led to a range of feelings—guilt, feeling sorry for oneself, helplessness, anxiety, and depression. More often than not, these were deep-seated feelings, ones that had been felt for many years. The thoughts triggered emotions that then led to behavioral responses—not speaking up, agreeing to an activity that was too complicated, over-preparing for a work task, assuming no one wanted to meet them and, therefore, leaving a social event early, finishing someone's sentence, and so forth. In therapy, we discussed the relationship between thoughts, feelings, and behaviors.

Burns identified 10 types of cognitive distortions. The most common among my clients were the "overgeneralization, fortune-telling, and magnification/catastrophizing." Some of the more common thoughts were "My boss will never like my work," "I can't do anything right," "I am simply incompetent," and "My colleagues will soon realize that I am not as good as they think I am."

The Burns's triple column technique was the basis for the homework (Burns, 1980, pp. 60, 62). The clients would write down (codify) their more common automatic thoughts, categorize these by the type of cognitive distortion, and then enter the rational response. For example, if the thought is "My boss thinks I am incapable of doing the assignment so she will probably not ask me to do it," a rational and empowered response might state: "I have been doing these types of projects for the past 2 years and always get praise for successful outcomes. I treat this assignment like all others—just doing my job." In short, this written activity provides a logical formula for identifying the automatic negative thought, labeling it, refuting it, and replacing it with a positive statement about oneself. Clients were asked to limit themselves to three automatic thoughts per assignment.

These thoughts were ones we had already discussed in session. I generally pointed out the patterns of self-reference that were overly self-critical and questioned the basis for such thinking. Through discussion, we would unravel the thought, going back to early life encounters with parents or siblings who, through various types of engagement, introduced negative feedback and even bullying behavior. It was my role to discuss with clients the connection between the contemporary individual(s) contributing to their self-doubts and the historical figures. This cognitive process was helpful and a necessary step to the written activity.

References

Beck, A. T. (1975). *Cognitive therapy and the emotional disorders.* Madison, CT: International Universities Press.

Burns, D. (1980). *Feeling good.* New York: New American Library.

Web Surfing to Reach Your Vocational Fantasy

Therapist: Edward S. Beck, EdD, CCMHC, NCC

Affiliation: Susquehanna Institute, Harrisburg, Pennsylvania; Rosemont College, Philadelphia, Pennsylvania

Major work:

Beck, E. S., Seiler, G., & Brooks, D. K., Jr. (1987). *Training standards for mental health counseling*. Alexandria, VA: American Mental Health Counselors Association.

Dr. Beck is the author of more than 20 articles on standards, ethics, and professional affairs. He was the 1992 Counselor of the Year of the American Mental Health Counselors Association and received the Practitioner of the Year for 2000 from the International Association of Marriage and Family Counselors of the American Counseling Association.

Population for whom the technique is appropriate: Computer-literate high school, postsecondary/trade school, college, young adult, and career-changing adults
Cautionary notes: None

Note: Research assistance provided by Jessica R. Smith, Albright College, Summer Intern Susquehanna Institute

In the 21st century, one's vocational choices will be limited only by one's inability to fantasize and master the ever-growing and improving database of occupational and placement information. In the early 1990s, a daily update of the help wanted ads in the local newspaper was considered to be the most comprehensive list of jobs. Until the mid-1990s, you might have gone to the local newsstand and bought a national or big city newspaper and learned of positions in other areas.

The World Wide Web has become by far the most comprehensive source of career information, placement information, and sources of jobs all over the world. People who work, need career information, and need access to jobs (which is most, if not all, of us) must learn how to master the technology and learn to fantasize vocationally (Beck, 1998) using the technique of web surfing. Getting clients to overcome their fear of technology may be a major obstacle in helping them get the information they need and become linked to the up-to-date, accurate career information and job listings that are available in unprecedented numbers. Clients need to be motivated to learn how to web surf with fanciful abandon to find that information. The payoff for the client to learn this technique is that they have a lifelong researching skill, not just for careers, but also for other information.

After all the tests and assessments, after all the career-decision-making focus techniques, comes the homework. It's "get busy" time to research the client's occupation. There are several important key databases for up-to-date career information that clients should explore.

Perhaps the client wants to make a quick online search by reading Richard Bolles's *What Color Is Your Parachute?* Web site at http://www.jobhuntersbible.com. Next she may want to look to the Bureau of Labor Statistics home Web site at http://stats.bls.gov to obtain the various links to national and regional information on careers and the economy. If she is looking for jobs with equal opportunity employers, she might find the information at http://www.blackcollegian.com (the career and job site for African American college students) very helpful.

If these pages do not get your client where she wants to be, she may want to catch a linked wave to the *Occupational Outlook Handbook* home page at http://www.bls.gov/oco, where she will find specific information about jobs, earnings, employment outlook, training and qualifications, and sources of relevant information. From there she may want to see what is available at America's Job Bank http://www.ajb.dni.us/index.html or go to the 250,000 job listings at www.monster.com or perhaps look for a federal job at www.jobsfed.com. There are hundreds of valuable career development sites on the Internet. Clients can use all the major search engines to look for jobs and career development information. Many employers want résumés sent electronically via e-mail to get quick feedback. This approach is efficient, economical (free in most instances), and, above all, fruitful and fun. It is homework that could and should be done on a regular basis throughout one's life to help achieve one's vocational fantasy.

Reference

Beck, E. S. (2011). Vocational fantasy: An empowering technique. In H. G. Rosenthal (Ed.), *Favorite counseling and therapy techniques* (pp. 47–49). Philadelphia: Accelerated Development/Taylor & Francis.

Reviewing Therapy Notes

Therapist: Judith S. Beck, PhD

Affiliation: Director, Beck Institute for Cognitive Therapy and Research, Bala Cynwyd, Pennsylvania; Clinical Assistant Professor of Psychology in Psychiatry, University of Pennsylvania, Philadelphia

Major works:

Beck, J. S. (1995). *Cognitive therapy: Basics and beyond.* New York: Guilford Press.

Beck, A. T., Freeman, A., Davis, D., & Associates. (2004). *Cognitive therapy of personality disorders* (2nd ed.). New York: Guilford Press.

Dr. Beck is a Distinguished Founding Fellow and Past President of the Academy of Cognitive Therapy.

Population for whom the technique is appropriate: Appropriate, when adapted, for clients of all ages, with any problems or diagnoses, in individual, group, couples, or family therapy, inpatient or outpatient

Cautionary notes: Provide a rationale for reviewing therapy notes and collaboratively design the homework.

A top homework priority in cognitive therapy is having clients review their therapy notes regularly (Beck, 1995). Throughout each therapy session, I continually ask myself, "What do I wish my client would remember this week (and in the future)?" Because research has shown that clients forget almost everything they hear in a doctor's office, I try to have clients record anything I want them to remember. Many clients write in a notebook or on index cards (or I will do the writing for them if they are unable or unwilling). Other clients prefer to listen to a short audiotape or CD with a summary of important points that we compose jointly toward the end of the session.

Sometimes I have to be creative in suggesting ways clients can remember what we covered. Clients who cannot read may have a supportive friend or family member who can read therapy notes to them. They can draw pictures to prompt their memory of important ideas. Clients may be able to borrow an iPod, CD player, cassette player or play their audio recording several times a day in the car.

At the beginning of treatment, most clients do not know what would be beneficial for them to record. When we finish discussing a problem or issue, I generally ask the client, "Can you summarize what we've just talked about?" or "What's the main message here?" or "What do you want to remember about this [problem/discussion]?"

If clients compose a reasonable summary, I ask them to write it down (or I write it down for them). If not, I usually say something such as, "That's good, but I wonder if it might be more helpful to phrase it like this: ..." If I judge that the flow of the session will be interrupted or the client will react negatively, I wait until the end of the session to suggest that the client record the most important points.

How do I judge what is important for clients to record? At the very least I ask patients to record their homework assignment. (In fact, I often ask them to start a written assignment in session and complete it for homework.) A second category is the steps involved in skills they have learned during the session, so they can practice them each day at home. In the future, especially under stress, they may forget to do, or forget how to do, tasks they have learned. A third category involves helping clients integrate their modified thoughts and beliefs. Clients often find it useful to write them in a "new idea/old idea" format. For example:

Old idea—If others are unhappy, it's my fault and it means I'm bad.

New idea—People may or may not be unhappy because of me. It's impossible to please everyone all the time. "Bad" people deliberately hurt other people over and over again for their own pleasure.

Old idea—If I don't reach my full potential, I'm a failure.

New idea—Success and failure are on a continuum. If I try to achieve my full potential at work, I will sacrifice reaching my potential in terms of family, friends, leisure, personal affairs, and so on.

A fourth category is more behavioral, aiding clients in remembering what to do in particular situations or when they are in distress.

If my mood is starting to spiral downward and I can't respond to my negative thoughts, try four or five of the following:

1. Leave the situation, if appropriate.
2. Call Peter or Sue.
3. Do quick hard exercises (bike, walk, exercise video).
4. Self-soothe: Bathe, meditate, do relaxation exercises, or listen to upbeat music.
5. Distract: Watch television or read *People* magazine.
6. Read coping cards.
7. Do a dysfunctional thought record.

If these don't help enough and I'm at risk of suicide, call my therapist (phone #_____) or go to _____ Hospital emergency room.

If I don't want to take my medication, remind myself:

- I have suffered long enough.
- I haven't gotten better by *not* taking medicine.
- I'm starting off slowly, so as to minimize side effects.
- I won't ever know if medication will be effective unless I try it.

It's a sign of strength if I do something that goes against my grain but is potentially helpful.

Reading these cards only when the client is in distress is unlikely to be sufficient. Clients should read many of them on a regular basis. Reviewing them at breakfast, lunch, and dinner, for example, and on an as-needed basis, makes it more likely clients will heed them or believe them when they are under stress.

Reference

Beck, J. S. (1995). *Cognitive therapy: Basics and beyond.* New York: Guilford Press.

Together Time

Therapists: Dorothy S. Becvar, PhD, and Raphael J. Becvar, PhD

Affiliations: Dorothy S. Becvar is a Licensed Marital and Family Therapist, a Licensed Clinical Social Worker, an AAMFT approved supervisor, and a national board certified counselor for the Haelan Centers. She is also a Professor of Social Work at St. Louis University.
Raphael J. Becvar is a Licensed Marital and Family Therapist, a Licensed Psychologist, and an AAMFT approved supervisor in private practice in St. Louis, Missouri.

Major works:

Becvar, D. (1997). *Soul healing: A spiritual orientation in counseling and therapy*. New York: Basic Books.
Becvar, D., & Becvar, R. (2008). *Family therapy: A systemic integration* (7th ed.). Boston: Allyn & Bacon.
Becvar, R., & Becvar, D. (1998). *Pragmatics of human relationships*. Iowa City, IA: Geist & Russell.
Together and separately, the Drs. Becvar are the authors of more than 80 professional publications.

Population for whom the technique is appropriate: Couples
Cautionary notes: None

Regardless of the presenting problem, we have found in our work with couples who have been together for some time that there is the tendency for them to have settled down too much and to have forgotten how to enjoy one another. Whether married or not, the magic has gone out of the relationship and the focus primarily is on what is going wrong rather than what is going right. The more the members of the couple attempt to solve their problems, the more stuck they become. Perhaps one member has become a workaholic or has had an affair. Or perhaps what is described is constant conflict, the inability to communicate effectively, or both. Ultimately, sometimes as a last-ditch effort, sometimes in an attempt to prevent further deterioration, they decide to come to therapy.

After having the clients tell their stories, which generally consist of laundry lists of problems they are experiencing, we ask them to describe their desired solutions. We then ask them to recount their experiences in the families in which they grew up and to describe how and when they met, the early period of their courtship, and how the relationship has evolved over time. We often ask each to tell the other what it was that attracted them in the first place and what it was they fell in love with. We now have a good sense of where they have been and where they would like to go. Ideally, we also have created a context that enables the couple to feel somewhat hopeful about what is possible.

Generally we have found by this point that, like most couples in trouble, the clients are not spending much time together and that when they do, fuses are short and tempers flare easily. Therefore, toward the end of the session we often make the suggestion that they spend 15 to 30 minutes with each other at some point every day during the coming week. We may need to spend time in the session allowing the members of the couple to negotiate when they might take this time. We often need to remind them that there are 24 hours in every day, and it is up to them to decide how these hours are to be used. We emphasize the potential benefits to be derived from making their relationship a priority.

Once a time has been selected, we recommend that it be considered inviolate. We also suggest the following guidelines:

1. There is to be no discussion of problems during their together time.
2. There is to be no discussion of work, children, money, or other mundane, perhaps "hot," issues during their together time.
3. As much as is possible, there are to be no intrusions from children, phone, television, newspaper, and so on, during their together time.
4. The members of the couple are to take turns being in charge of their together time.
5. The person in charge of the together time picks an activity she or he believes the other would enjoy.

To help get the couple started, we may provide ideas for activities, which include playing a game, taking a walk, giving a back rub or foot rub, dancing, or listening to music. We remind them that having fun does not have to cost a lot of money. We also suggest that rather than "working at" the relationship, which implies drudgery, what is more important is taking time to be creative about their relationship.

In making the assignment for together time, we are careful to assure the couple that we are not ignoring their problems. Rather, we explain that our goal is to enable them to generate some positive energy so that they will be able to deal with their problems more effectively. We remind them that they didn't get where they are overnight and that it will take some time to achieve their goals.

Although we don't say so, we believe that there is a limited amount of energy available to any relationship system. It is our belief that the more energy that is devoted to positive interactions, the less energy will be available for negative interactions. It also is our hope that the members of the couple will rediscover what it was that brought them together in the first place. As they begin to see each other in a more favorable light, it is hoped they will be less tuned into and sensitive about every little misstep. As therapy proceeds, we often build on these assumptions by expanding the assignment for together time to include a date night.

The basic guidelines for a date night are the same as those previously specified. The difference is that the person in charge must invite the other person out for a date, specifying only time and appropriate clothing. For example, "I would like to take you out on Saturday night about 8:00 p.m. Please wear your jeans and bring a sweater." Where they actually are to go and what they will be doing, however, is kept as a surprise until the appointed time. If a babysitter is required, the person in charge also needs to make the appropriate arrangements.

We like to help couples shift their attitude from one of being wary that the other is "out to get" him or her to being suspicious that the other is trying to make him or her happy. We have found that helping clients to create together time is often useful in this regard. And as they begin to enjoy each other more, they are better able to achieve their desired goals.

Community Volunteerism: Identifying Influences and a Plan

Therapists: Marla Berg-Weger, PhD, LCSW, and Julie Birkenmaier, PhD, LCSW

Affiliation: Licensed Clinical Social Workers and Faculty, Saint Louis University School of Social Work, St. Louis, Missouri

Major works:

Berg-Weger, M. (2005). *Social work and social welfare: An invitation*. Boston: McGraw-Hill.

Birkenmaier, J., & Berg-Weger, M. (2007). *The practicum companion for social work: Integrating class and field work* (2nd ed.). Boston: Allyn & Bacon.

Dr. Berg-Weger has additional publications in the areas of driving and older adults, family caregiving, and social work education. Dr. Birkenmaier has published work in the areas of community development, financial empowerment, field education, and older adults.

Population for whom the technique is appropriate: Older adolescents and adults of all ages experiencing a transition in their lives or mild depression

Cautionary notes: Not appropriate for individuals in a high state of immediate crisis or clients with severe and persistent mental illness. This technique is most useful as termination approaches and long-term strategies for mental health are being formulated.

Introduction

Many individuals and families facing stress from change or loss struggle with an inadequate social support network and isolation. Furthermore, many individuals and families without strong ties to a community fail to enjoy the fulfillment and satisfaction that could be gained through making contributions to a community. Volunteering for community institutions and activities can expand one's social supports through contacts with helping institutions, neighbors, and other community leaders. In addition, involvement in one or more aspects of a community can enhance one's mental health by facilitating an active and positive contribution to one's environment.

When individuals face a multitude of stresses, volunteering in the community may not appear to be an immediate aid. In fact, clients may not consider volunteerism to be important. However, volunteering can alter a client's perspective on his or her issues and provide other benefits, such as new purpose and direction in life, successes on which to build, and even employment contacts. The extent to which one's family of origin considered community involvement and volunteerism important may strongly impact an individual's perception of community involvement. The use of a genogram can facilitate a discussion regarding family patterns of volunteerism.

This exercise can assist clients to do the following:

1. Reflect on their previous contribution(s) toward the community.
2. Develop an understanding of the degree to which their caretakers/family of origin were involved in community affairs and how this may have shaped their perception of the importance of community involvement.
3. Develop an appreciation of the importance of contributing to communal efforts.
4. Generate a plan to contribute to community efforts.

Application

Note that participation in the betterment of the community can include contributions toward the following:

A religious institution or tradition (church, synagogue, mosque)

Educational institutions (elementary, secondary, or higher education)

Cultural institutions (e.g., theater, visual arts, or musical organizations)

Advocacy/political affairs (e.g., helping with political campaigns, working voting polls, being involved in groups advancing political causes)

Organizations (e.g., volunteering in the office, organizing or participating in fundraising, serving on the board of directors)

Charitable efforts (e.g., organizing a food or clothing drive, working in a shelter, delivering materials to the poor, helping to build homes for the poor, serving in a soup line)

Neighborhood efforts or events (e.g., helping during a neighborhood block party, being an officer in a neighborhood organization)

Reflect on Previous Contributions to the Community

Questions such as the following can elicit the individual's perception and history of involvement in community affairs.

1. Outside of your current commitments (e.g., work and maintaining a home), what else occupies your time?
2. How much satisfaction do you gain from activities that consume your free time?
3. How do you feel about your community/neighborhood environment?
4. What do you think would improve your community/neighborhood environment?
5. What kinds of volunteer efforts have you had in the past? Currently?

Develop an Understanding of the Impact of the Patterns of Community Participation by the Family of Origin

The use of a family genogram can be useful in organizing an inquiry into contributions to the community by the client's family of origin. Make certain that the information included in the genogram is current. If you have previously introduced the idea of identifying dysfunctional patterns through the genogram, you may wish to introduce the idea that you will be revisiting the genogram by discussing the contributions made by various individuals (usually adults) to the community. Underscore the importance of identifying both individual strengths and weaknesses to get a complete picture of the individuals that compose the client's family of origin. Tell the client that you would like to hear about the community participation by members of the family of origin. As you discuss each adult on the genogram, ask the client to think about any contribution the individual made (or makes) to their community. Contributions may be small or large. If the client never saw an individual make a contribution to the community, ask whether he or she ever heard anyone comment about an activity carried out by an individual in the family. If the client cannot think of anything, it may be helpful to probe by asking such questions as, "Did he/she ever help in the neighborhood or church?" "Did he/she ever help organize anything at his/her child's school?"

After this exercise, ask the client questions about the perception of his or her family of origin regarding community participation, such as, "Did anyone in your family ever talk about contributing to the community?" "Did it seem important as you were growing up?" "How do you think your experiences in your family concerning community involvement shaped your life?"

Develop an Appreciation of the Importance of Contributing Toward Communal Efforts

To build on the previous discussion of the client's perception of volunteerism, ask questions about the benefits of volunteerism. If the client was able to identify some community contributions by family members, attempt to elicit their thoughts about the benefits of volunteerism by asking such questions as, "What do you think [relative's name] got out of volunteering?" "What kept him/her involved?" With clients unable to identify any family members who were involved in the community in a positive fashion, share your thoughts about the importance of community participation as an aspect of good mental health. Point out the possible benefits gained by making positive contributions to one's environment and the possible increase in social supports. Inquire about the client's thoughts concerning the possible positive effects of volunteerism on his or her mental health and the type of involvement that would be of most interest to him or her.

Generate a Plan

Develop a detailed plan for the client to volunteer toward the betterment of the community and incorporate volunteering into the treatment plan according to the plan.

Lights, Camera, Action!!! Making New Meanings Through Movies

Therapist: Bob Bertolino, PhD

Profession: Licensed Professional Counselor, Licensed Marriage and Family Therapist, and Licensed Clinical Social Worker (all in the state of Missouri); National Certified Counselor; Certified Rehabilitation Counselor

Affiliation: Assistant Professor, School of Health Professions, Department of Rehabilitation Counseling, Maryville University, St. Louis, Missouri; Senior Clinical Advisor, Youth In Need, Inc., St. Charles, Missouri

Major works:

Bertolino, B. (2010). *Strengths-based engagement and practice: Creating effective helping relationships.* Boston: Allyn & Bacon.

Bertolino, B., Kiener, M. S., & Patterson, R. (2009). *The therapist's notebook for strengths and solution-based therapies.* New York: Routledge.

Bertolino, B., & O'Hanlon, B. (2002). *Collaborative, competency-based counseling and therapy.* Boston: Allyn & Bacon.

Author or coauthor of 10 books and numerous book chapters and journal articles

Population for whom the technique is appropriate: Adolescents; also can be expanded for use with families of adolescents

Cautionary notes: If the movie has an "R" rating, be sure to obtain parental consent for the adolescent to watch the movie.

In working with adolescents, it is commonplace to hit the proverbial "brick wall." That is, oftentimes adolescents have heard the same lecture, speech, or rant from parents, teachers, law enforcement officials, and, yes, even therapists. As a result they tune out such people or respond with a hardy case of the "I don't knows" when asked about a particular view, action, or pattern of behavior. To counter this I often use the following assignment.

The use of stories maintains a rich tradition in many cultures. Movies extend the tradition of stories and captivate people of all ages. I have found movies to be particularly useful with adolescents in helping them to gain new perspectives. Whereas adolescents can become accustomed to others telling them how to feel, see the world, and act, movies allow for adolescents to create their own new experiences, views, and actions.

To use the approach, first clearly identify the concern that is to be addressed. By "clearly," I mean be sure that you have a behavioral description of the concern. That is, gravitate away from vague, nondescriptive terms and phrases such as "oppositional," "out of control," and "misbehavior" and determine what it looks like when the adolescent is *doing* the problematic behavior. For example, if a father defines the problem as his son being "oppositional" and "disrespectful," inquire as to what the son *does* when he's being oppositional and disrespectful. We can then learn that the son "yells and uses profanity" and "makes fun of others." The clearer you are about the concerns facing the adolescent or family or both, the more specific you can be with the movie that is assigned.

From there, I suggest the task of having the adolescent watch a movie that I have assigned. I have assembled a list from which to choose that tends to encapsulate many of the issues facing adolescents and families. For example, if I discovered that this child was picked on because of his weight, interests, and so on, I might use the movie *Angus* because it explores the life of an adolescent struggling with similar issues. The only instructions I give to the adolescent are to watch the movie, in its entirety, uninterrupted. I then inform the parent(s)/guardian of the task and ask him/her/them to rent or purchase the movie. I do not given a reason why a particular movie was selected, and I ask only that the adolescent be prepared to discuss the movie at the subsequent session. To set this up I usually say, "There's something in the movie for you and you'll know what it is. I'd like to talk about it next time." This *presupposes* that the adolescent will find some meaning regarding some aspect of the movie.

At the next session, I ask the adolescent, "What stuck out for you in the movie?" or "What did you notice about the movie?" By asking such questions, I am allowing the adolescent to speak about what stuck out or resonated with him or her, without giving my ideas and thoughts. Most often, the adolescent will describe a situation or character. Sometimes I don't even need to initiate the discussion as the adolescent is chomping at the bit to tell me what he or she experienced. From there we have a conversation about what stood out for him or her, be it a character, scene, or situation. I then search for new views that an adolescent may have developed as a result of watching the film by asking questions such as the following:

What stood out most for you about that character/scene/situation? How come _____ did what he/she did?

How do you think _____ got the idea that that was a good thing to do?

In your experience, where do people get the idea to act like _____ did in the movie?

How would you have felt if you were _____ in the movie?

What do you think it would have been like to be in that situation if you were _____ in the movie?

If an adolescent responds with "I don't know" or "Nothing," when asked what stood out for him or her, I select specific characters, scenes, or situations and ask some of the aforementioned questions. I then ask questions that either (a) build on a positive outcome that occurred in the movie, or (b) search for possible alternative views and actions that the adolescent might consider in the future.

Would you have done the same as _____ did in the movie? If so/not, how come?

What could he/she have done differently?

What would you have done if you were _____ in the movie?

What would you do if you found yourself in that situation?

Would you want to be seen as being like _____ in the movie? If so/not, how come?

To be seen in that way, what would you need to continue to do or do differently?

Because there are multiple meanings that adolescents can derive from movies, there are many opportunities for them to create new views and learn more positive actions and ways of dealing with adversity or problems in the future. Further, movies provide an excellent way of fostering the therapeutic relationship and an alternative pathway for indirectly addressing problematic views, behaviors, or both, of adolescents when direct methods just don't seem to work.

I recommend that therapists put together their own lists of movies to assign. As a starting point, here are a few that I suggest for adolescents. Remember that different adolescents will derive different meanings from different movies.

Title	Themes
Angus	Adolescent deals with adversity and trying to be "normal" only to discover that there is no such thing as normal. He can only be himself.
Simon Birch	Adolescent with physical disabilities learns to cope, make friends, and, ultimately, find hope.
The Mighty	Two boys, each facing adversity, befriend each other and learn to face the challenges that life presents them.
Dangerous Minds	A teacher who won't give up and a group of "unruly" students learn from each other about adversity, culture, family, education, poverty, and the possibilities for the future.
Stand and Deliver	Another teacher who won't give up helps his students to learn despite numerous roadblocks, including others' stigmatizing views and the challenges of everyday life in a poverty-stricken society.
Good Will Hunting	A brilliant, young adult struggles with responsibility and direction in a world full of possibilities.

Disrupting Enabling

Therapist: Claudia Black, PhD

Profession: Psychologist

Affiliation: Keynote Speaker/Trainer/Author Claudja Inc., dba Mac Publishing; Senior Clinical and Family Services Advisor, Las Vegas Recovery Center; Senior Editorial Advisor, Central Recovery Press

Major works:

Black, C. (1999). *Changing course.* Bainbridge Island, WA: Mac Publishing.

Black, C. (2001). *It will never happen to me* (2nd ed., rev.). Bainbridge Island, WA: Mac Publishing.

Black, C. (2006). *Family strategies.* Bainbridge Island, WA: Mac Publishing.

Author of 15 other books, 20 DVDs, and 7 CDs

Population for whom the technique is appropriate: Addicted clients wanting help in stopping their addictions and its manifestations, their partners, adolescent and adult-aged family members

Cautionary notes: This exercise is contraindicated unless the addict shows some motivation for treatment and recovery, as he or she will have an investment in the enabling and will demonstrate resistance. While counselors, friends, and family may be concerned that the addict will not have the insight to respond to the exercise, addicts are very aware of how others enable them. They count on it and learn to manipulate others to engage in enabling behaviors. If the addict has any motivation for recovery, he or she will engage in the exercise. Therapist needs to use discretion regarding maturity of adolescent-aged children and be assured that such children are, and will be, supported for engaging in this exercise.

Description

Addictive behavior is often supported by the enabling behavior of loved ones. Enabling behavior is any action that supports the delusion that addiction is not the problem and aids the addicted person in avoiding responsibility for his or her addiction related behavior. Be it a substance or behavioral addiction, family members and concerned others act out of fear and love in ways that make it easier for the addict to continue living in active addiction. The enabling behavior is a normal, natural response when a loved one is confronted with the frightening consequences of addiction, but its effects are contrary to their desire for the addict's self-destructive behavior to stop. Addiction counselors work diligently to explain enabling, and although family members may grasp the concept intellectually, they often slip back into their familiar and practiced behaviors.

This exercise serves as a form of intervention with enabling family members, strongly motivates families to stop shielding the addict from the consequences of his or her behavior, and also disrupts the addict's conscious manipulations.

The greatest power in this exercise lies in the family hearing the addict acknowledge how he or she has been enabled, as well as the message(s) the addict received from the enabling behavior. While family members enable to protect, it becomes painfully apparent they have been consciously used and manipulated. To hear this from the very person they thought they were helping strengthens their willingness to stop the enabling behavior. It fuels an appropriate and rightful anger—not righteous, but rightful. Family members understand at a deeper level that they have been participating in the addictive process in a manner that supports the continuation of active addiction.

The addict completes the writing assignment once for each family member and/or concerned other who is participating in the therapy process. Each participating family member/concerned other will only complete the assignment once.

The Exercise

A handout is given (often as a take home assignment, as time is needed to seriously consider the response) wherein they complete the following sentence stem exercise multiple times.

Addict's sentence stem is:

> One of the ways you enabled me was _____ (fill in the blank) ...
> and that behavior tells me _____ (fill in the blank)

The full sentence stem needs to be repeated minimally 3 to 5 times per family member. Each time it is repeated, the first part of the sentence stem "one of the ways you enabled me was" needs to be different from the previous response. Many times the response to the second part, "that behavior tells me," is repetitive of other responses. If so, it is simply reinforcing the point.

Examples:

- One of the ways you enabled me was loaning me money when I said I needed it for food. I used it for drugs. That behavior tells me I can get what I want from you by lying.
- One of the ways you enabled me was by not telling anyone how I really broke my leg (falling down the stairs when loaded). That behavior tells me you'll keep secrets for me so I can keep using.
- One of the ways you enabled me was when you lied to my boss about my whereabouts. That behavior tells me you'll cover for me.

Family member's/concerned others' sentence stem is:

> One of the ways I enabled you was _____ (fill in the blank) ...
> and that behavior tells you and me _____ (fill in the blank)
> and I commit to _____ (fill in the blank)

Family members repeat the entire sentence stem multiple times, filling in the blanks differently each time.

Examples:

- One of the ways I enable you is by not telling you when I find your stash and that behavior tells you and me that I am not willing to confront you about your addiction. I commit to no longer staying silent. I will tell you when I find your stash.
- One of the ways I enable you is when I sit and listen to you berate me verbally when we are out with friends and that behavior tells you and me that I am not deserving of respect. I commit to telling you in front of others that I don't want to be spoken to in that manner and if you do not immediately stop, I will physically leave.
- One of the ways I enable you is by cleaning up the physical messes you make when you are drunk (toss clothes, vomit, etc.) and that behavior tells you and me you don't have to be responsible for yourself or deal directly with the consequences of your own behavior. I commit to no longer cleaning up the wreckage of your behavior and will tell people why it is there.

The addict and one family member at a time are brought together, to sit facing each other. They each read their completed list. The addict always goes first, reading his or her list slowly. There is no dialogue. Then the family member takes his or her turn. The addict then shares another list with another family member, and the family member shares. This continues until all participants have had a chance to share.

This exercise is but one element in a process to positively impact a family addressing active addiction. The goal is to assist family members in recognizing their part of living in active addiction, motivating them to step outside the shadow of the addictive behavior patterns. Although family members do not have the power to stop the addict from his or her addictive behavior, they do have the ability to change their own behavior in ways that afford them more personal esteem and dignity, and allows the addict to be confronted with the unmitigated consequences of his or her own behavior—a critical factor in the motivation to attain healthier behaviors.

Trioing

Therapist: Richard N. Bolles, BA, STM

Affiliation: JobHuntersBible.com LLC

Major works:

Bolles, R. N. (2007). *The career counselor's handbook.* Berkeley, CA: Ten Speed Press.

Bolles, R. N. (2010). *What color is your parachute? 2010 Edition: A practical manual for job-hunters and career-changers.* Berkeley, CA: Ten Speed Press.

Bolles, R. N., & Bolles, M. E. (2005). *Job-hunting on the Internet.* Berkeley, CA: Ten Speed Press.

Richard Bolles's book *What Color Is Your Parachute?* is the best-selling job-hunting book of all time. Millions of people have now read this work, which has been translated in 20 languages!

Population for whom the technique is appropriate: Students as young as 17 years of age and adults

Cautionary notes: The purpose of this technique is to help people build their self-esteem, by identifying their own gifts—particularly their favorite gifts. It presumes the ability to write stories about one's own life. However, with those populations who cannot write but are able to tell stories about themselves, this technique also can be done without writing. It also presumes that the participants come from a culture where the concept of "individual achievement" is known and accepted. Those societies or cultures that allow people to speak only of what the community accomplished, wherein they were but one insignificant member, may have difficulty with this technique. Although, as Bernard Haldane has demonstrated, replacing the word "achievement" or "accomplishment" with "good experiences" often solves this problem in such cultures.

Description of the Technique

I first invented this technique in 1973 with John C. Crystal and published it in 1974. It builds upon the base of ideas laid out previously by Bernard Haldane (1947) regarding "motivated skills" and Crystal's "work autobiographies." In the case of the latter, Crystal had his students or clients write a detailed biography of their own lives, paying particular attention to their work experiences, which he subsequently analyzed for the particular gifts, talents, or skills that appeared again and again in that autobiography of his clients.

The problem was how to allow the clients to do this analysis, so that they might discover for themselves their own unique gifts or skills. We tried the obvious, first, which was to ask them to do the analysis independently. Here we discovered an interesting fact. Of course, some people were much better at this task than others, which was to be expected. But our surprise findings were that those who excelled at identifying the gifts or skills of others were blind to their own skills in their own autobiographies.

We moved, consequently, to having people work in pairs, helping each other identify the other's gifts. But as one member of the pair tended to be better at the task than the other member, they lapsed into a "teacher-pupil" relationship, which was greatly helpful when it was the teacher's turn to help the pupil, but not the other way around. The "teacher," blind to his or her own skills, often found little or no help from the pupil.

Therefore, we finally settled on a "trio" as the minimum group that could give true help to every member. And, when we worked with a much larger group, we broke that larger group into trios at the minimum, with perhaps one or two having to be "quartets" if the number in the group was not an exact multiple of three.

The technique, as it finally evolved into a finished form, which has now been used quite successfully worldwide goes like this:

1. Sitting quietly together, each member of the trio writes a one-page story of some incident in their life when they were truly enjoying themselves and felt some sense of achievement. (Alternatively, they may simply tell their story to a pocket tape recorder, if they have one.) A "good story" will typically have these parts to it:

a. A goal: what you wanted to accomplish

b. Some kind of hurdle, obstacle, or constraint that you faced in achieving that goal (self-imposed or otherwise)

c. A description of what you did, step by step (how you set about to achieve your goal, despite the hurdle or constraint)—told simply, as to a 5-year-old

d. A description of the outcome or result from this step-by-step description

e. Any measurable/quantifiable statement of that outcome that you can come up with, in terms of money (saved or earned), time, numbers, and so on

2. Still sitting quietly together, each member of the trio writes down, in the margin of the paper on which they told that story, the gifts or skills they see that they used there (e.g., inventing, analyzing, organizing, creating, and so on).

3. When all three have finished these first two steps, the actual "trioing" begins. We will call the members of each trio A, B, and C. A begins by reading his or her story. B and C listen attentively, and on a blank sheet of paper, each jots down the skills that they hear A using, in A's story. They are free, at any time, to ask A to pause while they jot down what has occurred to them, and they are also free to ask A for further clarification, if A moved too swiftly in telling the story, without giving all the step-by-step information.

4. When done telling/reading the story, A then proceeds to tell the other two what gifts or skills A heard in his or her own story.

5. When done, A gets a pen or pencil in hand and prepares to jot down the information that B and C are now about to give. B goes first, and reads off to A the list of skills that B compiled as he or she was listening earlier to A's story. Some of these will, of course, duplicate skills that A already listed. We have discovered this is all to the good, as it lends A confirmation of what he or she may only tentatively have identified. On the other hand, much of B's list may be skills that never occurred to A in that story. A must jot these down—asking B to pause, when necessary—and

do so without argument or questioning. This is, at this point, essentially a process of brainstorming, and A must jot down even those skills that A is not sure he or she has.

6. When B is done, it is C's turn to repeat precisely the process described in Step 5.
7. When C is done, this completes the first third of the trioing. It is now time for B to step to center-stage, and do all that A did in Steps 3 through 6. A and C now, of course, are the listeners.
8. When this is all done, it is now time for C to step center-stage and do all that A and B did in Steps 3 through 6. This time, A and B are the listeners.
9. When all three have thus taken their turn, they have completed the first round of trioing. On a subsequent day (preferably), it is time for the second round in which they repeat (either in the same trio or a new one) Steps 1 through 8. Each member of the trio, of course, writes a completely new story of some time in their life (work related or not) when they were really enjoying themselves and had a distinct sense of achievement or accomplishment.
10. On a subsequent day (preferably) it is time for the third round, in which they repeat Step 9.
11. On subsequent days, they should repeat Step 9 two to four more times, until a minimum of five rounds, a maximum of seven, have been completed. What will be discovered are two things:
    a. Each person's "blindness" to their own gifts, talents, skills, or "strengths" will diminish with each succeeding round. That is, each person will get better and better at seeing his or her own skills, without the aid of the other two members of the trio. Indeed, it may be said that this is the main goal of trioing—to increase participants' self-esteem by teaching them how to get over their "blindness" to their own gifts.
    b. By doing trioing for a minimum of five to seven rounds, patterns will begin to emerge. Each will discover that he or she uses the same skills again and again, in story after story. That is because these are their favorite skills,

and whenever anyone tries to write about the times they were enjoying themselves, as here, it will always turn out that they enjoyed themselves because they were able to use their favorite skills or gifts. They have only, now, to ask themselves, among their 10 favorite skills, which is their absolute favorite, which is next, which is next, and so on. Then they will be able to go out into the world with not only a stronger self-esteem but also some practical information that can guide them in the work they choose and the activities where they will find the greatest sense of accomplishment and the greatest sense of fun, at the same time.

References

Crystal, J. C. and Bolles, R. N. (1974). *Where do I go from here with my life?* Berkeley, CA: Ten Speed Press.

Haldane, B. (1947). A pattern for executive placement. *Harvard Business Review, 25*(4a), 652–663.

Meditational Working Through

Therapist: John D. Boyd, PhD, ABPP, ABPH

Affiliation: Independent Practice, Licensed Clinical Psychologist, Charlottesville, Virginia

Major works:

Boyd, J. D. (1978). *Counselor supervision: Approaches, preparation, practices.* Muncie, IN: Accelerated Development.
Grieger, R. M., & Boyd, J. D. (1980). *Rational emotive therapy: A skills-based approach.* New York: Van Nostrand.

Author of numerous book chapters and journal articles on psychotherapy and clinical hypnosis

Population for whom the technique is appropriate: Adolescents and adults in group, individual, or couples therapy who are coping with chronic emotional distress
Cautionary notes: Emotional stability, including affect containment and modulation, should be established prior to using this technique.

Note: Diplomate in Counseling Psychology and Clinical Hypnosis

Subcortical/Subconscious Theory

Psychodynamic and neocognitive-behavioral psychotherapy now recognize that chronic emotional distress and symptomology often are precipitated by subcortical mental processes (e.g., drives, impulses, primitive affect, imagery, classical and operant conditioning) and subconsciously stored information (i.e., traumatic memories and other pathogenic learning experiences). When processes and information in the subcortical mind are not readily accessible to the conscious, cortical mind and its problem-solving operations, emotional disturbance is refractory to psychotherapy and heavily defended from conscious awareness and disclosure within treatment.

Psychotherapy

Regardless of theoretical approach, effective psychotherapy begins with the building of a trusting alliance between therapist and client, the establishment of emotional stability in the client, and then a slow, careful uncovering of subconscious material through a variety of techniques. When the client gains a substantial amount of conscious insight and emotionally can tolerate emergent subconscious material, the working through process can begin.

Working Through Process

Techniques within this stage of psychotherapy are directed at changing subconscious processes and stored information so that emotional disturbance dissipates. Working through takes place within therapy and via homework. The client enters a deeper state of consciousness (i.e., meditation, self-hypnosis, introspection) and meditative steps are followed.

Future Image and Motivational Rationale

There are two prerequisites for working through homework: (1) a goal-oriented future image and (2) a motivational rationale. The image is an internal representation of how the client would like to feel, think, and act—a realistic and psychologically healthy replacement for the disturbed emotions, schematic beliefs, meanings, and actions that brought the client to therapy. Accompanying the future image must be a motivational rationale consisting of the courage to encounter and experience unwanted emotional symptoms within meditation, faith in one's ability to coordinate problem-solving processes of the bicameral mind, and trust in the transformational healing of integrating, reorganizing, and synthesizing subconscious and conscious information. Transformational healing produces a new adaptive synergy and personality changes that lead to an actualization of the future image, or an approximation thereof.

Meditation Steps

As practiced in therapy, the working through homework assignment consists of entering the meditative state in whatever manner has been learned, focusing on the desired future image and experiencing it, then turning inner attention to an experiencing of the disturbed symptoms and spending 20 minutes of meditation time while relying on the aforementioned bicameral processes of transformational healing. Subconscious and cortical changes move the client from disturbance and toward the future image. The exercise is concluded by leaving inner work and concentrating on becoming alert, then recording the meditative experience in a diary or log, along with emerging cognitive organization (e.g., insights, ideas, concepts).

Outcome

Meditative experiences, cognitive alterations, and dream content mark the *subtle* course of transformational change, which is usually discovered after symptoms have abated. Clients are surprised to find that emotional disturbance has resolved without fanfare or exhilarating breakthrough experiences.

The working through homework technique depends upon corresponding work within therapy, and the therapist is called upon to assist in the evolvement of intrapersonal meaning. However, the client always remains in charge, being the principal agent and validator of changes.

Case Example

An elderly widowed client entered brief psychotherapy (six sessions) because she had been emotionally distressed (alexithymia and dysphoric mood) throughout life regarding blank spots in her memory of childhood, a wanderlust preoccupation, and an inability to emotionally experience love for her children. Her vague future image was to be a better mother and somehow satisfy her travel compulsion. Meditation within therapy brought forth painful memories of parents who were unable to nurture and preferred a precocious, attractive sibling. Dreams reflected these same memories, and meditative homework led the client to the insight that continual travel was a quest to find a home where she felt loved. As painful affect was repeatedly experienced within meditation, she realized that her own children had suffered emotional neglect and she felt a provocative, deep love for them. A contentment with her present residence developed quickly, and she began to seek more frequent contact with her adult children during which she offered and experienced emotional intimacy.

A Dangerous Assignment

Therapist: Peter R. Breggin, MD

Affiliation: Psychiatrist, Ithaca, New York; Former National Director, Center for the Study of Psychiatry and Psychology, Bethesda, Maryland; Faculty Associate, Department of Counseling and Human Services, Johns Hopkins University, Baltimore, Maryland

Major works:

Breggin, P. R. (1998). *Talking back to Ritalin: What doctors aren't telling you about stimulants for children.* Monroe, ME: Common Courage.

Breggin, P. R. (2000). *Reclaiming our children: A healing solution for a nation in crisis.* Cambridge, MA: Perseus.

Breggin, P. R., & Cohen, D. (1999). *Your drug may be your problem: How and why to stop taking psychiatric medications.* Cambridge, MA: Perseus.

Population for whom the technique is appropriate: Any population

Cautionary notes: It may backfire.

Based on the therapy principle, "Do unto others as you would have others do unto you," I rarely assign homework to my clients. I do, however, urge them to think about what they are learning in therapy, to select what's useful for them, and to apply what is useful to their daily lives between sessions.

There is, however, one exception: a homework assignment that I guarantee will improve my clients' lives and the lives of almost everyone they touch. If only as an experiment for a week or two, I suggest that they try being nice to everyone they meet. I explain, "Before we get together again, try being courteous and kind to everyone you deal with, even people you find unworthy or aggravating."

Some religions speak of greeting the God within each person we meet; the Quakers talk about addressing "that of God," which is in each of us. Basically, I urge my clients to experiment with treating all other people with respect and even reverence.

Naturally, like most of us, my clients are tempted to dismiss "being nice" as utopian, unmanly, embarrassing, and even dangerous. Rarely does anyone gratefully declare, "That's a great idea, Peter. An application of universal truths to my personal life. I can't wait to put it into action."

For some of my clients, the practice of being nice has transformed their lives. They find, first, that they feel stronger and better when they are continually drawing upon their innermost capacity to be nice. Ultimately they find themselves tapping the soul's energy source—the spiritual stuff we call love. As they experiment with being nice, and even loving, they begin to feel good about actually living by their highest ethical and spiritual values. They also notice that other people—family, friends, cab drivers, waiters and waitresses, and sometimes even their doctors and lawyers—tend to treat them better in return.

My clients also find that this new principle of relationship rarely gets them into trouble. To the contrary, they experience much less conflict with people. And when someone occasionally tries to mistreat them, they enjoy the inner satisfaction of maintaining their own more positive perspective. They are also better able to spot potentially dangerous people.

When we create a welcoming aura around ourselves, it seems to throw a bright, contrasting light on anyone who approaches us with negative attentions. By contrast, when we are internally obscured by the dim light of negativity, we are less likely to recognize, and to protect ourselves from, the hostility of others.

There is one grave danger in recommending that our clients try being nice as a regular practice in their lives: It can backfire on us. Our clients may notice when we, as therapists, aren't being so courteous and respectful toward them all the time. Any day now, one of my patients could say to me, "Peter, I do my homework, now you do yours." Naturally, I will be tempted to protest that it's utopian, naive, dangerous—and besides the rule doesn't apply to therapists because ... well, just because.

When I do apply the principle in my own therapy practice—when I do greet each of my clients as an expression of God, as someone to be treasured as highly as any other human being on this earth—it seems to help both of us feel and act to the best of our ability. It's mutually therapeutic. I urge all therapists to make it homework for themselves.

Pursuing the Pursuit of Happiness: A Homework Assignment for Couples

Therapist: Patricia Bubash, MEd

Affiliation: Licensed Professional Counselor, Rockwood School District, retired; Member, St. Louis Psychoanalytic Association; Past President, St. Louis Association for Counseling and Development

Major work:

Bubash, P. (2008). *Successful second marriages.* Gilroy, CA: BookStand Publishing.

Population for whom the technique is appropriate: Couples of any age in a married or committed relationship who are experiencing dissatisfaction in the relationship

Cautionary notes: None

Dr. Joe Pfeffer, in writing on the topic, "The Powerful Pursuit of Happiness," noted in his observation of this task the following: "The *act* of striving for happiness may actually be what brings us that particular contentment we are searching for rather than the actuality of 'having' whatever it is that we perceive as 'happiness.' It is *the* striving, working toward a tangible or nontangible that creates happiness."

His insightful view of the term *happiness* and the act of striving can be utilized in a counseling activity with a discontented married couple. Frequently, couples having problems find themselves without a common goal or mutual interest. As in any relationship, where there is team effort, each person becomes the cheerleader for the other, providing encouragement and support. A partnership evolves out of this shared commitment.

A marriage that brings contentment and satisfaction to both spouses will be the marriage that incorporates a common goal, or a common striving.

And, if this goal or interest is of the variety of nonmaterialistic, then it is even more rewarding for the twosome.

Unlike the couple who has invested their efforts into acquiring "things," happiness and contentment will be elusive. If the success and happiness of a relationship is based solely on the goals of a bigger house, a more expensive car, buying a new big flat screen TV, or membership in an expensive country club, eventually, expectations will run out: shades of *The War of the Roses*. This 1989 movie starring Michael Douglas and Kathleen Turner exemplified the downfall of a marriage that started out with common goals but ended up with only the desire to acquire more and more things and losing sight of each other and the love they once had for each other. Their happiness was short-term, but the couple going for togetherness in helping to achieve a skill, good health, and personal development will find long-term regard and accomplishment for each other.

In my interviews with couples for my book, *Successful Second Marriages*, I observed that those couples who shared a common goal—whether it was a planned vacation, an exercise class, a hobby, or simply volunteering as a couple for an agreed organization—displayed contentment, respect for each other, and satisfaction with their relationship.

After the initial interview with a couple coming for marriage counseling, I would give each spouse a sheet of paper, asking that they put the words *Pursuit of Happiness* as the heading for the activity. I would ask them to list three personal goals. A personal goal could simply be to join an exercise club, write a book, or compete in a marathon; whatever is important and desirous to them. My examples would tend to be nonmaterialistic.

Once they had written their lists, I would ask them to exchange them. As they discussed and shared what was on their partner's list, I would ask of each to determine which goal was a priority. Once this had been determined, then each partner would write on the other's goal sheet three concrete items he or she would do for their partner to provide the encouragement and support that would help both in accomplishing a personal goal.

The premise of this assignment is to bring the couple to a place of focusing on the "partnership" of their marriage. Helping each other reach a goal is the real pursuit of happiness: the act of striving together. It is not the tangible things that provide a contented marriage but, as stated by Dr. Pfeffer, "the act of striving" that gives us the most happiness or satisfaction. Striving as a couple, encouraging each other, and then sharing in the accomplishment of each other, is the bonding of a marriage.

At the next session we would take account of what progress had been made by each partner.

1. Any or all of the three steps completed?
2. How far along were they in reaching the goal of each one?
3. Had they experienced any changes in their rapport with each other?

Reference

Pfeffer, J. (2009, August). The powerful pursuit of happiness. *Java Journal*, p. 9.

The Letter From the Future

Therapist: Christine Byriel, MPF*, EAP†

Affiliation: Licensed Clinical Social Worker; President, Psykotera-peutisk Institute (Institute of Psychotherapy), Copenhagen

Major works:

Byriel, C. (1998). *Men hvordan skal jeg få det sagt?* [But how can I get myself to say it? Introduction to assertiveness] (3rd ed.). Copenhagen, Denmark: C.A. Reitzels Forlag.

Byriel, C. (1999). *Kom godt igennem din skilsmisse* [Get through your divorce in one piece]. Copenhagen, Denmark: Atelier.

Byriel, S., & Byriel, C. (1996). *"Se mig!—Hør mig!" Introduktion til stemmens lyd, krop og psyke* ["See me—Hear me!" An introduction to voice as health and healing]. Copenhagen, Denmark: C.A. Reitzels Forlag.

Christine Byriel is also author of two other books and five works of research in the health care field.

Population for whom the technique is appropriate: Adolescents and adults

Cautionary notes: None

A principal characteristic of my work is that I never know in advance precisely how to help my clients live a richer life. I always work from personal experience, never from some therapeutic prescription, because life in the therapeutic consultation room is just as colorful, unpredictable, and surprising as life outside it. With a background in a formal professional education and supervised practical training, I have found the most valuable teaching experience as a therapist is in my communication with my clients, and the homework I prescribe springs like a fountain from the mutuality generated in the therapeutic relationship.

---

* MPF signifies membership in the Danish Association for Psychotherapists.
† EAP stands for membership in the European Association for Psychotherapy.

To be able to feel and express what is inside us, and to discover a sense of the life we desire for ourselves, are competences whose development I regard as the principal goal of the therapist's work. Most of those who consult me are cut off from essential parts of their own emotional lives. They have difficulty expressing their real selves in word and action and have a rather uncertain notion of the possibilities life might have to offer them. Some clients, moreover, are locked in the misconception that they have no capacity for bringing about change, that life has in fact little else to give them than negative and destructive experiences. They have created a life that seems futile. My work helps find the keys to the doors that lead to the unused rooms, to unlock the treasure that lies hidden in each of us. By far, most clients need to be guided back to a wisdom and strong imagination that were present in their childhood. Regardless of how that childhood turned out, often personal values and competences will lie hidden under the ruins of the life that has been so painfully crippled. We need to penetrate the fantasies and wishful dreams of the child into the right-hand side of the brain, which possesses the golden formulas that cause the mountain to open or the darkness to recede.

Our ability to focus and direct our consciousness and attention is the only way we have to bring about change. This ability can be strengthened, and as a therapist I view it as one of my crucial tasks to support consciousness in its work, so that my clients become able to direct their attention toward healing and personal growth. Training this ability in many respects resembles the process involved in every other kind of learning experience. Remember, for instance, what it was like to learn to ride a bicycle. We see a bicycle and wish to own it. We fantasize about the way it will carry us far and wide, and we sustain that dream despite innumerable moments when we literally bite the dust. Our parents, sisters, and brothers run like mad to ward off the worst disasters and provide support. And then one day we discover, in one breathless moment, when our consciousness is concentrated on the point of physical equilibrium, that we are riding without help. That is the first victory. Our frustrations and bruises are forgotten in the exultation at being able to move on our own. Gradually more skills are added through processes of learning similar to that first and decisive one. All human beings are able to learn new skills and all are able to focus their consciousness upon things rewarding and gratifying in life *or* upon those that are black and morbid. Whichever direction we take will be the result of our own personal choice. We choose freely, every time, whether our decisions concern matters of great and lasting importance or others small and trivial—in other words, in all actual and concrete situations where we interact with other people, adopt or discard a concept, embrace or reject a particular topic, move toward or away from new ways of thinking—and we choose the emotions with which we respond to these.

Our free will resides in our choices, but this must not be taken to mean that we are free to do anything we want exactly when we want it. We cannot, for instance, force others—whether spouse, partner, colleague, or client—to think like us or act like us, through an act of will. Neither can we create a perfect world simply by "wanting" it, but we can decide our own course of action. We have the right to determine when and how we react, which words we use, what we decide from one moment to the next, and in what way we pay attention to ourselves and others. Every single moment of consciousness about our own selves is a moment of freedom to choose.

Self-consciousness requires us to be alert to encodings originating in childhood: These are the inculcated habits and adult value standards, which may have become automatic, unconscious, and thus fossilized and obsolete. This makes us respond to our environment in predetermined and counterproductive ways, in a life of self-fulfilling predictions. The seed of behavioral change lies elsewhere: in the will to change.

It is this seed that I, as a therapist, must nurture and protect.

The only place we can safely and responsibly assert our willpower lies in our relation to ourselves. If we are not children or victims of violence, we cannot be robbed of our autonomy unless we have given others the opportunity to do so. It is our own inner faith, anxiety, hope, sympathy, or apathy that leads us into self-sacrifice or toward a richer life. When we believe that our life is destined for futility or misery, we behave like victims of others and will find our lives affected in a negative direction; it is like sitting on one's new bicycle and telling oneself that one shall never be able to ride it.

The homework task I will share with the reader generates a powerful attitude. In the course of my 30 years of work as a psychotherapist, I have had frequent confirmation that this particular homework task has been a practical turning point.

Assume Power Over Your Future (Instructions to the Client, Step I)

Your task is to work with yourself at the level of fantasizing. You have done it before as a child. As an *adult*, you must now fantasize about your future and evoke a mental image of yourself in the context of the life you aspire to live. Explore more and more aspects and shades of the life your imagination calls up.

The imagination is the mother of action; it always precedes the thoughts and conceptions that determine the course of our lives. All man-made development comes from visual images of that which is to be created. We know that our thoughts and fantasies have a decisive influence upon the quality of our relation to ourselves as well as to others. Each of us creates our own interior version of the world, which influences the way we see and experience it. We have the freedom to choose whether that fantasy is to be black and painful or bright and prosperous. As a child, too, you created your image of the world. This image was created by the adults you were dependent upon. It was their world that shaped your interior map. You had no alternative, since you had no other models. Others materialized later, when you discovered how other families lived among themselves. Today you have grown up, and you are completely free to create your own image, and this has to be a positive one. Both you and the outside world have changed. Children cannot change their world. Adults can.

You create your life even while you live it, not in the past or the future, but while it happens.

Transforming one's fantasies into concrete results requires talent, a strategy, exercise, and scope for change. But the principal enabling circumstance is the way we imagine ourselves as a success. In this way you can exorcise your own negative images of both yourself and others.

Write the Letter From Your Own Future (Instructions to the Client, Step II)

The purpose of this task is to explore your awareness of the way your fantasies, thoughts, and perceptions work to determine your future life—the life that you want in the long run. You set up a positive goal.

You must plan a moment when you know you can be alone for quite some time. You must find a place where you expect you'll feel good. It must be a place where you have never been before, a place unconnected with frustration or pain. *Your place of the future!*

You may choose to sit down by the sea or a lake, in a church you have never been to before, or a quiet museum where no one will disturb you. Perhaps it's a café, or a restaurant. Imagine—at this very moment—that you are sitting there sometime in the future.

You need to bring pen and paper and an object that means something special to you, something symbolic of what is good and beautiful in your life. It could be a piece of jewelry, a stone, a photograph, a book, or something that anchors you in the positive side of your personal history.

Then follows a choice, for you must call up your own future in your mind's eye. Now choose whether you wish to encounter yourself in 5 or in 10 years.

Next, you must enter a fantasy in which your dreams of a good life have come true. Your future life is as you have wished it to be. Your task is to be very egocentric and make certain that in your fantasies you are the very center of the world (as in your child-hood dreams).

You need to think in positive images and concentrate on light and warmth. In other words, no self-censoring! When you have attuned your consciousness to your interior and positive energy and evoked a positive image of yourself in that future life, you must write a letter *from* the person you are in your vision of the future and addressed to a close relative or friend, who has not heard from you in the period in between.

Even today you have found time to relate the choices you have made and the roads you have taken the past 5 or 10 years that have brought you to the life you lead today, a life with which you are happy and content.

Now, don't blame yourself if you have to attempt the exercise several times before you manage it. If it is a new thing for you to enter completely into a fantasy, it will take some practice before you succeed.

Put aside the letter and pray your imagination and inner resources help you open the door to the world that contains your new life.

The exercise is simple, but the task has nonetheless meant a personal turning point for those clients who have completed it. Try it yourself, and you will inevitably find that it has a positive effect!

Editor's note: Special thanks to Marianne Borch of Odense University in Copenhagen, Denmark, who provided the initial translation of this article from Danish.

Love Thy Neighbor: Facilitating Social Interest in All Clients

Therapist: Jon Carlson, PsyD, EdD

Affiliation: Distinguished Professor, Division of Psychology & Counseling, Governors State University; Director, Lake Geneva (Wisconsin) Wellness Clinic

Major works:

Carlson, J., & Dinkmeyer, D. (2003). *Time for a better marriage.* Atascadero, CA: Impact Publishers.

Carlson, J., Watts, R. E., & Maniacci, M. (2006). *Adlerian therapy: Theory and practice.* Washington, DC: APA Books.

Kottler, J., & Carlson, J. (2004). *The mummy at the dining room table.* San Francisco: Jossey-Bass.

Population for whom the technique is appropriate: People of all ages

Cautionary notes: None

The law of social interest well practiced can free the latent powers of a human being and help him to overcome the egocentric aim out of which all neurosis is born. Adler believed that when the law of social interest is understood and every human being's education based upon it—the love of our neighbour (which is the goal of all true religions) will become "as natural as breathing or the upright gait."

Bottome
(1937, p. 150)

This homework strategy touches at what Alfred Adler referred to as *social interest.* He felt that social interest is what every mentally healthy person strives for. It involves showing an interest in others and reaching out in a socially responsible manner to provide help and service to others.

In this activity, the therapist instructs the client to engage in a socially useful or helpful action. This type of assignment changes the focus from the client's ego (or self) and forces the client to think of helping others. By engaging in behavior that helps others, the client is bolstered by the positive feelings that are a result of giving to others and develops new ways to connect with the social world. After all, researchers have recently documented that happiness results from giving and not having (Gilbert, 2006).

The therapist simply asks the client, *"If you needed to do community service what activity would you pick?"* Perhaps it would be providing free babysitting, mowing an elderly neighbor's grass, volunteering at church or synagogue, or helping out at the local nursing home. The specific activity is not as important as the gesture or intention of the person. *"For this week it is important for you to provide some service for another person who is not in your immediate family."*

This is a generic homework assignment that I use with most clients in my practice. Whenever I am stuck in a therapy session, I ask the client to get socially involved in whatever way is meaningful for him or her.

References

Bottome, P. (1937). *Alfred Adler: Apostle of freedom.* London: Faber & Faber.
Gilbert, D. (2006). *Stumbling on happiness.* New York: Vintage Books.

Client-Centered
Homework in Groups

Therapists: Marianne Schneider Corey, MA, and Gerald Corey, EdD, ABPP

Affiliation: Marianne Schneider Corey is a Licensed Marriage and Family Therapist and a Consultant.
Gerald Corey is a Licensed Psychologist and Professor Emeritus of Human Services and Counseling at California State University, Fullerton.

Major works:

Corey, G., Corey, M. S., & Callahan, P. (2010). *Issues and ethics in the helping professions.* Pacific Grove, CA: Brooks/Cole.

Corey, M. S., & Corey, G. (2008). *Groups: Process and practice* (4th ed.). Pacific Grove, CA: Brooks/Cole.

Corey, M. S., & Corey, G. (2010). *Becoming a helper* (3rd ed.). Pacific Grove, CA: Brooks/Cole.

Gerald Corey is the author or coauthor of 15 counseling textbooks as well as numerous journal articles. Dr. Corey and his wife Marianne Schneider Corey have conducted mental health and counseling workshops all over the world. The Coreys received the Association for Specialists in Group Work's Eminent Career Award in 2001.

Population for whom the technique is appropriate: Mainly adults

Cautionary notes: This approach works best once the group facilitator has established a collaborative and trusting relationship with the members of the group.

Perhaps one of the most useful techniques to assist group members in getting the most from a group experience is designing homework assignments that they can carry out both during group sessions and outside the group. Because a group meeting is relatively brief, engaging in homework is one of the best ways to maximize the learning of any group experience. We do not have one favorite technique;

instead, we strive to build into all of our groups a process that motivates the members to identify what active and specific steps they can take to bring about the changes they desire in their lives.

The Purpose of Homework in Group

In our view, the group is not an end in itself; rather, it is a place where people can learn new behaviors, acquire a range of skills in living, and practice these skills and behaviors, both during the group session and outside of the group. Homework is a means to maximizing what is learned in the group and a means of translating this learning to many different situations in daily life. Members should be encouraged to devise their own homework assignments, ideally at each of the group sessions. Homework leads to the involvement and active participation of each member.

Although we often suggest to members an activity for them to consider doing outside of the group, we avoid being prescriptive and telling members what they should do for homework. Our suggestions are presented in the spirit of assisting members in increasing the chances of their getting what they want from the group experience. Any homework in our groups is client centered in the sense that it is based on what the client wants. As much as possible, homework is designed collaboratively with the group members. Frequently we will ask, "What can you do between today and next week to practice what you are learning in here?" Or we may say, "You are getting clearer of what you want with others in your life. Can you think of some specific tasks you are willing to set for yourself during the week that will move you closer to what you want?"

Journal Writing as Regular Homework

In our groups we strongly encourage members to make it a practice to engage in regular journal writing in between the group meetings. We ask the participants in our groups to spend even a few minutes daily in recording in their journals certain feelings, situations, behaviors, and ideas for courses of action. Members can also review certain periods of time in their lives and write about them, which will assist them in clarifying what they want to explore in a group session. Writing in a free-flowing style without censoring can be of great help in getting a focus on feelings.

Members are encouraged to bring their journals to the group and share a particular experience they had that resulted in problems for them. They can then explore with the group how they might have handled the situation better. These journals are for the benefit of the members to help them focus on ways they want to involve themselves in the group.

Another way to use journals is as a preparation for encountering others in everyday life. For instance, Jenny is having a great deal of difficulty talking with her husband. She's angry with him much of the time over many of the things he does and does not do. But she sits on this anger, and she feels sad that they don't make time for each other. Jenny typically doesn't express her sadness to him, nor does she let him know of her resentment toward him for not being involved in their children's lives. To deal with this problem, she can write her husband a detailed and uncensored letter pointing out all the ways in which she feels angry, hurt, sad, and disappointed and expressing how she would like their life to be different. It is not necessary that she show this letter to her husband; in fact, we caution her not to share this letter with him. The letter writing is a way for her to clarify what she feels and to prepare herself to work in the group. This work can then help her to be clear about what she eventually wants to say to her husband as well as how she wants to say it.

Still another technique is for members to enter in their journals spontaneously their reactions and experiences to the first few meetings. They can reflect on questions such as the following: How do I feel about being in this group? How do I see people in the group? How do I see myself in it? What are some ways that I most want to use the time in the group sessions? What would I like to leave this group having learned or experienced? By devoting time outside the group to reflect on these questions, the members increase their chances of deriving the maximum benefit from their participation in the group.

The process of writing in a journal allows members to keep track of what they are experiencing in each of the group sessions, and often it is a catalyst for members to engage in new behavior within the group. At the midpoint of a group, people can take time during the week to write down how they feel about the group at this point, how they view their participation in it so far, what they are doing outside the group to attain their goals, and how they'd feel if the group were to end now. By discussing these topics in the group, participants are challenged to reevaluate their level of commitment and often are motivated to increase their participation in the group.

We caution group members to exercise care as they write in their journal so they do not breach the confidentiality of anyone in the group. They are told not to write any names of participants or specific identifying information of others. We suggest they focus on themselves and their own reactions, rather than writing about what others say or do in the group. We suggest to members that they keep their journals in a secure place so that others will not have access to their personal writings and reflections.

Designing Realistic Homework Assignments

Homework assignments can be performed during the group sessions as well as outside of the group. For instance, Henry indicates that he tends to remain silent in the sessions and does not bring up what he would like to talk about during a meeting. More often than not, at the end of a group session, Henry thinks of what he wished he had said earlier. We might suggest an assignment that Henry make a commitment a week in advance to be the first person to speak at the following meeting.

Often members do some very intense exploration about significant relationships in groups. Although talking about a relationship in the group meeting can be very therapeutic and members gain insights into the dynamics of a relationship, this is usually only the beginning of change. Members then need to decide if they are interested in dealing with a person in their lives and talk to them differently. For instance, Rosa decides she wants to approach her mother in a different manner than she typically does—without arguing and getting defensive. She can first practice what she hopes to be able to express to her mother and can benefit from the feedback and support from other members. Rosa stands a better chance of actually being different with her mother if she is clear what she wants with her mother and also has received input from other members based on her behavioral rehearsal in group.

We always stress to members how important it is that they show up to a following meeting, even if they have not done all that they had agreed to do, or even if their homework resulted in disappointing outcomes. Measures can be discussed that will help members when the assignments they have given themselves do not materialize as they had expected. At times, even with hard work and commitment, members will not get what they expected from their encounters. We talk about how some regressions are to be expected and how members can best cope with unexpected outcomes. The chances of disappointing outcomes are lessened if members have given themselves homework that is manageable. It is essential to tailor homework to each member's developmental level and to guide them in formulating realistic plans. Our hope is that members will identify and carry out small steps rather than attempt to do too much too quickly. As members engage in self-direction through the process of carrying out homework, they increase their responsibility for taking action to get what they want and they enhance their sense of empowerment.

Marriage Counseling Test Homework Assignment

Therapist: Raymond J. Corsini, PhD, deceased

Affiliation: Retired Private Practice Clinical and Industrial Psychologist

Major works:

Corsini, R. J. (1994). *Encyclopedia of psychology.* Toronto, Ontario, Canada: Wiley-Interscience.

Corsini, R. J., & Wedding, D. (2007). *Current psychotherapies.* Pacific Grove, CA: Brooks/Cole.

Painter, G., & Corsini, R. J. (1990). *Effective discipline in the home and school.* Muncie, IN: Accelerated Development.

Author and editor of over 25 books and numerous professional articles

Sadly, Dr. Corsini passed away Nov. 8, 2008 at the age of 94.

Population for whom technique is appropriate: Clients in marriage or couples counseling

Cautionary notes: None

Harold and Wanda came to see me and said that they were on the brink of divorce. They started the usual defense of themselves and attack of the other, but I stopped them and asked them what I considered a crucial question: "Do you have good will toward each other?" After consideration, they both agreed.

I then said that I had a particular way to operate and wanted to put it into effect right now. So, would they please only talk to me? They agreed.

I looked at Wanda and said, "What one thing that cannot be denied would you want Harold to either stop doing or start doing?"

She thought for a moment and then said, "I want him to stop picking on my mother."

I then turned to Harold and said, "Please tell me what she wants you to stop doing." He began with what was seemingly a long story of his complaints about Wanda's mother, but I interrupted him saying, "All I want to hear from you is what she said." He then replied, "She wants me to stop talking about her mother." "Not quite right," I said, "Shall I repeat her words?" He then said, "She used the word 'picking.'"

I then turned to Wanda: "Do you think that he knows what bothers you the most?" And finally she said, "He knows damn well what bothers me."

Then I asked him to tell me one thing that Wanda did that bothered him the most.

The answer was one word: "Smoking."

I turned to Wanda and just looked at her. She started again with what might have been a long statement, but I stopped her and said, "I only want to know if you know what bothers him the most."

She replied, "Does he want me to stop smoking completely or merely refrain from smoking in front of him?"

I looked at him and he said, "It would be better if you stopped altogether, but it would be enough if you would stop smoking in my presence. You know I …"

I broke in by saying, "That's enough."

I then said to Wanda, "What does he want?"

"I should not smoke in front of him," she replied.

I asked Harold if she understood his complaint and he replied in the affirmative.

I wrote a note that I would later read out loud to them.

I turned to Wanda and asked her for another complaint, and after fumbling a bit she asked him not to call her "fat ass."

He then agreed after some sparring about the word and tried to tell me she should reduce, but I wanted to hear none of that.

Eventually, as the end of the session drew near, I was ready for a summation, and said, "I am going to name the things that each of you agreed bothered you, and I am going to ask you whether you will agree to stop them or to start them, as the case may be, from now until next week."

I started with Harold: "Will you promise not to pick on Wanda's mother for one week?" He agreed. Then I turned to Wanda," Will you promise not to smoke in Harold's presence for one week?"

And then I continued with Harold agreeing not to call her fat ass, with Wanda agreeing to have dinner ready by 6:15, with Harold agreeing to take her out to dinner one night this week, and with Wanda agreeing to stop calling her sister long distance more than once this week.

They agreed to do exactly that for one week.

It is not that important for you to know whether they lived up to their agreements, but it is important to understand the theory behind the method, how to interpret the reactions of the couple that first session, and how to interpret the next session and the value of the technique of this imaginary couple. The basic idea is that if the couple indicates that they care for each other, that gives the marriage counselor something to work for and to find out whether they will mention complaints. The counselor is looking for behaviors that occur often and are clear-cut and unarguable. The counselor secures no more than three complaints and has the other party repeat the complaints. Later—when all complaints are in—the couple is asked to repeat them again, and each one is asked whether they will agree to do or not do the offenses for a week.

At this point the situation becomes a litmus test for you as the marriage counselor. You will make decisions about whether the person is ready with complaints or not, how reasonable they are, whether the person states the problem he or she had heard in a reasonable manner, and whether they agree to stop or say that they will "try to" stop."

And the next week we may find that both stop 100% or that one did and the other didn't, and so on.

I would take the following step if anyone did not follow the directives of their homework: "Harold, last week you promised to not call Wanda a fat ass, and yet she states that you have continued to use this derogatory term." Often the client will grumble that it is not important or something like that. "It is important to her and to me as your counselor. I will not go further unless you show respect for your promise and for her."

So I may go over the entire six items for each of them—sticking to the letter of the word. Do not move forward until each has agreed the other has lived up to the agreement.

What may occur, and I have had this happen, is that one party lived up to the agreement and the other did not in every case. In that latter case I would say, "Both of you listened to the other person's complaints. I only accepted those complaints that seemed reasonable to me, which occurred frequently, and those that the other person showed that he or she understood and then agreed to stop. One of you did stop. The other did not. To me, this indicates that the one who did not want to stop does not want the marriage to continue. This matter may seem unimportant, but I will not go ahead with you. I suggest you seek a better marriage counselor."*

I call this the Marriage Counseling Test and have had excellent results with it, when both people are reasonable. The couple is able to succeed in a situation that had been impossible and, thus, will be more ready to cooperate having gained evidence of the good will of the other. Then the therapist may seek a further set of agreements, if this is indicated, or may intervene in other ways.

Editor's note: Ethical guidelines for some professionals dictate that the therapist provide referrals in this situation. Check the ethical standards for your profession prior to implementing this technique.

Positive Action Tags: Utilizing Therapeutic Symbols in Family Therapy

Therapist: Richard H. Cox, PhD, ABPP

Affiliation: President and Professor Emeritus, Forest Institute of Professional Psychology, Springfield, Missouri

Major works:

Cox, R. (Ed.). (1973). *Religious systems and psychotherapy.* Springfield, IL: Charles C Thomas.

Cox, R. H., & Esau, T. G. (1974). *Regressive therapy: Therapeutic regression of schizophrenic children and young adults.* New York: Brunner-Mazel.

Author of numerous chapters in books and articles in professional journals

Population for whom the technique is appropriate: This technique is appropriate for all families. It may be used to increase family health and to restore dysfunctional families.

Cautionary notes: There are no known cautionary notes other than wearing a jewelry-type chain around one's neck.

Family dysfunction is normal from time to time, becomes chronic in others, and becomes acute in many. The technique described is beneficial for workshops, family therapy, and other group activities where human dignity is the subject of concern. The world of brief psychotherapy and reduced mental health benefits requires that therapists find ways to intervene more rapidly and utilize the family to help itself. This technique works best with families of Judeo-Christian heritage, although words certainly may be found for all religious faiths, because all share common human dignity concerns.

Method

First, discuss common interpersonal respect and how to practice human dignity. Particularly address how the lack of given virtues cause family disruption, disrespect, and dysfunction. The therapist should seek specific family concerns that demonstrate how a given virtue would have helped if practiced in a dysfunctional situation. Have a family member discuss how they would have felt if a given virtue had been extended to him or her, and attempt to get someone else to discuss how he or she felt when a given virtue was withheld from the situation (i.e., when someone was impatient).

Second, find a phrase, poem, or passage such as a Bible verse that spells out the ingredients in interpersonal dignity. Most families have some context from which a therapist can draw a "common belief" listing of virtues. As an example, refer to the Bible, which states that the fruit of the Spirit is "love, joy, peace, patience, kindness, and faithfulness" (Galatians 5:22). There are many such phrases in religious and secular literature that can be used to demonstrate the universal nature of how to treat other human beings.

Third, have small metal plates made (like army "dog tags") and place them on neck chains. Instruct each family member to wear a "Positive Action Tag" for one week and agree to practice the virtue on that tag every day with all other family members. Dad, for example, agrees to practice "patience" with all other family members for the week.

Fourth, at the next family session, have each member discuss their experience with practicing their designated virtue on their Positive Action Tag. Each family member confers with the other members of the family on how he or she felt practicing the virtue and how it felt when a virtue was practiced on them. They may also note how their friends related to their "new piece of jewelry" as well as the explanation they gave their friends about their jewelry. Many beneficial results have been reported from the open discussion of the "tags" with friends. It becomes a public "confession" of sorts and a public "commitment" as well. Such peer group reinforcement is very helpful.

Fifth, family members should exchange Positive Action Tags for the following week. Tags are exchanged by drawing them out of a hat. Family members have no choice in the tag they get. (You can make up your own rules as well, or ask the family to do so.

Families that are severely dysfunctional do not do well making up their own rules!)

Although there are seemingly corny aspects to such a homework assignment, I have found it revolutionary in demonstrating both the absence of such virtues in common day-to-day home life and in positive reward demonstrations on a daily basis in practicing "common dignities" of interpersonal communication and interaction. It is important for the therapist to find a body of accepted literature with which the family can identify, such as religious belief systems. It is difficult for family members to state their unwillingness to at least attempt to practice what they believe. The day-to-day constant reminder of the dog tag causes them to recognize their own promise on a daily basis and explain to others who may see the tag what it means, thus further imprinting their commitment to family change.

How many family members there are and how many virtues have been chosen to be practiced will determine the number of sessions needed or the number of virtues to be discussed in any one session. In the illustration given, one virtue can be utilized per week for 7 weeks and a final week of summary therapy, thus making the process amenable to brief 8-week therapy.

Self-Monitoring as Client Self-Report and Self-Intervention

Therapists: Susan R. Davis, PhD, and Scott T. Meier, PhD

Affiliations: Susan R. Davis: Licensed psychologist, Southern Illinois University-Carbondale, Private Practice

Scott T. Meier: Licensed psychologist, Professor, Department of Counseling, School, and Educational Psychology, SUNY Buffalo

Major works:

Davis, S., & Meier, S. (2001). *The elements of managed care: A guide for helping professionals.* Pacific Grove, CA: Brooks/Cole.

Meier, S. (2008). *Measuring change in counseling and psychotherapy.* New York: Guilford Press.

Meier, S., & Davis, S. (2010). *The elements of counseling* (7th ed). Pacific Grove, CA: Brooks/Cole.

Population for whom the technique is appropriate: College students and adult outpatients

Cautionary notes: Some knowledge about cognitive-behavioral theory, particularly self-efficacy theory, enhances the use of this technique.

Our favorite homework assignment is self-monitoring, where clients record information about themselves outside of the therapy session. Self-monitoring is a combination of self-report and behavioral assessment: The client observes himself or herself on some dimension and records that information as it occurs. The client then brings the observational record for discussion at the next therapy session.

We prefer that the type of information recorded depend on a problem the client has discussed in a particular session (e.g., "I want to study more"). That is, the information the client records is idiographic or specific to that person (i.e., the client wants to increase the number or length of study sessions), not a generic problem from a manual or workbook. This enhances the client's motivation to do the self-monitoring homework in that the task has "face validity"; that is, the client understands what and why he is recording a particular behavior (e.g., recording whenever he studies and for how long).

The focus of self-monitoring is typically a behavior. That is, what is recorded is an overt behavior such as number of cigarettes smoked, alcoholic drinks consumed, or number of conversations initiated. The target of self-monitoring, however, could also be thoughts or feelings. A client might record, for example, whenever she has an intrusive thought or a depressed feeling.

Self-monitoring has been shown to be a useful method for both assessment *and* intervention. Research indicates that the recording of behavioral problems such as smoking decreases the observed behavior independent of other interventions. Self-monitoring appears to be a *reactive* method of obtaining data: Because the individual becomes more aware of the observed behaviors, he is more likely to change those behaviors. And typically the behavior change is in a desired direction, such as decreased smoking or increased social interactions.

Self-monitoring homework can usefully be paired with graduated exposure to a feared or difficult situation. A college-age client who describes being shy, for example, might agree to self-monitor the number of conversations he initiates with fellow students during the next week. If that number is zero, the homework for the following week might be to continue self-monitoring and also initiate at least 1 conversation, for any length of time.

An important aspect of this homework is that it should be designed to maximize the chances of success for any particular client. That is, the homework task chosen must be one that the client is very likely to be able to complete. Our shy client is more likely to successfully initiate a conversation with one fellow student in 1 week than with 10 fellow students. Similarly, a shy adult who moves into a new neighborhood might first try taking a short walk, gardening in the backyard for 30 minutes, or initiating a 5-minute conversation with a neighbor.

One way to enhance the possibility of success is to ask the client explicitly whether the proposed homework is something worth trying. Rather than the therapist's persuading the client that she can succeed at some task, it is more useful to adjust or change the task so that the client leaves the session with a sense of competence for performing the behavior in question. In the unlikely event that the client does not successfully perform the task, the failure can be portrayed as a consequence of the task chosen—not the client—and explicitly discussed as such in the next session. The basic philosophy is to produce conditions around the homework task that increase the client's self-efficacy for performing the behavior in question.

References

Bandura, A. (1997). *Self-efficacy: The exercise of control.* New York: Freeman.

Nelson, R. O. (1977). Assessment and therapeutic functions of self-monitoring. In M. Hersen, R. M. Eisler, & P. M. Miller (Eds.), *Progress in behavior modification* (Vol. 5, pp. 263–308). New York: Brunner/Mazel.

"As If": Enacting Desired Schema Change

Therapist: Keith S. Dobson, PhD

Affiliation: Professor, Clinical Psychology, University of Calgary, Alberta, Canada

Major works:

Dobson, D. J. A., & Dobson, K. S. (2009). *Evidence-based practice of cognitive-behavioral therapy.* New York: Guilford Press.

Dobson, K. S. (Ed.). (2010). *Handbook of cognitive-behavioral therapies* (3rd ed.). New York: Guilford Press.

Population for whom the technique is appropriate: All clients with personal agency; may not be appropriate for minors or dependent adults

Cautionary notes: None

Description

The "as if" technique is a part of the range of techniques employed in cognitive therapy. Its purpose is to assist clients in their exploration of an alternative schema or self-concept, as well as the behavioral expression of that schema. This technique can be extremely powerful and can generate considerable momentum toward therapeutic change, but it also carries significant risks, as described later.

Steps of the Technique

The technique is predicated on several requirements or steps. First, it must be established that the client has, over the course of his or her personal history, developed a schema that is dysfunctional and causes the client personal distress. Because it typically takes some time to fully understand the operation of dysfunctional schemas, by implication the "as if" technique tends to be used in the middle to later stages of therapy. Second, once the dysfunctional schema has been identified and its consequences are fully appreciated by the client, the therapist and client need to work to identify a viable alternative schema that the client would like to develop. This step can take some time, as there is sometimes a tendency to completely reject the original negative schema and desire to be nothing like one was before, which is often unrealistic. Thus the alternative that is developed has to be a realistic and adaptive pattern, which can be sustained over the long term. For example, if a client has a self-schema of being an unlovable person, based on a history of early childhood abuse, social rejection, and adult victimization, then developing an alternative self-schema of being intrinsically worthwhile and loveable may not be realistic; in contrast, developing the perspective that the client could be loved by someone might be a more viable view to try to develop.

The third step of the "as if" technique is to work with the client to imagine, in as much detail as possible, the implications of the new schema. Would the client talk differently to himself or herself? Would he or she dress differently? Would he or she carry himself or herself in a different manner? What ways of interaction with others are implicated? Does the social circle itself need to be modified? What occupational or career implications might exist? In a sense, the general question being asked is "What are the intended outcomes?" How would the client know if the technique has been a success or not? The result of this analysis might implicate a "tweaking" of the client's current manners and behavioral patterns to be more consistent with the new schema that is being developed, or it might require a major shake-up of these patterns, if the goal is a more radical change in the self-schema. Sometimes this review motivates clients to make changes, if they can actually imagine these changes. In other cases, clients can become anxious about the implications of the changes, or even despondent about the magnitude of the implied change that they desire.

In the fourth step of the "as if" technique, the client and therapist design an experiment in which the imagined ways of being are enacted. This enactment can include imaginary interactions with others, role plays with the therapist, discussions with people in the client's life in which these changes are discussed, or actual enactment of the changes in the client's day-to-day lived experience. In some cases the enactment can be introduced in a progressive or step-wise manner, whereas in other cases the enactment may be fully executed from the outset. This step is the core of acting as if the new schema was already in place and as if the client expects others to respond to him or her from this perspective. In reality, such a shift is often not radical, but rather takes weeks or months of experience before the new sense of self may emerge. What is important during this time is that the client actively monitors his or her thoughts, feelings, and behaviors, to see how adequately he or she is fulfilling the expectations of the desired schema, and the extent to which he or she permits the new experiences to be incorporated into the changing view of self.

The final stage of the "as if" technique is evaluative. Did the changes that were enacted lead to the desired change? If so, in what areas, and why? How will the client maintain these benefits? If the desired change did not occur, what problems emerged? Do these problems warrant a shift in the strategy and another attempt, or a complete abandonment of the technique? If the technique will be re-attempted, it will be important for the client and therapist to "back up" to the beginning, and in light of the new information that has been gathered, redesign and implement the "as if" technique.

Advantages and Challenges

As noted, the "as if" technique can be powerful. If the method is well designed and effectively implemented, it can provide information to the client that he or she would never obtain if living according to the preexisting schema. For example, a client whose self-view is being dependent on others might never plan a trip alone, or have the experience of independence, without the development of a deliberate strategy.

Although these ideas are sometimes confused, it is important to note that the "as if" technique is different from the idea of "Fake it, until you make it." In the latter case, the sense of "faking it" implies that the client really has not committed to the change that is being attempted and does not really take responsibility for the outcome. In contrast, with the "as if" technique, there should be a true endorsement of the change as a desired goal that will be worked toward. In this sense, the client needs to commit himself or herself to the effort and to experience it as fully as possible. It is in part because of this aspect of the technique that it also carries large risks. For example, a client who comes to understand that his or her current intimate relationship also causes him or her personal grief, and who decides to live alone, is risking that the decision turns out to be one to regret. That client may experience some degree of distress, as he or she comes to experience being alone. Indeed, just the act of behaving as if a new schema were in place could lead to some sense of distress or disequilibrium. Further, in this case the client is making a decision that affects his or her partner and could cause interpersonal dispute or problems. In an extreme form, this technique might lead to career, lifestyle, or major interpersonal changes.

Given the aforementioned considerations, it is important that the therapist who uses the "as if" technique ensure that the client fully appreciates the implications of either doing or not doing the enactment part of the technique. It is the client's right to make changes in his or her life, and although the therapist can guide the exploration and decision-making process, it is critical that the therapist ensures that it is the client who makes the decision to act or not, and what specific steps to take. The therapist also needs to ensure that his or her involvement in the case can last long enough that any untoward outcomes of the "as if" technique can be evaluated and potentially mitigated.

In summary, the "as if" technique can be a powerful, even if sometimes risky, strategy to achieve change in schemas that cause the client distress or dysfunction. The technique should be employed in the context of a comprehensive case conceptualization and as part of an ongoing program of care, rather than as an isolated treatment method. It requires some time to organize, plan, execute, and evaluate, and it should be undertaken only with the client's expressed informed consent. The outcomes of the technique, however, can be profound and can, in the extreme, lead to a deeply transformed sense of self and possible agency in the world.

The Zig-Zag Technique

Therapist: Windy Dryden, PhD

Affiliation: Professor of Counseling, Goldsmiths College, University of London

Major works:

Dryden, W. (1999). *Rational emotive behavioural counselling in action.* London: Sage.
Dryden, W. (1999). *Rational emotive behaviour therapy: A personal approach.* Bicester, UK: Winslow Press.
Ellis, A., & Dryden, W. (2007). *The practice of rational emotive behavior therapy* (2nd ed.). New York: Springer.

Dr. Dryden is author or editor of 118 books and editor of 13 book series.

Population for whom the technique is appropriate: Adults and older adolescents

Cautionary notes: This technique is best used with clients who see intellectually that their healthy beliefs are logical, true, and constructive and want to increase their conviction in these beliefs as a way of achieving their therapeutic goals.

One of the major goals of rational emotive behavior therapy (REBT) is to help clients to identify, challenge, and change their unhealthy (irrational) beliefs and acquire and strengthen their conviction in their alternative healthy (rational) beliefs. Albert Ellis (1963), the founder of REBT, has distinguished between intellectual insight (defined as a lightly and occasionally held conviction in a healthy [rational] belief) and emotional insight (defined as a strongly and frequently held conviction in a healthy [rational] belief in ways that significantly promote healthy emotions and constructive behavior).

Once a client has achieved intellectual insight into a healthy belief, which means, in this context, that she (in this case) understands that her unhealthy belief is inconsistent with reality, is illogical, and is unconstructive and that her healthy alternative belief is consistent with reality, is logical, and is constructive, the next step is to help her to weaken her conviction in the former and strengthen

1. Write down your healthy belief in the top left-hand oblong.
2. Rate your present level of conviction in this belief on a 100-point scale with 0% = no conviction and 100% = total conviction, and write down this rating in the space provided on the form.
3. Respond to this healthy belief with an attack that is directed at the healthy belief. This may take the form of a doubt, reservation, or objection to the healthy belief. Make this attacking statement as genuine as you can. The more it reflects what you actually believe, the better. Write down this attack in the oblong on the right.
4. Respond to this attack as fully as you can. It is really important that you respond to each element of the attack. Do so as persuasively as possible and write down the response in the second oblong on the left.
5. Continue in this vein until you have answered all your attacks and cannot think of any more.

   If you find this exercise difficult, you might find it easier to make your attacks gentle at first. Then, when you find that you can respond to these attacks quite easily, begin to make the attacks more biting. Work in this way until you are making really strong attacks. When you make an attack, do so as if you want yourself to believe it. And when you respond, really throw yourself into it with the intention of demolishing the attack and raising your level of conviction in your healthy belief.

   Don't forget that the purpose of this exercise is to strengthen your healthy belief, so it is important that you stop when you have answered all your attacks. Use as many forms as your need and clip them together when you have finished.

   If you make an attack that you cannot answer, stop the exercise and we will discuss how you can best respond to it in the group.
6. When you have answered all your attacks, rerate your level of conviction in the healthy belief as before. If you have been successful at responding to your attacks, then this rating will have gone up. If it has not increased or has done so by only a little, we'll discuss the reasons for this in group.

FIGURE 3.2 How to complete a zig-zag form.

her conviction in the latter. Doing so helps her to gain emotional insight into her healthy belief, which in turn facilitates the achievement of her constructive emotional and behavioral goals.

One of my favorite techniques to help clients to gain emotional insight into their healthy beliefs is known as the zig-zag technique. It is based on the idea that one can strengthen conviction into one's healthy belief by responding effectively to attacks on this belief expressed as a doubt, reservation, or objection.

In using this technique, I give my clients clear written instructions as to how to use this technique for homework and, in the case of the written form of the zig zag, I provide them with a

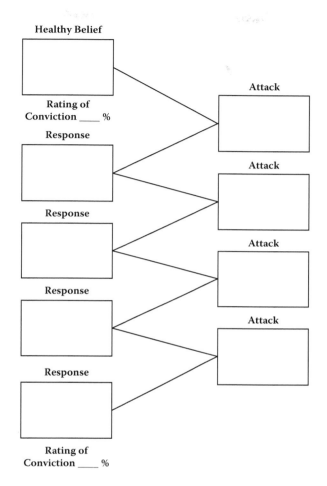

Healthy Belief

Rating of
Conviction _____ %

Response

Response

Response

Response

Rating of
Conviction _____ %

Attack

Attack

Attack

Attack

FIGURE 3.3 The zig-zag form.

worked example that represents successful implementation of the
technique by a former client who has given permission for this to
be used for this purpose.

I now provide you with the following:

1. Written instructions on how your clients can complete a
   written zig-zag form (Figure 3.2).
2. A blank zig-zag form (Figure 3.3).
3. A worked example of how one of my clients successfully
   completed the written zig-zag form (Figure 3.4).

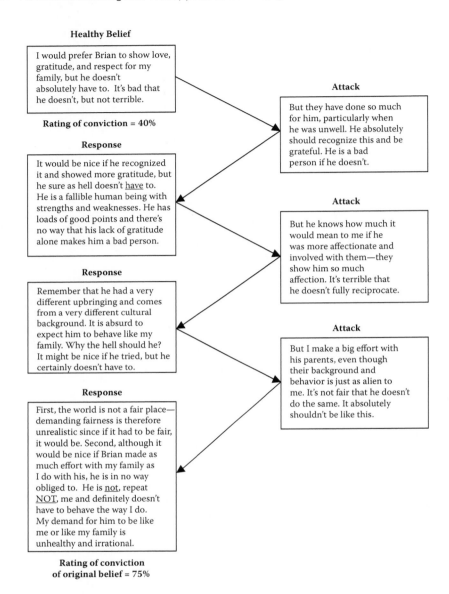

Healthy Belief

I would prefer Brian to show love, gratitude, and respect for my family, but he doesn't absolutely have to. It's bad that he doesn't, but not terrible.

Rating of conviction = 40%

Response

It would be nice if he recognized it and showed more gratitude, but he sure as hell doesn't <u>have</u> to. He is a fallible human being with strengths and weaknesses. He has loads of good points and there's no way that his lack of gratitude alone makes him a bad person.

Response

Remember that he had a very different upbringing and comes from a very different cultural background. It is absurd to expect him to behave like my family. Why the hell should he? It might be nice if he tried, but he certainly doesn't have to.

Response

First, the world is not a fair place—demanding fairness is therefore unrealistic since if it had to be fair, it would be. Second, although it would be nice if Brian made as much effort with my family as I do with his, he is in no way obliged to. He is <u>not</u>, repeat <u>NOT</u>, me and definitely doesn't have to behave the way I do. My demand for him to be like me or like my family is unhealthy and irrational.

Rating of conviction of original belief = 75%

Attack

But they have done so much for him, particularly when he was unwell. He absolutely should recognize this and be grateful. He is a bad person if he doesn't.

Attack

But he knows how much it would mean to me if he was more affectionate and involved with them—they show him so much affection. It's terrible that he doesn't fully reciprocate.

Attack

But I make a big effort with his parents, even though their background and behavior is just as alien to me. It's not fair that he doesn't do the same. It absolutely shouldn't be like this.

FIGURE 3.4   Zig-zag technique: An example.

1. You will need to use a hand-held, good-quality tape recorder with good-quality tape for this exercise. A good micro- or minicassette will suffice.
2. Find a time and a space when you won't be interrupted and cannot be overheard. Put your answering machine on or take the phone off the hook. You will need to set aside about 20 or 30 minutes for this task.
3. Begin the recording process by stating your healthy belief on tape, noting verbally your level of conviction in it, using a 0% to 100% scale.
4. Try and get yourself to return to your unhealthy belief by attacking your healthy belief.
5. Respond to this attack in a forceful and persuasive manner, making sure that you answer all elements of the attack.
6. Go back and forth in this matter (making sure that your responses are more forceful and persuasive than your attacks) until you can think of no more attacks.
7. Rerate your level of conviction in your originally stated healthy belief.
8. Listen to the recording and note the following:
   • Instances where you went off the point. Formulate an alternative response that would have enabled you to keep to the point.
   • Instances when you failed to respond to an element (or elements) of an attack. Formulate a response to the unanswered element.
   • Instances when you sounded unpersuaded by your response to an attack. Formulate more persuasive ways of responding to this attack in both tone of voice and content of argument.

FIGURE 3.5   Instructions on how to use the tape-recorded version of the zig-zag technique.

4. Written instructions on how your clients can use the tape-recorded version of the zig-zag technique, which I suggest that they practice after they have gained competence in completing the written version (Figure 3.5).

Reference

Ellis, A. (1963). Toward a more precise definition of "emotional" and "intellectual" insight. *Psychological Reports, 13,* 125–126.

REBT Self-Help Form and Reading Materials

Therapist: Albert Ellis, PhD, deceased

Affiliation: Licensed Psychologist; President, Albert Ellis Institute, New York

Major works:

Ellis, A. (1994). *Reason and emotion in psychotherapy* (Rev. & updated ed.). Secaucus, NJ: Carol Publishing Group.
Ellis, A., & Dryden, W. (2007). *The practice of rational emotive behavior therapy* (Rev. ed.). New York: Springer.
Ellis, A., & Harper, R. A. (1997). *A guide to rational living* (3rd ed.). North Hollywood, CA: Wilshire.

Dr. Ellis was the author of over 75 books and 1,200 articles. He was the founding father of rational emotive behavior therapy (REBT).

Dr. Ellis, one of the true luminaries in our field, passed away on July 24, 2007 at the age of 93.

Population for whom the technique is appropriate: Adolescent and adult clients

Cautionary notes: This technique is not suitable for younger adolescent clients and for adults with severe reading difficulties.

Almost all my adolescent and adult clients are given several copies of the rational emotive behavior therapy (REBT) Self-Help Form during their first therapy session, together with a dozen pamphlets describing the basic principles and practices of REBT, which also have been discussed with them during the first session. Usually, their first homework assignment is to start reading the pamphlets, as well as one or two of my self-help books, such as *A Guide to Rational Living, How to Stubbornly Refuse to Make Yourself Miserable About Anything—Yes, Anything!, How to Control Your Anxiety Before It Controls You,* or *The Albert Ellis Reader.*

The clients are asked to start reading the pamphlets and preferably one of the books and to complete one or two of the REBT

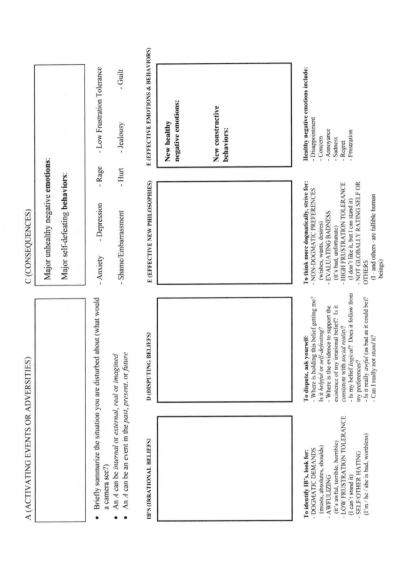

FIGURE 3.6 REBT Self-Help Form. Copyright Windy Dryden & Jane Walker, 1992. Revised by Robert Ellis, 1996.

Self-Help Forms (Figure 3.6) about an important disturbed feeling or behavior that they currently experience. They are told that we will go over the filled-in-form together during the next therapy session and that I will check it to see if they have filled it out accurately and started to learn how to find and dispute their main irrational beliefs that help create their disturbances and whether they have figured out their effective new philosophies and effective emotions and behaviors.

Clients often are asked to use the REBT Self-Help Form as a continuing assignment and are encouraged to fill out one of the forms and bring it in for discussion in their therapy sessions when they have an important emotional or behavioral problem.

Behavioral Assignments for Individual and Couples Therapy: Corrective Suggestions for Behavioral Change

Therapist: Robert W. Firestone, PhD

Affiliation: Clinical Psychologist, the Glendon Association, Santa Barbara, California

Major works:

Firestone, R. W. (1997). *Combating destructive thought processes: Voice therapy and separation theory.* Thousand Oaks, CA: Sage.

Firestone, R. W. (1997). *Suicide and the inner voice: Risk assessment, treatment, and case management.* Thousand Oaks, CA: Sage.

Firestone, R. W., & Catlett, J. (1999). *Fear of intimacy.* Washington, DC: American Psychological Association.

Author of three other books, audiovisual mental health training materials, and the Firestone Assessment of Self-Destructive Thoughts (FAST; Firestone & Firestone, 1996) test, which discriminates suicidal from nonsuicidal clients

Populations for whom the technique is appropriate: Adult and adolescent clients in individual or group psychotherapy and couples who have learned to use the techniques of voice therapy in individual or couples therapy

Cautionary notes: None

Introduction and Background

Voice therapy is the process of giving language or spoken words to thoughts and attitudes, antithetical toward self and hostile toward others, that are at the core of an individual's maladaptive behavior and lifestyle. The methods bring internalized destructive thought processes to the surface with accompanying affect in a dialogue format such that a client can confront alien components of the personality.

As described in previous works (Firestone, 1985, 1988, 1990, 1997a, 1997b, 1998; Firestone & Catlett, 1999), the primary technique consists of asking clients to verbalize their negative thoughts *toward* themselves in the second person, "you," as though they were talking *to* themselves instead of the first person, "I," statements *about* themselves. Putting self-attacking statements in this form often releases strong feelings followed by spontaneous insights. Expressing voices in the second person also facilitates the process of separating the client's point of view from negative thought processes that had been incorporated during the developmental years.

The techniques of voice therapy traditionally have consisted of three components: (1) the process of eliciting and identifying negative thought patterns and releasing the associated affect; (2) discussing insights and reactions to verbalizing the voice; and (3) counteracting self-destructive behaviors regulated by the voice through the application of appropriate corrective suggestions. (For an in-depth discussion of Step 1, see Firestone, 1998; for discussion of Step 2, see Firestone, 1997a.) In this phase of treatment, client and therapist attempt to interrupt maladaptive behavior patterns through collaborative planning and suggestions for behavioral change that are in accord with each individual's personal motivation. Plans for behavioral change fall into two categories: (a) corrective suggestions that help control or interrupt self-feeding habits and disrupt addictive attachment and (b) corrective suggestions that expand the client's world by taking risks and gradually overcoming fears related to pursuing wants and priorities. It is important to note that these steps are not necessarily undertaken in the order delineated here. Even in the beginning phase, corrective suggestions are used to encourage clients to avoid the addictive substances and habits they use to suppress feeling. I often suggest the following activities or assignments at various stages in the treatment process:

The Techniques of Voice Therapy

1. In the initial session, I usually encourage the client to write a personal history that includes a description of important childhood events, current relationships, personal and

vocational concerns, and aspirations. This history assists therapists in understanding the unique aspects of their clients' backgrounds, as well as their priorities and goals, and helps the client develop an overall picture of his or her present situation. In compiling a personal account or review of their lives, clients are better able to formulate the problems that brought them to therapy and incidentally gain insight into the antecedents or sources of their distress.

2. To help clients to become familiar with the process of self-attack, I suggest that they become aware of specific times when they start to experience self-critical thoughts. It is important to identify situations and experiences that trigger painful mood swings and psychological disturbance. It is also important for clients to recognize negative thoughts and attitudes as they are occurring. It is not necessary for them to either agree or disagree with these negative thoughts; it is sufficient to simply recognize them as attacks when they occur, rather than accept them at face value or as accurate self-appraisals. Merely acknowledging that one is involved in a process of self-attack often is effective in countering the influence of destructive thinking on one's overall mood and behavior.

3. As noted, maintaining a daily journal can be an important adjunct to therapy in that it helps clients identify specific events or circumstances that precipitate a self-attacking thought process. Writing down thoughts that act to inhibit clients' positive or assertive behaviors can facilitate changes in attitudes that allow them to challenge their fears. Voice attacks that deride the pursuit of love and satisfaction in relationships are among the most common reported by clients. These voices warn individuals against investing themselves emotionally in caring for another person and emphasize the possibility of being hurt or victimized. When clients record their seemingly self-protective thoughts in a journal, or reveal them to a close friend or spouse, they discover that these negative predictions are generally illogical or inaccurate.

In most cases, I recommend that clients keep track of their destructive thought processes through talking, on a daily basis, with a reliable friend who is empathetic and understanding. I encourage them to disclose their self-critical thoughts and cynical attitudes toward other people, while not necessarily analyzing them, during these conversations. This technique alone can be of significant value.

4. As a supplemental exercise to identifying destructive thoughts that influence addictive behaviors, clients are encouraged to become aware of the times they feel compelled to indulge in destructive habits. I propose that they make a conscious decision to decrease their involvement in, or entirely abstain from, most addictive habits (smoking, drinking, overeating, or any habitual response that becomes compulsive) and to focus on the feelings (anxiety, anger, sadness) that may emerge. For example, if a client decides to stop smoking, I recommend maintaining a journal, a daily log, of the feelings that arise subsequent to giving up the addictive behavior pattern. In general, the process of recording emotional reactions at times when the temptation to smoke, drink, or overeat feels overwhelming helps clients maintain their resolution to abstain.

5. In couples therapy, partners learn to disclose their destructive thoughts toward themselves and their partners. Through the process of identifying specific self-attacks, as well as judgmental, critical thoughts about the other, each partner becomes better able to relate openly to the other. Hostile, cynical attitudes toward the other are verbalized in the *third person* format, as though someone else were giving negative information to the individual about his or her partner. For example: *"He's* so cold and uncommunicative. *He's* going to reject you sooner or later." *"She's* so melodramatic and acts so helpless. Why get involved with *her?"*

In our individual sessions or couples groups, men and women develop the ability to listen to each other with understanding as a result of participating in individual sessions or couples groups. Both partners reveal self-depreciating thoughts and angry attitudes toward the other in a forthright exchange of views. At times, we focus on one partner's individual work while the other listens. Tracing the source of their self-attacks and hostile attitudes toward their partner to early family interactions helps them gain a fresh perspective on each other's problems. As a result, they tend to feel more empathy for their mates and compassion for themselves.

In applying this procedure as a homework assignment, I often recommend that the partners spend up to a half hour a day engaged in a similar form of communication. It is important that each partner strive to "give away" their negative attacks without blaming the other and to attempt not to react to the voice statements of the other as personal criticism, even when they have some basis in reality. The partners try to be sincere and sensitive when giving away their negative thoughts and attempt to relinquish their critical views and grudges.

6. A modified version of the exercise described in Item 5 helps people interrupt negative thoughts that often emerge prior to, during, or following a sexual encounter. Partners' feelings of affection, sexual excitement, and attraction are easily dispelled by negative thoughts about their own body—for example, *"Your penis is too small." "Your breasts are too large, too small, the wrong shape,"* or sexual performance, for example, *"You're not going to be able to keep your erection." "You're not going to have an orgasm."* When men and women make the transition from an affectionate embrace to a sexual caress, often their respective "voices" may gain in ascendance and can significantly reduce sexual desire as well as positive personal feelings.

In these cases, I recommend that partners give away their self-critical thoughts and cynical attitudes toward their partner during the sex act. At the point where one or both partners are aware of losing feeling and becoming more involved in a cognitive process, they can stop making love temporarily and communicate with their partner by carrying out this exercise. They are instructed to maintain physical contact while saying their self-attacks and critical thoughts about each other. By interrupting their lovemaking for a certain period of time to share these thoughts and express their anxieties, they are able to sustain a level of feeling and preserve their affectionate and close feelings for one another.

Conclusion

In the voice therapy model, corrective suggestions regarding specialized activities that the client can undertake in the interval between sessions are different from those used in behavioral or cognitive-behavioral therapies. They derive from the types of negative prescriptions the client has discovered for himself or herself in the sessions and are not directives imposed by the therapist. Our suggestions bear a direct relationship to the maladaptive behavior patterns that are influenced and controlled by clients' negative thought processes. Therapists must be cognizant that clients' acceptance of corrective suggestions tends to arouse considerable anxiety and resistance and may precipitate an onslaught of voice attacks that need to be dealt with by the experienced clinician.

Because the procedures of voice therapy challenge clients' core defenses and basic self-concepts, the process of initiating important behavioral changes that expand their boundaries and expose their misconceptions about self become apparent. I believe that the potential for therapeutic progress is not merely a function of identifying negative thought patterns and uncovering repressed material; indeed, personal growth ultimately must involve constructive behavioral changes that oppose self-limiting or self-destructive patterns and lifestyles. Working on themselves outside the therapy office environment helps clients begin the process of eliminating behaviors that are opposed to self-actualization and initiating behaviors that are more consistent with their personal goals.

References

Firestone, R. W. (1985). *The fantasy bond: Structure of psychological defenses.* New York: Human Sciences Press.

Firestone, R. W. (1988). *Voice therapy: A psychotherapeutic approach to self-destructive behavior.* New York: Human Sciences Press.

Firestone, R. W. (1990). Voice therapy. In J. Zeig & W. Munion (Eds.), *What is psychotherapy? Contemporary perspectives* (pp. 68–74). San Francisco: Jossey-Bass.

Firestone, R. W. (1997a). *Combating destructive thought processes: Voice therapy and separation theory.* Thousand Oaks, CA: Sage.

Firestone, R. W. (1997b). *Suicide and the inner voice: Risk assessment, treatment, and case management.* Thousand Oaks, CA: Sage.

Firestone, R. W. (1998). Voice therapy. In H. G. Rosenthal (Ed.), *Favorite counseling and therapy techniques* (pp. 82–85). Philadelphia: Accelerated Development/Taylor & Francis.

Firestone, R. W., & Catlett, J. (1999). *Fear of intimacy.* Washington, DC: American Psychological Association.

Firestone, R. W., & Firestone, L. A. (1996). *Firestone assessment of self-destructive thoughts manual.* San Antonio, TX: Psychological Corporation.

What We Can Change and What We Can't: Responding to the Negative Voice

Therapist: Arthur Freeman, EdD, ABPP

Affiliation: Psychologist, Department of Psychology, Philadelphia College of Osteopathic Medicine, Philadelphia, Pennsylvania

Major works:

Beck, A. T., & Freeman, A. (2006). *Cognitive therapy of personality disorders.* New York: Springer.

Freeman, A., Pretzer, J., Fleming, B., & Simon, K. M. (2004). *Clinical applications of cognitive therapy* (2nd ed.). New York: Plenum.

Gilson, M., & Freeman, A. (1999). *Beating the BEAST of depression.* San Antonio, TX: Psychological Corporation.

Dr. Freeman has published over 60 books that have been translated into numerous languages. He has lectured in more than 30 countries.

Population for whom the technique is appropriate: Adolescent through adult patients in cognitive-behavior therapy (CBT)

Cautionary notes: None

The CBT patient is socialized to the importance of homework as an essential part of the therapy. Several points are stressed: Homework provides a laboratory experience for the patient; homework offers continuity between therapy sessions; homework affords the patient practice at skills not easily done within the therapy session; homework brings the therapy work into the "real" world; homework provides an opportunity for data collection; success in the real world serves to empower the patient; and, finally, when therapy sessions are finished, everything becomes homework.

Structuring the homework is very important. It must be collaborative, fully explained to the patient, and seen by the patient as a potentially valuable experience. The homework must come organically from the session material; that is, there must be a connection between what has gone on in the therapy session or what is planned for the next therapy session.

The first homework assignment is useful for patients who see themselves as overwhelmed by the enormity of their perceived life problems. Typically, the patient verbalizes, "There's nothing I can do. So much has to change."

When asked by the therapist, "Just how many things must you change?" The patient responds, "About a million."

The sequence of the homework is as follows:

Therapist: I would like you to make a complete list of all of the things that you believe that you must change. The list should be as complete as you can possibly make it. Leave nothing out, and please break large problems into several parts, if possible. (Note: This is not meant as a paradoxical intervention, rather as an opportunity for data gathering.) Please number each problem or subpart.

When the patient brings in the list, he or she will see that although it may be substantial, it shows far fewer than a million problems.

The therapist can then discuss the total number of problems. The second, and most important, part of the homework follows:

Therapist: What I would like you to now do is to redo the list and assign each item to one of four categories.

1. Things that can easily change
2. Things that can be changed with some (mild to moderate) difficulty
3. Things that can be changed with great (severe) difficulty
4. Things that cannot change

In scaling problems in this way, the patient will likely see that the vast majority of problems fall into the first three categories.

Clinical Example

Rose was a 42-year-old woman who sought therapy because of "low self-esteem." At intake she had a Beck Depression Inventory score of 32, placing her at the level of severe depression. She reported feeling badly about herself since she was an adolescent. The theme for many of Rose's statements was that she was defective in many ways. The session between Rose and the therapist follows:

Therapist: What do you see as MOST wrong with you?
Patient: Everything.
Therapist: Everything?
Patient: Yes, everything.
Therapist: How many "everythings" are there? What's your guess—count all of the "everythings" wrong with you.
Patient: Oh, I don't know. Too many to count.
Therapist: Stay with this for a moment more. Humor me. If we could hire an accountant to do a count of all of the things wrong with you ... you know, an auditor ... what would he or she find?
Patient: A million.
Therapist: A million?
Patient: Probably.
Therapist: And most of those things wrong with you, would they be related to how you look?
Patient: Yeah, probably.
Therapist: Hmmmm. I wonder ... I wonder what would happen if you could get an actual count of all of the things wrong with the way that you look. What do you think you would find if we could figure out a way to do an actual count?
Patient: I would probably be even more depressed and upset.
Therapist: Or maybe not. Whether or not you would be even more upset is something we can measure. Would you be willing to try an experiment to gather the information for the therapy?
Patient: It depends what it is. I don't know.
Therapist: Here's my idea. What if ... Do you have a full length mirror at home?

Patient: Oh God.

Therapist: Wait. Wait. What if you could be alone. You totally undress, stand in front of the mirror …

Patient: Yuck.

Therapist: … and you have a pad and pen with you. And then you start to make a list, starting from your toes to your head of all of the things wrong with you … with the way that you look.

Patient: I'd be there a very long time.

Therapist: That's also something that you can evaluate and that we can discuss.

Patient: (Exasperated) What's the purpose of my doing that? To feel worse?

Therapist: There are three reasons to try it. First, as always, to collect information. Second, to see what the real number of flaws and faults are. Last, to then decide what can be done about them. Would you be willing to try this … as an experiment?

Patient: I really don't want to.

Therapist: That wasn't my question. I didn't ask whether this would be fun, whether this would be enjoyable, or whether this was something that you wanted to do. My question was … is … would you be willing to try this as a way of gathering data for us to work on?

Patient: Okay. What are you suggesting I do?

Therapist: Simply stand naked in front of the mirror, and make a list of the million things wrong with your body and how you look. Then bring the list in at the next session.

Patient: This is the dumbest homework I've ever done.

At the next session, the patient brought in her list. It included the following:

1. My toes are crooked.
2. My feet are too big.
3. I have fat ankles.
4. I have heavy calves and thighs.
5. My hips are too wide.
6. My stomach bulges out.

7. My breasts are too small.
8. My shoulders are big.
9. I have a double chin.
10. My lips are too thin.
11. My face is too round.
12. My eyes are small and piggylike.
13. My eyes are a washed out color.
14. My hair is a mousy color.
15. My hair is ugly.
16. I'm too short.
17. I'm overweight.
18. I look like I have only one eyebrow.

Therapist: What do you think of this list?
Patient: I think that the whole thing was stupid.
Therapist: Were you surprised by what you found and wrote down?
Patient: No.
Therapist: Nothing surprised you?
Patient: No. It's all of what I thought.
Therapist: Well I must admit that I'm surprised.
Patient: Why?
Therapist: There are 18 things on the list. You had led me to believe that there were a million. I had expected a carton of information. Here it's all on one sheet of yellow paper.
Patient: Yeah, that's true. But there are still 18.
Therapist: You're 999,982 items short of your prediction.
Patient: Okay. That's true. But 18 is hard to live with.
Therapist: Okay … now let's do the fun part of this experiment. I would like you to take this list and divide it into four separate lists. First, things that can change easily. Second, things that can be changed with some (mild to moderate) difficulty. Third, things that can be changed with great (severe) difficulty. Fourth, things that cannot change.

The patient then did this in the session. Her revised list looked like this:

1. My toes are crooked.

Patient: There's nothing I can do.

Therapist: You could have the most crooked ones broken and reset by an orthopedic surgeon.

Patient: That's bizarre!

Therapist: I agree. But it could be done. Where would you place this one?

Patient: This is surely a three.

The scaling was done, with discussion, on the remaining 17 with the following result:

2. My feet are too big. (4)
3. I have fat ankles. (3)
4. I have heavy calves and thighs. (2)
5. My hips are too wide. (4)
6. My stomach bulges out. (3)
7. My breasts are too small. (2)
8. My shoulders are big. (4)
9. I have a double chin. (2–3)
10. My lips are too thin. (2)
11. My face is too round. (2–3)
12. My eyes are small and piggy-like. (1)
13. My eyes are a washed out color. (1)
14. My hair is a mousy color. (1)
15. My hair is ugly. (1)
16. I'm too short. (3)
17. I'm overweight. (2–3)
18. I look like I have only one eyebrow. (1)

What Rose saw rather quickly was that the majority of the points on her list could be changed, but many would take time, money, or pain to alter. Other items were against her beliefs (e.g., breast enhancement).

The session focused on things that she could change rather quickly, for example, changing her hairstyle, hair color, getting colored contact lenses, or losing weight.

This scaling technique places the change possibilities on the patient. If she does not like something, she can change it. Or the client can decide if she is willing to work to change. The one caveat is to be careful of being sidetracked by the patient arguments such as, "Why should I have to do this? It isn't fair. Other people are born beautiful. I was cheated."

Work on what can be changed, not the unfairness of nature, the world, genes, or what "they" will think.

Responding to the Negative Voice

One of the key interventions in cognitive therapy is helping the patient to become aware of her internal dialogue. Given that we all carry with us both a collection and a selection of the voices of the past, it is for each of us to determine which voices are most active and dominant and which voices are passive and latent. The active voices govern day-to-day behavior—for example, how to dress, adherence to social conventions, appropriateness of response, and so on. In times of stress, the passive or latent voice often will come forward, govern behavior, and then return to the passive and latent position. Cognitive therapists call these "automatic thoughts" because they just seem to appear, often without any conscious control. The purpose of the following technique is to bring the unspoken voice to the level of awareness, and to then help the patient to respond adaptively to the mal-adaptive, irrational, negative, or distorted ideas.

This technique has some similarities to the famous "empty chair" technique so well known from Gestalt therapy.

The therapist will hear from the patient, most often from the first contact, the automatic thoughts related to self ("I'm no good." "I'm fat and ugly." "I'm defective."), to their idiosyncratic world ("It's unfair." "They're unfair." "All men are lousy."), and to the future ("My pain will never end." "I will always be unhappy." "Things are hopeless."). The effects of these thoughts are translated into action, such as avoidance for the anxious individual or inaction for the depressed individual. As the individual "listens" to the internal voice without challenge, she is affected in myriad ways.

For the next homework, I use the following lead-in: "Let's suppose that you are arrested and charged with a crime. The district attorney presents 90 witnesses over a 9-day period, all of whom testify to some aspect of your guilt, after which the prosecution rests.

"Your attorney for the defense then gets up and makes the following statement: 'Your honor, ladies and gentlemen of the jury, my client is a generally nice person and is probably innocent.'" I then ask the patient, "Given this defense, what are your chances of an acquittal?" The patient will likely say, "No chance!"

I continue. "Now let's suppose that the district attorney presents those same 90 witnesses over a 9-day period, but your attorney presents 50 witnesses over a 5-day period, all of whom testify to your innocence. Now what are your chances of an acquittal?"

To this the patient will likely answer, "Well, now I have a chance because there is some defense."

The final part of the introduction is the following: "The district attorney presents those same 90 witnesses over a 9-day period, but your attorney says, 'Your honor, ladies and gentlemen of the jury, we have only one witness for the defense. Please have the Pope take the stand.'"

The Pope takes the stand and says that you could not have committed the crime because you were having dinner that very night at the Vatican with the Pope and several of the cardinals.

The patient is then asked, "Now what would be your chances of an acquittal?" The patient will likely answer that her chances are even better because she now had a very credible and powerful defense.

I then tell the patient that the next homework will have the effect of helping them to build a powerful and credible defense against their dysfunctional thinking.

The equipment necessary for this homework is an audiocassette or digital recorder.

1. The therapist will have developed a list of the patient's automatic thoughts regarding a specific inter- or intrapersonal life issue.
2. The thoughts are listed in a sequence. The patient then practices the negative self-statements.
3. The therapist then helps the patient to develop adaptive responses.
4. The therapist and patient can practice responding to the dysfunctional thoughts.

5. The patient is then helped to record each of the dysfunctional thoughts on tape with a 5-second pause between each thought. The thoughts are stated in the third person. For example: "You're no good" (*pause*). "Nothing you ever do will work" (*pause*). "You have no worth" (*pause*).
6. The patient is then encouraged to use the tape in the car on the way to work, practice the adaptive responses for a period of time each day.

The result will be that the patient will have practiced adaptive responding so that when the automatic thought emerges, the patient will be able to respond, thereby reducing the patient's negative reaction to the automatic thoughts.

One of the most common patient reactions is he or she has problems offering the adaptive reactions when he or she doesn't believe the adaptive response. It should be pointed out to the patient that at the beginning he or she does not have to believe the response to the automatic thought. With practice and an ongoing assessment of the response to the adaptive responding, the patient will start to believe the response.

Ultimately, the patient also will become so well practiced in the response that he or she can react quickly in responding to the automatic thought.

Naive, Cynic, Realist

Therapist: Chris Frey, MSW

Affiliation: Frey and Tobin Counseling Associates, St. Louis, Missouri; Licensed Clinical Social Worker; Academy of Certified Social Workers

Major works:

Frey, C. (1997). *Men at work: An action guide to masculine healing.* Dubuque, IA: Islewest Publishing.

Frey, C. (2006). *Double jeopardy: A counselor's guide to juvenile male sexual offenders/substance abusers.* Alexandria, VA: American Correctional Association.

Frey, C. (2006). *Double jeopardy: A workbook for treating juvenile male sexual offenders/substance abusers.* Alexandria, VA: American Correctional Association.

Population for whom the technique is appropriate: Adults

Cautionary notes: Therapists and counselors need to understand the issues behind a client's worldview; the experiences that have formed a naive or cynical stance on relationships and personal health.

Many clients describe life and relationships in absolute terms. At one end of the spectrum is the client who continues to be surprised that some people can repeatedly act in harmful, insensitive ways. These clients often carry a significant amount of covert anger, wondering why their family, friends, and coworkers don't appreciate them, wondering when they will be rewarded for their sacrifices and niceness. This naïveté can result in resentment, guilt, confusion, and a series of unfulfilling relationships.

At the other extreme is the client who, based on previous painful experience, has decided to view the world, personal relationships, and, at times, even self, from a foundation of mistrust. These clients are angry, often overtly, falsely believing they are insulated against hurt and pain by their cynicism. These people are often seen by others as "takers," which becomes most problematic in intimate relationships. They often see themselves as wise, having learned the ways of the world through hard, true lessons.

Both the naive person and the cynical person tend to believe in a one-dimensional world with overgeneralized, somewhat rigid views of good and bad. In the extreme, clients from both perspectives were often seriously emotionally wounded, perhaps at a time in childhood when being naive was a natural and normal state of being.

The primary goal of the naive, cynic, realist homework assignment is to assist clients in moving toward a more flexible, mature view of self and others. The assignment helps instill hope and personal growth without rose-colored glasses so the clients can build more effective support systems and adopt a more realistic view of themselves.

As clients arrive at an understanding of their typical point of view, more toward naive or cynical, one method for introducing the homework is a discussion, in session, about individuals who represent the realist perspective. These are people who learn life's hard lessons and then put them to work in intimate relationships, their work, perhaps even in their community. These people are described as works-in-progress, dealing with anger, trust, trauma, and any number of the critical recovery issues that affect people. I often refer to realists by using the 12-step slogan: progress, not perfection.

Clients may then be able to identify individuals they have known through life that carry this energy: family, friends, teachers, mentors, colleagues. The therapist or counselor may offer stories from his or her own experience, or examples of public figures. I have suggested Martin Luther King Jr., Victor Frankl, and my mentor, Dr. Bob Brundage, who maintained his compassion and creativity in a career devoted to the chronically mentally ill, as excellent examples of powerful realists. Each of these individuals saw the shadow and gold in humanity, including their own.

I then ask the clients to identify themselves along the following continuum:

Naive Realist Cynic

The client is then presented with a series of questions to consider outside of the session. As with most homework, I encourage the client to choose methods of completing the work that will be the most meaningful and fits best with his or her learning style:

writing by hand or computer, drawing and writing along the continuum, discussing the assignment with another person, or simply considering the questions.

The questions vary with the needs of the person and may include the following:

- Pick several stages of your life. Place yourself along the continuum at each stage. Have you moved over time? What events and people impacted your movement at each stage?
- Where do you place yourself today?
- Whose point of view, among significant people and influences, is the most similar to your own? Do you view the perspective of these people as positive and productive? If so, in what ways? If not, in what ways?
- What life experiences strengthened your belief in the style you currently live in?
- How does your point of view affect your anger? Hurt? Confusion? Guilt? Fear? Personal relationships? Other relationships?
- How well is your current point of view working in your life?
- If you would benefit from changing your perspective, what direction would you move in?

Upon the client's return to session, the homework can lead in any number of directions. I have often used this assignment in combination with exercises on trust building for the cynic and boundary setting for the naive person. In various forms of trauma resolution and family-of-origin work, clients may return with greater insight into specific events and past relationships, and this insight can lead to other forms of healing. From the here-and-now perspective, this homework can highlight patterns in unsuccessful relationships and lead clients toward present-oriented change strategies. As therapy continues, formerly naive clients can view themselves in more forgiving terms while seeing others with greater clarity. As the cynical person recovers, individuals who merit some degree of trust can be identified, self-righteous anger diminishes, and the client can begin to find safe spaces within an often challenging world.

Affective Deficit: Relationship Conditioning

Therapist: Sterling K. Gerber, PhD

Affiliation: Professor, Eastern Washington University, Cheney, Washington

Major works:

Gerber, S. K. (1986). *Responsive therapy: A systematic approach to counseling skills.* New York: Human Sciences Press.

Gerber, S. K. (1999). *Enhancing counselor intervention strategies: An integrational viewpoint.* Philadelphia: Accelerated Development/Taylor & Francis.

Population for whom the technique is appropriate: Married couples or couples with long-term commitment to partners

Cautionary notes: Failure to follow the procedure exactly and over a prolonged period of time may result in increased emotional turmoil and stress in the relationship.

Affective deficit (see Gerber, 1999) is a condition wherein the client is unhappy, unfulfilled, or insecure because of the failure to establish one of two affective states. The first corresponds to a lack of noncontingent, personal validation. It is established by children in functional families during childhood and adolescence. Successful accomplishment of Maslow's third level of need (love and belonging) may reference the same condition. Clients present complaints such as, "I don't understand what is wrong with me. As I survey my life, everything seems to be okay. I have an adequate income, a nice house, a good partner, well-socialized children. Yet something is missing. I'm not happy. I feel unfulfilled."

The second type of affective deficit occurs in long-term relationships wherein there is a lack of consistent emotional security. This represents a failure to bond on an emotional level, often because of engaging in a sexual relationship, sharing common living arrangements (often including having children), or both, prior to, or in conflict with, accomplishment of the emotional relationship bond. It is to this condition that the prescribed homework pertains.

Clients often present with what appears to be surplus dynamics, that is, the presence of conditions that militate against a satisfying relationship. They may note communication problems, a mismatch in love language, selfishness of the partner, having fallen out of love, inability to reach resolution of financial conflicts or of career disjunctiveness, or all of these. In short, they may generate many targets of complaint, not realizing that what is at the base of their unhappiness is not what's wrong with their relationship but rather what is not right with it.

They approach each other with what may be analogous to the distrust and skittishness of a wild animal in response to a trainer or of an abused pet (or child for that matter) toward its owner. The process of creating a predictably safe, supportive relationship by painstakingly being in the presence of the wild animal and progressively decreasing the distance until proximity and contact are tolerable may be descriptive of the conditioning of a mutually supportive and secure relationship between two people.

Another frame for perceiving the dynamics is to consider Gestalt splits within each partner, with some dynamics well established and others unaccomplished. For example, the couple may have predictable sexual patterns that are mostly satisfying, problem resolution techniques that usually work, and social front skills that project an ideal relationship. At the same time they may withhold emotional commitment, maintain a stance of insecurity or protective distance, and nurse a precipitous "cut-and-run" strategy.

A third way of describing the way this works, particularly useful in explaining it to clients, is a metaphor using the automobile battery. For anyone who has experienced depleted batteries and the processes of getting them charged, the analogy is quite cogent. The process of slow charging a battery is to "trickle" charge it over an extended period of time. This approach has the advantage over the quick charge method in that it provides a longer period of performance following the charge. By "charging the relationship battery" a little bit every day, it will withstand brief periods of high drain and quickly bounce back to a working capacity. This homework strategy is a way of slow charging the relationship battery.

Although this approach can be instituted within all couples counseling, it is especially useful for those wherein the partners show emotional ambivalence to one another—the sending of simultaneous or alternating "come closer–go away" messages. There are three critical elements to this procedure. First, the partners are instructed to spend 5 minutes (by the clock) twice a day in close physical (some skin to skin), nonsexual contact. This may be snuggling or cuddling in bed prior to rising, sitting together on the couch and holding hands, or any other mutually comfortable interaction. Kissing or other actions that have become associated with sexual interaction are to be avoided, as is progressing from the 5-minute conditioning period directly into sexual behavior.

The second critical aspect is for the couple to have neutral or pleasant conditions or interaction accompanying the touch. Neutral conditions may include watching a portion of a television program or reading books. Pleasant interaction may include non-inflammatory conversation, sharing positive experiences from earlier in the day, or communicating agenda for the coming day. Focusing on problems or on interpersonal concerns is to be conducted at other times and in other settings.

Third, it is necessary for this activity to occur twice daily, every day, for a prolonged period. Some positive effect may be apparent in as early as 3 weeks. Maximum effect comes from habituating the routine and continuing it indefinitely.

Positive early effects may be inhibited in couples wherein one or both partners are accustomed to being touched only as a prelude to, or as part of, sexual interaction. Another frequently encountered problem is the unwillingness of one or both partners to put aside, for 10 minutes a day, their need for debating, winning, or dominating. One might assume, parenthetically, that a couple that cannot neutrally or pleasantly do little or nothing, and do it together and in contact one with another, has a poor prognosis for doing the things together that involve negative or problematic elements.

This strategy is seldom sufficient in and of itself to resolve all of the problems in malfunctioning relationships. It provides a good basis for cooperation and for emotional satisfaction of the partners, upon which the facilitation of understanding and acceptance of differing communication styles, establishment of mutually acceptable ground rules, and honoring and tolerating individuality may be accomplished.

Reference

Gerber, S. K. (1999). *Enhancing counselor intervention strategies: An integrational viewpoint*. Philadelphia: Accelerated Development/Taylor & Francis.

Sun–Cloud–Tree: A Magnifying/ Minifying Technique for Creating Change

Therapist: Samuel T. Gladding, PhD

Affiliation: Wake Forest University, Winston-Salem, North Carolina; Licensed Professional Counselor (North Carolina)

Major works:

Gladding, S. T. (2008). *Groups: A counseling specialty* (5th ed.). Upper Saddle River, NJ: Prentice Hall.
Gladding, S. T. (2009). *Counseling: A comprehensive profession* (6th ed.). Upper Saddle River, NJ: Prentice Hall.
Gladding, S. T. (2010). *Family therapy: History, theory, and practice* (5th ed.). Upper Saddle River, NJ: Prentice Hall.

Dr. Gladding is the author of numerous other books, chapters, and journal articles.

Population for whom the technique is appropriate: Elementary school to geriatric age groups and family/couples in therapy
Cautionary notes: This technique is not as effective for individuals who process information primarily through concrete means.

Sun–Cloud–Tree can be used in a group or family counseling session or as homework between sessions. The technique is designed to illustrate to clients how magnifying or minifying one of three elements in a picture can change the overall nature of the picture. More importantly, it is designed to help clients realize that magnifying or minimizing parts of their behavior can change the way they are functioning and how others respond to them.

Group or family members are each given a sheet of 8½ × 11 inch blank white typing paper. They are also given a box of crayons or markers, which should ideally give them a wide selection of colors from which to choose. Group or family members are told by the counselor to draw on their sheet of paper a sun, a cloud, and a tree in that order but to arrange these elements as they wish. They are given between 3 and 5 minutes to complete their drawing.

Next, group or family members are given a second piece of blank white paper and provided with the following instructions: "Look at your first drawing of a sun, cloud, and tree. Now make another drawing on this second sheet of paper that magnifies or minifies one of the elements in your first drawing. For example, you might make the sun you drew bigger or smaller."

Group or family members are then given between 3 and 5 minutes to draw their second picture.

After the two drawings have been made, the counselor asks each group or family member to display the first drawing and tell the group or family something about how he or she felt in regard to the drawing. For example, did the drawer like the way the elements were arranged? Then the group or family member is asked to hold up the second drawing for the display and tell the group what he or she did to magnify or minify an element in the picture. The group or family member is asked to describe how the second picture differs from the first and how he or she feels about that difference. For example, the drawer may feel more comfortable about the second drawing because the cloud may have been magnified, blocking out some of the "heat" of the sun. If necessary or desired, the process of magnifying or minifying the other elements in the picture can be done so that the drawer gets an even better idea of what changes come about in such a process.

When all of the group or family members have shared their pictures, the counselor then asks each one to pick a behavior he or she currently displays, such as talking fast or slow or looking interested or disinterested. This action should be one that is typical in that person's behavioral repertoire. The behavior is then shown to the group or family by the person who afterward is asked to magnify or minify it. The person then discusses with other group or family members how such a modification of the behavior felt. In turn, the individual receives feedback from the group or family about how such a modification was perceived.

After feedback, group or family members are asked to think about and write down on a list other behaviors they would like to modify by either magnifying or minimizing them. As a homework assignment, they are given the task of modifying one or more of the behaviors on their list. They are asked to be sure to solicit feedback from people outside the family or group as well as those within the family or group on the display of their new modified behaviors. Group or family members are then challenged to examine from time to time other behaviors that they may wish to modify. They are reminded that they may magnify or minify such behaviors as they did in their drawing of Sun–Cloud–Tree.

Getting Rid of the Seven Deadly Habits of Unhappy Couples

Therapist: William Glasser, MD

Affiliation: Board certified, psychiatrist and psychiatry, since 1961. President, William Glasser Institute, Los Angeles, California

Major works:

Glasser, W. (1998). *Choice theory.* New York: HarperCollins.
Glasser, W. (1999). *The language of choice theory.* New York: HarperCollins.
Glasser, W. (2000). *The compatibility connection, A great relationship—A matter of choice not fate.* New York: HarperCollins.

Dr. Glasser is the founding father of reality therapy and is one of the most influential psychiatrists of all time.

Population for whom the technique is appropriate: Adolescents and adults
Cautionary notes: None

In my 1998 book, *Choice Theory,* I explained that all we do from birth to death is behave and that all of our purposeful behavior is chosen. Further explained in *Choice Theory* is that the overwhelming cause of all psychological problems—for example, everything listed in the *Diagnostic and Statistical Manual of Mental Disorders, Fourth edition (DSM-IV)*—is the psychology we practice whenever we have trouble getting along with other people. This ancient practice, which I call *external control psychology,* is, essentially, the only psychology the world uses.

This means that almost everyone who comes, or is sent, to a therapist is suffering from his or her use of external control psychology or someone else's use of it on them. Unless they learn a new psychology the same as, or equivalent to, what I call *choice theory,* therapy has little chance for success. Based on this belief, reality therapy, the therapy I created in 1965 and brought up to date in *Reality Therapy in Action* (2000), has, as a major goal, teaching clients to replace external control psychology with choice theory psychology.

When we use external control psychology, we believe that whatever we choose to do in our relationships is right. And because it is right, it is not only permissible, it is our moral obligation to try to control the way the person we are having trouble with behaves. In a wide variety of ways, we try to force him or her to embrace our "right" way because his or her "right" way is "wrong." It is also our moral obligation to resist anyone who tries to force his or her "right" way on us. As is often the case in marriage, couples use this psychology on each other when they disagree. Because both partners know what is "right," trouble ensues.

As we continue to use external control on others or they use it on us, we harm what we all need—good relationships with the important people in our lives. And because it is essentially the only psychology we know, there is no evidence in the 21st century that any large group of people anywhere in the world is getting along significantly better with each other now than 100 years ago. External control psychology is a plague on all humanity.

Choice theory is a new psychology that explains that we can control only our own behavior. If we are willing to accept the consequences, no one can control us. So whenever we are having difficulty with another person, for example, a wife having difficulty with her husband, all she can control is what she does; she cannot control what he does. But choice theory also explains that, because we can only control our own behavior, when we are having difficulty with another person we should try to choose behaviors that keep us close or bring us closer. External behaviors that do just the opposite harm the marriage.

To help both partners in a couple, in therapy I will explain that there are seven deadly external control habits that eventually will destroy the happiness in any relationship. It is almost certain that they are both using one or more of these habits in their marriage: (1) criticizing, (2) blaming, (3) complaining, (4) nagging, (5) threatening, (6) punishing, and (7) rewarding to control or bribing.

Their homework would be for the wife, separate from her husband, to write down examples of when she uses one or more of the seven habits consistently in the marriage, and for the husband, on his own, to do the same. Before they show each other what each has written, they should read my book, *The Language of Choice Theory* (1999), together and discuss it.

Once they believe they understand the difference between using external control language and choice theory language, they should together discuss how they could rewrite the examples they had written down. Their task would be to change them from external control to choice theory language. As they do this, they will see the value of removing these seven deadly habits from their lives and their marriage will improve significantly.

Further homework would be to read my entire book, *The Compatibility Connection* (2000), to find out more about the "marital solving circle" and other things they could do at home to improve their marriage. If they can then put this information to work in their marriage, they will eventually eliminate the seven habits altogether. This may seem to be a lot of reading, but to move from an unhappy to a happy marriage is more than worth the effort.

References

Glasser, W. (1998). *Choice theory*. New York: HarperCollins.

Glasser, W. (1999). *The language of choice theory*. New York: HarperCollins.

Glasser, W. (2000). *The compatibility connection, A great relationship—A matter of choice not fate*. New York: HarperCollins.

Glasser, W. (2000). *Reality therapy in action*. New York: HarperCollins.

Circle of Trust: Support for Grief

Therapist: Linda Goldman, MS

Affiliation: Certified Professional Counselor; Certified Grief Therapist; Certified Grief Educator; Private Grief Therapy Practice and Consultant, Chevy Chase, Maryland

Major works:

Goldman, L. (1994). *Life and loss: A guide to help grieving children.* Muncie, IN: Accelerated Development.

Goldman, L. (2001). *Breaking the silence: A guide to help children with complicated grief* (2nd ed.). New York: Brunner-Routledge.

Goldman, L. (2009). *Great answers to difficult questions about death: What children need to know.* Philadelphia: Jessica Kingsley.

Population for whom the technique is appropriate: Children 5 years of age through the teen years; can be modified with age-appropriate language

Cautionary notes: Young children may need adult support for cutting, pasting, and supplying needed photos and materials. Encourage children to follow each step, but do not force them. This strategy can be conducted as one long assignment or several separate smaller assignments.

Children need to know they have people they can count on when grief arises. Too often, at the time of crises, their overwhelming feelings and sudden change of life structure can create insecurity and uncertainty about themselves and those around them. Sometimes they feel they have no one to turn to that will listen and care. The following homework assignment can be useful as a preventive tool to be set in place when needed, as a technique to create awareness of present support during a grief period, and as a vehicle for discussion and communication about thoughts and feelings children carry for people in their lives.

1. Ask children to paste their picture in the center of his or her circle of trust.

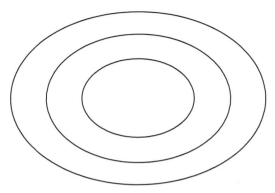

FIGURE 3.7 **Pictoral representation of the Circle of Trust.**

2. Children read or have read to them the following:

"There are people in my life that I care about and I trust with my feelings. I can call them if I need to talk or ask for something. My very most trusted people are: _____ Their phone numbers are: _____ ."

Write their name, draw their picture, or paste a photo around your picture in the innermost circle.

3. Children read or have read to them the following:

"There are even more people in my life I can depend on– family, friends, teachers, neighbors, God, or even pets like my dog or cat. They are _____. Their phone numbers are_____ ."

Write their name, draw their picture, or paste a photo of them in the middle circle.

4. Children read or have read to them the following:

"Sometimes there are people I like in my life, but I am not sure I can call them for help. They could be the school nurse, a friend's mom, or the gym teacher. They are _____. I would _____ or would not _____ like to be able to call them. I will ask them for their numbers and tell them why I would like their phone number."

Write their name, draw their picture, or paste a photo in the outer circle.

5. Children read or have read to them the following:

"Sometimes people are outside of my circle of trust. I may feel that they have disappointed me, made me angry, or given me a reason not to trust them. Maybe Dad never calls after the divorce, Uncle Tom is an alcoholic, or Grandma has Alzheimer's.

These people are _____.

I can't trust them with my feelings because _____."

Write their name, draw their picture, or paste a photo outside your circle of trust.

Effective Intervention With Psychotherapeutic Business Cards

Therapist: Paul A. Hauck, PhD

Affiliation: Clinical Psychologist, University of Utah; Private Practice

Major works:

Hauck, P. A. (1994). *Overcoming the rating game: Beyond self-love, beyond self-esteem.* Louisville, KY: Westminister John Knox Press.

Hauck, P. A. (1984). *The three faces of love.* Louisville, KY: Westminister John Knox Press.

Hauck, P. A. (1998). *How to cope with people who drive you crazy.* London: Sheldon.

Author of 13 other books

Population for whom the technique is appropriate: Adolescents and adults who are troubled by emotional disturbances such as depression, anger, jealousy, passivity, anxiety, low self-esteem, and procrastination

Cautionary notes: None

To respond to Dr. Rosenthal's request for a contribution to this book, I first thought it would be an excellent opportunity for me to write about my work on the three principles of human interaction and the three rules of assertion. These have been my major formulations over the past several years, with which I have attempted to teach people to face their interpersonal problems. I point out that our problems with people are usually the result of three behaviors: (1) We get the behavior we tolerate, (2) others will not change unless we change first, and (3) what must be changed is our excessive toleration.

To achieve this last condition of intolerance the three rules of assertion must be understood: (1) If people do good things to you, do good things to them; (2) if people do bad things to you, reason with them on two separate occasions; and (3) if people do bad things to you a third time and reasoning with them has not helped, do something equally annoying to them, but it must be done without feelings of anger, guilt, other-pity, fear of rejection, fear of physical harm, or fear of financial harm.

I was all set to elaborate on these two sets of ideas when I entered my group therapy room recently and was informed by several of my group members that they had been very grateful to me for what I had been able to do for them and their families by another therapeutic technique that is less well known but that seems to have great promise. This is the technique I will elaborate on at this point.

It all began some years ago when one of my clients asked me to write down one of the ideas I had given him so that he could use it when he got home. He returned a week later to say that he had lost the paper and would I therefore be kind enough to write it down again so he could stick the paper on his refrigerator. I wrote down one or two of the major irrational ideas that he was using to disturb himself. In a later session, he told me that the paper helped and would I please write another note stating another irrational idea that he found helpful but that he always forgot.

He eventually suggested that I print these ideas on a card that he could keep in his wallet. I gave it some thought and decided that the listing of the irrational ideas (as phrased by Albert Ellis) would be an excellent card to pass out, but it would be even better if I expressed them in a rational version rather than in the irrational version by which they are usually known.

I put this on a card measuring 3½ × 2¼ inches and he was delighted with it. But so were many other clients, who were then in a much better position to refresh their memories. In addition, they also were able to show their partners, family members, or friends what they were trying to do. Frequently their friends would either show interest in what my clients were learning and would talk about it, or they would find the ideas unacceptable, making my clients defend themselves as best they could. This gave them the opportunity to learn just how much they knew about the subject.

In time, I added other cards, all taken from the several books that I have published on depression, anger, worry and fear, self-rating, the crazymakers, assertion, parenting, love and marriage, and procrastination. There are now 10 cards summarizing different books, one attributable to Albert Ellis and Bob Harper and the rest from my own efforts.

These are the steps that lead to anger.

1. I want something.
2. I'm frustrated because you won't give me what I want.
3. That's uncomfortable and I can't stand to be uncomfortable.
4. I've changed my mind: I don't just want something, now I demand that I get whatever I want.
5. You are bad and worthless because you frustrate me.
6. To change you into a good person, I'm going to be very severe with you.

To talk yourself out of anger, use the following reasoning.

1. You're not upsetting me. I am. No one can disturb me emotionally unless I talk myself into it.
2. If I don't get my way, I'll only be disappointed.
3. If I never make another demand, I'll never get angry again.
4. Not getting my way is not horrible, awful, or the end of the world.
5. Not getting what I want is only uncomfortable and I can stand that.
6. You are not an evil, bad, or worthless person for frustrating me. You are a human being and have a right to be wrong.
7. Being frustrated is bad enough. Why should I make things much worse by getting mad?
8. I'm not a child. I'm an adult and don't need to have my way ever.

Any time you are accused of anything, immediately ask yourself three questions.

1. Is the statement true? And do you agree the behavior in question is undesirable? Then say, "Thank you," and try not to repeat those actions.
2. If the statement is true, but you don't think it's wrong to behave as you did, then ignore the accusations.
3. Is it false? Consider the accuser to be wrong, upset, immature, and so on, and that he or she has a right to an opinion different from yours. After a brief response, agree to disagree.

For more information on this subject, read *Overcoming Frustration and Anger* (1976), by Paul A. Hauck, PhD, published by Westminster John Knox Press, Louisville, KY.

FIGURE 3.8   The psychology of anger.

As an example, the card on anger is shown as Figure 3.8.

People who have a serious problem with anger often cannot simply be told in one therapy session what they ought to do differently. They need something with them that is very handy to which they can resort in an instant and to which they can check their thoughts for irrationalities. They assure me constantly that the cards are very helpful and make therapy more efficient.

Depression is described on another card for those who suffer feelings of guilt and pity. See Figure 3.9.

This is also an excellent way to get exposure of your ideas to the community at large. When people carry your card around with your name, address, and phone number, you give yourself free publicity. For example, my cards give my name and address first. On top it says, for example, The Psychology of Fear, Worry, and

---

Psychological depressions are caused by:

1. Self-blame
2. Self-pity
3. Other-pity

Self-Blame

1. No one makes you psychologically depressed. You do that by the things you say to yourself.
2. You are not worthless if important people in your life reject you.
3. Doing badly never makes you a bad person, only imperfect. We have a right to be wrong.
4. Guilt is created in two steps: (a) You did something bad, and (b) you decide you're awful.
5. Never blame yourself for anything. Instead, admit your responsibility for wrongdoing.
6. Self-blamers are conceited because they judge themselves more harshly than others who commit similar errors.
7. You can always forgive yourself since you are (1) deficient, (2) ignorant, or (3) disturbed.
8. Separate the rating of your behavior from the rating of your SELF.

Self-Pity

1. You don't have to have everything you want. The world was not made just for you.
2. Not getting your way is only disappointing or sad, not the end of the world.
3. Count your blessings.
4. You have put up with disappointments all your life; you can tolerate this one too.

Other-Pity

1. Caring for others is mature. Overcaring is neurotic.
2. All the pain you feel for the suffering of others does not relieve them of the slightest pain.
3. Healthy detachment by you helps others face up to their self-defeating behaviors.
4. You won't get burned out as a helper if you don't break your heart over others.

For more information on this subject, read *Overcoming Depression* (1976), by Paul A. Hauck, PhD, published by Westminster John Knox Press, Louisville, KY.

FIGURE 3.9 The psychology of depression.

Anxiety. Compliments of: Paul A. Hauck, PhD, Psychologist. My address and my phone number.

Figure 3.10 describes the psychology of fear, worry, and anxiety.

Let us never forget that along with having good therapy techniques, we also need to be businesspeople and know how to sell ourselves. If we have great ideas and can't get them across to the public, then what good are they?

These cards have been so successful that when I give seminars, I usually package the 10 cards in a small plastic packet and sell them at these presentations for $2 a package. They go like hotcakes because I see repeatedly that people are simply hungry for a short statement that hits an idea on the head and develops it logically on the front and the back of a card, which they can resort to at any time to assist them when their memories fail them.

To overcome the fear of (1) rejection, (2) failure, and (3) anxiety, consider the following:

1. Rejection does not hurt unless you make it hurt.
2. Unless you are a child, you do not need to be loved.
3. Being disapproved of is merely one person's opinion. Find someone else who accepts you.
4. Rejection by certain people is actually a compliment.
5. Rejection often results not from our faults, but from the neurotic habits of others.
6. Failure is not trying. Trying leads to learning. Learning leads to success.
7. Failure does not make you less of a person. Nothing does.
8. Most fears come from catastrophizing.
9. Anxiety attacks will make you shaky, but not crazy.

Other Techniques

1. Risk-taking: "Nothing ventured, nothing gained."
2. Antiperfectionism: Do poorly rather than nothing at all.
3. Exposure: The more you experience in life, the less fearful you become.
4. Relax by (a) exercise, (b) meditation, or (c) prayer.
5. Distraction: Think of something humorous or tranquil when you feel tense.
6. Antishame exercises: Do humiliating things until you ignore public opinion.

For more information, read *Overcoming Worry and Fear* (1976), by Paul A. Hauck, PhD, published by Westminster John Knox Press, Louisville, KY.

FIGURE 3.10 The psychology of fear, worry, and anxiety.

To achieve (1) cooperation, (2) respect, and (3) love, follow these three rules:

Rule 1: If people do something good to you, do something good to them (+ = +).
Rule 2: If people do something bad to you and don't realize they are behaving badly, reason with them, but only on two separate occasions (− = + × 2).
Rule 3: If people are inconsiderate a third time, do something equally annoying to them, but it must be without (1) anger, (2) guilt, (3) other-pity, (4) fear of rejection, (5) fear of physical harm, or (6) fear of financial harm (− = −).

If thoughtless behavior occurs again, you have four options:

Option 1: Tolerate without resentment.
Option 2: Protest (by using Rule 3).
Option 3: Separate or divorce.
Option 4: Tolerate with resentment.

Use any of the first three options because they can eventually lead to relief. Option 4 always creates more suffering.

The JRC

When do you have a right to protest? When you are less than just reasonably content (JRC). If you do not stand up for your rights over a long time, you will experience four consequences:

1. You will be unhappy.
2. You will become disturbed.
3. You will gradually fall out of love.
4. You will want to end the relationship.

If people will not change, decide to put up with the problem and tolerate it without resentment (Option 1), or use Option 3.

For a full explanation of these principles, read *The Three Faces of Love* (1984), by Paul A. Hauck, PhD, published by Westminster Press, Louisville, KY.

FIGURE 3.11   The psychology of assertion.

Incidentally, one of my cards actually covers the subject of assertion, which I referred to before; it is shown in Figure 3.11.

This is a fairly new technique that I have not seen repeated anywhere else. The Albert Ellis Institute staff in New York used their own versions of these cards, but I can also encourage all of you to find your favorite books that you refer to and make your own cards and pass them on to your people. I assure you they will be very grateful to you for giving them a means by which they can recall at will the very important lessons you're trying to teach them in the normal therapy session, whether it be individual or group.

The *I Love Lucy* Parenting Technique

Therapist: Lorna L. Hecker, PhD

Affiliation: Associate Professor, Marriage and Family Therapy Program, and Clinic Director, Marriage and Family Therapy Center, Purdue University Calumet, Hammond, Indiana; Editor, *Journal of Activities in Psychotherapy Practice;* Private Practice

Major works:

Hecker, L., & Associates. (2009). *Ethics and professional issues in couple and family therapy.* New York: Routledge.

Hecker, L., & Deacon, S., & Associates. (1998). *The therapist's notebook: Homework, handouts and activities for use in psychotherapy.* New York: Haworth Press. (Subsequently, *The therapist's notebook II* and *III* were also published.)

Hecker, L., & Wetchler, J. (Eds.). (2003). *Introduction to marriage and family therapy.* New York: Haworth Press.

Population for whom the technique is appropriate: Parents of children with behavior problems

Cautionary notes: None

When parents come to family therapy, they often are exasperated and are unable to see much hope of getting control of their unruly children. They feel hopeless and simply are not enjoying their parenting. They often see their children as the culprits, unable to see the impact of their behavior on their children. In strategic therapy terms, they often are contributing to the problem maintenance by their own attempts to solve the problem (Watzlawick, Weakland, & Fisch, 1974). Frequently, the way they approach the problem (nagging, cajoling, yelling, etc.) simply makes the problem worse.

The following intervention is a directive technique aimed at breaking inappropriate sequences of parent–child interaction.

When confronted with parents in this situation, I often use what I call the *I Love Lucy* technique. Most parents are familiar with the classic *I Love Lucy* television series and the iconic star, Lucille

Ball. If you recall, Lucy had a knack for being wacky. Invoking her image can usually bring a smile to people's faces if they think about her antics on the television show on which she played a housewife married to Ricky, a Cuban band leader. When parents are faced with typical children's behaviors that are exasperating to them, I ask them if they recall the *I Love Lucy* television show. Invariably they do, and I ask them if they can envision what Lucy would do in a situation such as theirs. For example:

Therapist: You both say that you are frustrated that your children leave stuff lying all over the house, and you are tired of yelling at them and nagging them about it. Imagine for a minute, if Lucy were in your situation, what do you suppose she would be doing?

Mother: I don't know; maybe she would gather up their socks for the Salvation Army.

Therapist: That's a great idea! What about the book bags you complain about being on the floor all the time; what do you imagine that Lucy would do with those book bags?

Father: She might run them up the flag pole.

Therapist: Wow, I never thought about that. Boy, they sure would think twice about leaving them out again, wouldn't they? What do you suppose Lucy would say when they confronted her, demanding to know where their book bags where?

Mother: I think she would act really stupid about it and pretend like she didn't know what they were talking about. Maybe say that perhaps they were stolen by an intruder.

Therapist: You're right! She would!

The parents are instructed as homework to handle a problem that arises during the next week as they imagine Lucy would. The therapist can help brainstorm ways that the parents can react to exasperating situations as if they were Lucy. For example, the therapist might ask: "When Brian comes in after curfew, what do you normally do?" When the parents respond with what they normally do, the therapist queries if the technique they are using works. Usually, it does not. Then the therapist can ask the parents to prepare for the Lucy approach by saying: "When Brian comes in late for curfew, what would you imagine Lucy doing?" The therapist should encourage creativity in parents' responses and help come up with some outlandish interventions. It is not really as important that the parents adopt your responses as it is for them to think about things they might do themselves to be Lucy. Using the curfew example, the therapist might brainstorm ways that the patients could be Lucyesque in their responses to Brian. It might be suggested to the parents that they do one of the following:

- Wait up for Brian in Halloween costumes and not say anything to him when he arrives.
- Put a bucket of water over the front door to douse him when he comes in.
- Pretend they are having sex on the living room floor when he comes in, quickly get dressed, and act embarrassed.
- Be asleep in his bed when he gets home, murmuring about how they worried he had run away.
- Set all the clocks back so it appears he is coming in on time and congratulate him on his promptness. Tell him you bought him his favorite ice cream because you knew he wouldn't let you down by being late.

It can be a lot of fun to brainstorm outlandish interventions with the parents, but, most importantly, in the brainstorming process the parents' sense of competence gets triggered. They begin to "plot" benevolently against their child, which reinforces that they are indeed in charge of the hierarchy in the family. This can be extremely empowering to fatigued parents. Parents typically respond one of two ways: They become enthralled with the idea of becoming Lucy, have fun with it, and respond differently to their children, or they say "I could never do that" in response to the suggestions but come up with one of their own.

I find it important to caution parents that Lucy was never malevolent and that they should only undertake being Lucyesque if they can do it in the same loving and fun way that a good Lucy would do.

Invariably this intervention empowers parents, reminds them that they are indeed in charge of their children, and gets them to have fun with parenting. I have had parents put book bags on rooftops, run underwear up flagpoles, and do some other extreme behaviors. Others respond in a less intense but effective fashion. In response, the problem behaviors disappear, the children begin to see their parents as both in charge and playful, and the parents' exasperation with "unruly" children resolves. In strategic therapy terms (Watzlawick et al., 1974), the parents have changed their part of the interactional pattern, thus triggering the children to act differently.

Reference

Watzlawick, P., Weakland, J. H., & Fisch, R. (1974). *Change: Principles of problem formation and problem resolution.* New York: Norton.

Meaning in Life Evaluation Scale—Homework Assignment for Clients in Logotherapy

Therapist: Rosemary Henrion, MSN, MEd, RN

Affiliation: Diplomate and Faculty, Viktor Frankl Institute of Logotherapy, Abilene, Texas; Private Practice, Biloxi, Mississippi

Major work:

Henrion, R. P., & Crumbaugh, J. C. (1997). *Rediscovering new meaning and purpose in life.* Abilene, TX: Viktor Frankl Institute of Logotherapy Press.

Author/coauthor of other articles in professional books and journals

Population for whom the technique is appropriate: Adolescents (over 15 years) and adults in individual, group, and family therapy who are in need of experiencing a meaningful and productive life

Cautionary notes: None

When Dr. Viktor Frankl, MD, PhD, developed his principles and concepts in logotherapy, he never expected to have a following and he never fantasized that Institutes of Logotherapy would be established in Europe, North and South America, and South Africa. His major intention was to share with other medical doctors how he survived horrific conditions in four concentration camps and maintained moments of meaning while there. Dr. Frankl began giving presentations on logotherapy in Europe in the early 1950s, and in the summer of 1961 Dr. Gordon Allport, PhD, invited Dr. Frankl to lecture at Harvard University. His lectures inspired many American professionals to focus on developing logotherapeutic programs for clients searching for meaning and purpose in their lives.

I use a number of homework assignments in the logotherapy program in which I have taught for a number of years. Each assignment corroborates with the steps in discovering a meaningful, fulfilling future, which makes this treatment modality a reality for clients. The clients become more enthusiastic as they progress through the program because they develop a conscious awareness of where they have been emotionally, where they are now, and where they may choose to take control of their future through prioritizing their values. Clients must reorder their values to experience the freedom of being in control of their lives. The Meaning in Life Evaluation (MILE) Scale is a significant tool that is used to accomplish this goal.

The Meaning in Life Evaluation (MILE) Scale

Instructions: Rate the following 20 values by beginning with the first value (wealth) and comparing it with the remaining 19 values. Place a check mark by the value that you prefer and leave the other value blank. This same procedure is repeated with each value as you progress through the 19th value. In psychology this method is known as the "paired comparison" in which you are forced to choose the value that you really wish for your future. On the other hand, if you were asked to rate the values that you prefer, you would most probably choose values that you think would please the therapist.

1. To be wealthy _____
2. To have authentic relationships _____
3. To have physical sex _____
4. To have a good name (high character) _____
5. To maintain youth forever _____
6. To gain intimacy _____
7. To be a great leader of people _____
8. To have good health _____
9. To have power _____
10. To be of great service to people _____
11. To be famous _____
12. To be physically powerful (males) beautiful (females) _____
13. To be an intellectual _____
14. To find adventure/new experience _____
15. To be happy _____
16. To understand the meaning of life _____
17. To fulfill spiritual goals _____

18. To experience peace of mind _____
19. To gain social acceptance/belonging _____
20. To gain a personal identity _____

After the clients have completed the list of preferences, they are instructed to add the raw score at the end of the line for each value. These scores are then added for the final total. The range is 0–19; if the clients have two 19s, they have done the MILE Scale incorrectly. The highest score (19) may be followed by more than one value, resulting in a tie. Clients then choose the value, thus prioritizing it next to the highest one, and the remaining value will be placed in a subsequent order. Consequently, the five top values will be the values that will be identified as goals for discovering new meaning and purpose. In other words, meaning and purpose in life are derived from values (Crumbaugh & Henrion, 1999).

In the logopsychotherapy groups, clients discuss how to progress in developing their goals for a meaningful and productive future. Through the values they choose, clients may creatively expand short- and long-term goals that bolster their self-esteem. The MILE Scale removes the focus from the problematic areas and refocuses on assets (*dereflection* is the term coined by Dr. Frankl). The approach also is preventive in that clients see the total picture (expanded awareness), gain courage and hope in the process, and are able to cope effectively with future losses, eliminating the feeling of despair (Dossey, 1991).

It is recommended that clients fill out the MILE Scale at least annually and specifically if they have had active goals for their values. They may proceed to higher values because the values they chose at this time may be of little or no significance to them the following year. Many clients frequently request a copy of the MILE Scale for spouses, relatives, friends, employers, and lovers. They find the MILE Scale intriguing.

References

Crumbaugh, J. C., & Henrion, R. (1999). (Rev. ed.). *Logotherapy: New help for problem drinkers*. Chicago: Nelson-Hall.
Dossey, L. (1991). *Meaning and medicine*. New York: Bantam.

Self-Concept Adjustment Strategy

Therapist: Joseph W. Hollis, EdD, deceased

Affiliation: Licensed Counselor and Health Service Provider in Psychology, State of Indiana; Professor Emeritus, Counseling Psychology, Ball State University, Muncie, Indiana. He helped found C-AHEAD, the Counselors Association for Humanistic Education. He also created Accelerated Development, Inc., a major publisher for counseling books and audio programs.

Major works:

Hollis, J. W. (1999). *Counselor preparation, faculty, programs, and trends* (10th ed.). Philadelphia: Accelerated Development/Taylor & Francis.

Rosenthal, H., & Hollis, J. W. (1993). *Help yourself to positive mental health.* Muncie IN: Accelerated Development/Taylor & Francis.

Dr. Hollis passed away Nov. 23, 2002 at the age of 80. He was the author of more than 15 professional books. He served as president for two state guidance associations and Accelerated Development, Inc., Philadelphia, Pennsylvania, and served as a board member for the American Personnel and Guidance Association.

Population for whom the technique is appropriate: If the work is done at home (between sessions), then the client must be old enough to write—generally 10 years old or older. If it is done during the counseling session with the counselor's instruction, then the child can be younger and the counselor can record what seems to be significant in working with the client. No upper age limit is imposed.

Cautionary notes: If the client is very upset, the technique as outlined may be too intense for him or her. The counselor needs to assess the emotional state of the client. If the client's inner look at self and inner look at what the client perceives that others think (i.e., see, believe) are too far apart and are upsetting him or her, then part of the technique may be used by the counselor while the counselor and client meet together. However, to list these concepts and wait until the next meeting may be too much for the client.

To use the technique, the counselor must have sufficient assessment of the client and must believe that he or she wants and is ready to consider modification to bring more agreement into what he or she sees in self and what others see in the client.

Procedure

1. Counselor states, "Each day I look into a mirror to see how I appear to others, for example, my eyes are bloodshot (red) or my face looks droopy, as if I just don't care."

    "Do you think you can look in the mirror and tell me how others might see you?"

    "It would be nice if you would write a list of those things you see in the mirror."

    "Can you do that? Remember these are the things you believe others see in you."

    "Think about it a little between now and when we meet for our next session."

2. "Next, I want you to identify those items that you listed that you like for others to see in you. Then place the letter 'L' in front of each thing that you like."

    "Now you can do that, can't you?"

3. "Next, place a 'D' in front of each of those items you dislike."

4. "We have no set number of items you like or dislike. Just write as many items as you think they perceive about you."

5. "Bring to the next session those notes that you wrote. We will discuss those so that I'll get to know you better."

6. "Then we can consider different things that we might do to help you become more the person you want to be."

This technique helps the client to open up and discuss those concepts held by others as the client perceives them and those held by himself or herself. Once these concepts are out in the open, the counselor and client can together explore means to help the client bring "what I am and what others think I am" into closer agreement. The achievement of that would be well worth the time. Secondary benefits would be that the client would learn how to look more realistically at things and learn how to bring the views (others and own) into closer agreement.

Learn How to Listen: Taking Home the Foundation Skills of Microcounseling

Therapist: Allen E. Ivey, EdD, ABPP

Affiliation: Distinguished University Professor (Emeritus), University of Massachusetts, Amherst; President, Microtraining Associates; Board of Directors, National Institute for Multicultural Competence

Major works:

Ivey, A. (2000). *Developmental therapy: Theory into practice.* North Amherst, MA: Microtraining. (Original work published 1986 by Jossey-Bass, San Francisco)

Ivey, A., Pedersen, P., & Ivey, M. (2000). *Intentional group counseling: A microskills approach.* Pacific Grove, CA: Brooks/Cole.

Population for whom the technique is appropriate: All types of clients and patients ranging from effectively functioning children, teens, and adults to long-term hospitalized and psychotic inpatients; depressed clients

Cautionary notes: The homework exercise is quite effective and often produces change rather quickly. It is, of course, dangerous to rely on a single treatment modality. Follow-up and systemic intervention is essential.

Attending behavior and the teaching of communication skills has been a central part of my homework assignments to clients for more than 45 years. If people listen to others, they gain support and people are attracted to them. If they talk about themselves and their problems, people tend to turn away.

Teaching listening skills is one of the most simple, yet most powerful, homework assignments possible. Extensive research and clinical practice have shown that the practice makes a difference in a client's life. The following discussion describes the origins of microcounseling and how we generated clinical applications of a seemingly "simple" skill. I would suggest that the simplicity of attending behavior is profound in its implications.

The following discussion outlines the origins of this homework assignment, how it evolved into a clinical treatment regime, and some specifics for action with individuals, families, and groups.

Origins of Microcounseling and Attending Behavior

In 1966, a group of us at Colorado State University received a grant from the Kettering Foundation to identify the observable behavioral skills of counseling and therapy (Ivey, Normington, Miller, Morrill, & Haase, 1968). At this point, videotape recording had not been used as a research tool in the counseling and therapy profession. Humanistic psychology and Carl Rogers almost totally dominated the scene, and behavioral psychology was in its infancy.

For 6 months we observed many interviews on video, reviewed the literature, and had endless discussions, but we found that breaking down the interview into component parts was not an easy task. In desperation, we invited our secretary, Janie, to present herself on videotape for training. A student volunteer served as her "client."

Fortunately, Janie's interview was a disaster. She spent most of the time looking at the floor, talked about herself, and asked random questions of the client. The client sat there awkwardly. "Eureka!" we thought as we reviewed the video, "Janie has shown us what is important behaviorally." With Janie at our side, we pointed out the need to maintain eye contact with the client, to lean forward with interest, and—most of all—to follow the topics presented by the client. The group of behaviors was, of course, titled "attending behavior," and we later added vocal tone as an essential component. Attending behavior has become a generic concept for the counseling and psychological professions since that time.

With this brief instruction, Janie returned to conduct a second interview with the client. Her behavior changed immediately, and we saw a smoothly flowing interview. We found we could count the number of eye contact breaks, classify her nonverbal behavior, and count the number of topic jumps. Janie, of course, was not a competent counselor after this one brief training session, but clearly something had changed.

The teaching session with Janie occurred on a Friday. Monday morning, Janie came into my office full of excitement. "My life has changed," she said and I wondered what was coming. "I went home, I listened to my husband, and we had a beautiful, wonderful weekend." One of the great strengths of microcounseling, we were to find, was that the concepts easily generalized to the "real world." Research and writing on the microskills continued over the years, and more than 400 data-based studies attest to its vitality and vigor (Daniels & Ivey, 2007; Ivey, 1971; Ivey & Authier, 1978).

Using Attending Behavior Clinically as Homework

The clinical implications of our experience with Janie became more central to my thinking. A student came to our campus counseling center presenting loneliness and depression. As Harold and I talked, I noted that he constantly spoke about what was wrong in his life and how impossible his situation was. His father had committed suicide when Harold was a teenager and he was totally lacking in support systems in the dormitory.

I asked Harold what he talked about with others in the dormitory. "I keep trying to tell them about my problems, but they won't listen to me. They seem to get bored and walk away." I thought of Janie and, on the spot, I engaged Harold in a practice session in attending behavior. I first demonstrated ineffective listening myself as Harold talked and we both laughed at the result. I asked Harold to list the behaviors of what I was doing as a poor listener. He came up with the same concepts of attending and listening that we had identified with Janie.

Harold and I then practiced attending behavior until he was able to listen to me effectively. I put him in the role of interviewer and he gradually understood the concept. The homework assignment I gave him at that point was to go back to the dormitory and deliberately attend to others and not talk about his own issues. He could save talking about problems for the interview with me.

When Harold came back for the next session, a new light was in his eyes. "I have a friend," he said. "It pays to listen. I found that if I put my attention on others that they stay around, but I also found that if I drift off and talk about myself, they are soon gone." We continued to work on Harold's issues over several sessions, but we also continued to work on his social skills through work on other microcounseling skills, such as questioning, encouraging, and paraphrasing.

Listening Skills With Hospitalized Inpatients

Since that time, I have found that the basic teaching model and concepts of microskills, and, particularly, attending behavior, are effective ways to produce significant change. From 1968 to 1972, I worked at the Veterans Administration Hospital in Northampton, Massachusetts, with long-term inpatients. At that time, medications were only being introduced and were not as effective as they are today.

Some of the patients I worked with had been in the hospital for 3 or more years. I used the teaching model of microcounseling in the following way with patients with diagnosed depression, schizophrenia, and other issues:

1. The patient was interviewed on videotape.
2. The videotape was then reviewed with the patient. Patients were asked to identify what they saw in the video—specifically, we were encouraging them to identify concretely specific verbal and nonverbal communication behaviors. To our initial surprise, patients typically picked variations of eye contact, body, language, verbal following, and vocal tone. But, they saw (e.g., "I look away a lot."). We used patient language rather than the more technical jargon of microcounseling. At the same time, "I look away a lot" would be operationalized behavior terms that both the therapist and the patient understood and recognized. Very important in this process is that the patient is learning his or her "own skills" rather than what is to be taught by the therapists.
3. A set of behavioral change goals based on review of the videotape was developed with the patient.

4. Practice on videotape on the patient's agenda continued until mastery was achieved.
5. Generation to the ward and to the patient's home setting was stressed.

The structure of training, of course, closely follows that which was discovered through work with Janie and later with Harold. The ineffective behaviors are noted nonjudgmentally with the aid of the client or patient. Role-played practice, ideally with videotape feedback, follows. Emphasis on generalization to the home setting follows, with specific action assignments.

I found that using this model alone was sufficient to enable many patients to move out of the hospital into the community (Ivey, 1973). Teaching social skills can make a difference.

One difficulty in getting acceptance of a seemingly simple treatment procedure such as this is its very simplicity. For example, as a visiting scholar at the medical school of the University of New South Wales, Australia, I worked with hospitalized inpatients in front of a one-way mirror with residents watching. The treatment was successful as always, but the residents gradually drifted away, because they found psychoanalytic and other complex and esoteric treatments more interesting. It is difficult for highly trained professionals to accept the idea that, at times, the simple and direct approach will be most effective.

Multicultural and Group Implications

Although it has been rewarding to see the concepts of microcounseling become increasingly generic to the helping fields, the lack of attention to cultural differences brings me considerable concern. Early on in our research, we noted that various cultural groups have differing styles of listening (Ivey & Gluckstern, 1974), but attending and listening skills often are still taught without attention to this fact. Generalization via homework assignments is very unlikely to occur until cultural distinctions are considered.

Groupwork and psychoeducation often use concepts of attending behavior as part of training. Most likely, you have participated in a variation of our experience work with Janie and our early writings when you have experienced the following group exercise:

- Two members are invited to role-play an effective interview or communication situation.
- Observers list what "went wrong," often to accompanying general laughter.
- Discussion follows on what needs to be done, and the concepts of attending behavior are generated out of group experience.
- Discussion of individual and cultural differences is essential, and often missed in training and homework assignments (sad to say, this is often omitted).
- Generalization (homework) to home, work, and family is stressed.

Homework assignments based on culturally appropriate communication skills can be and have been used in multiple settings from elementary schools to senior centers, from college counseling centers to psychiatric wards, from AIDS prevention volunteers in Africa to refugee training in Sri Lanka, and from assembly line workers to management executives. Translated versions of the microskills communication skills model exist in at least 16 languages.

Summary

Communication and communication skills are culturally based, and they are the foundation of effective counseling and psychotherapy. It makes only good sense to share the fundamentals of helping with our clients, families, and groups. The concreteness and specificity of the microskills model have demonstrated effectiveness and value for more than 45 years and extensive research. It clearly is not the sole answer to all the issues we face, but it appears to be a permanent part of the effective professional. It has great value for providing specifics for clients to use in their take-home assignments.

References

Ivey, A. (1971). *Microcounseling: Innovations in interviewing training.* Springfield, IL: Charles C Thomas.

Ivey, A. (1973). Media therapy: Educational change planning for psychiatric patients, *Journal of Counseling Psychology, 20,* 338–343.

Ivey, A., & Authier, J. (1978). *Microcounseling: Innovations in interviewing training, counseling, psychotherapy, and psychoeducation.* Springfield, IL: Charles C Thomas.

Ivey, A., & Daniels, T. (2007). *Microcounseling: Making skills training work in a multicultural world.* Springfield, IL: Charles C Thomas.

Ivey, A., & Gluckstern, N. (1974). *Basic attending skills.* North Amherst, MA: Microtraining Associates.

Ivey, A., Normington, C., Miller, C., Morrill, W., & Haase, R. (1968). Microcounseling and attending behavior: An approach to pre-practicum training. *Journal of Counseling Psychology, 16*(2).

Expanding Options With Reluctant Clients

Therapist: Muriel James, EdD

Affiliation: Licensed Marriage and Family Therapist; ITAA Clinical Member and Supervisor; Private Practice, Lafayette, California

Major works:

James, M. (1985). *It's never too late to be happy: The psychology of self-reparenting.* Reading, MA: Addison-Wesley.

James, M. (1998). *Perspectives in transactional analysis.* San Francisco: TA Press.

James, M., & Jongeward, D. (1996). *Born to win: Transactional analysis with Gestalt experiments* (25th anniversary ed.). Cambridge, MA: DaCapo Press.

Dr. James is the author of numerous chapters and journal articles and author or coauthor of 19 books, including the classic *Born to Win,* now in 22 languages.

Population for whom the technique is appropriate: Adolescents and adults

Cautionary notes: None

Some clients willingly accept homework assignments; others are more reluctant. I designed the following for the reluctant individuals, to be used in brief or ongoing therapy. Although written with the individual in mind, it can also be adapted to couples and families. In my experience, suggestions or questions that encourage thinking, instead of assignments that are designed to elicit compliance, usually are effective. They seldom elicit old reluctant responses associated with homework assignments from childhood.

The most common negative responses include despair because of feeling inadequate to accomplish specific homework, rebelliousness against being told what to do, or disinterest and boredom because the homework is not intellectually challenging or relevant. Negative responses can change when reluctant clients discover how to expand their options.

Method and Process

The first step in expanding options may begin during the last 15 minutes of the first therapy hour, and the basic goal of the first three minutes is to release natural human qualities of curiosity and hope. Persons who lack curiosity and hope are not hopeless. They need to experience their own power to make changes.

The process begins with the therapist asking a client, "Would you be interested in discovering other ways you could use to solve your problem when you are not here?" Starting with "Would you be interested … ?" usually elicits "yes" or "maybe" out of curiosity instead of responses that show despair, rebelliousness, or disinterest. The phrase "other ways" as part of the question indicates that the therapist is aware the client has probably tried but has been unsuccessful in resolving particular problems and there is hope of learning how to do so.

The second step follows immediately so that clients can become aware of how their childhood experiences might be relevant to current homework assignments. The therapist asks questions such as, "What was school like for you when you were a child?" and "What kind of homework did you have and how did you do with it?"

If responses in childhood indicate inadequacy, resentment, or boredom, one kind of effective intervention is a humorous comment about doing homework, as "work" at home. Sometimes it is more appropriate to inquire if they had a place that was more emotionally comfortable than home, a place where they could think clearly and without interruption. Answers may be clues to their current reluctance to think in positive ways about homework.

The third step involves recognizing the strengths they already have for solving problems. A therapist may say something casual such as, "You seem to have some positive capabilities. Would you be willing to make a list of some of them? Also a list of your accomplishments?" A client might respond with, "Who, me? I haven't accomplished anything." If so, the therapist can interrupt with "Hey, wait a minute. You got yourself here for our appointment. That was an accomplishment of sorts. How do you get out of bed? Do you just roll out of bed and land on the floor with a bang or do you put your feet on the floor and then stand up?" A smile often follows and the stage is set for a reinforcing comment such as, "See, you are able to do something right!"

Enticing reluctant clients to do something new is the fourth step in the process. Preferably it comes after some strengths have been acknowledged as having been used previously for survival or to climb toward other goals. By this time, clients know they have strengths but may not have been aware of them or how they could be adapted to solve current problems. In this step specific homework is suggested so that clients can use their personal strengths or create new ones.

To initiate the process with a client who is basically rebellious and resists advice, a preliminary statement, given without a smile, can be, "You probably wouldn't be interested in doing this, but if you were, you could make a list of some of your positive achievements and the personal strengths you need to use to achieve them." It is the phrase, "You probably wouldn't be interested …" that hooks rebellious clients who may want to prove therapists are wrong. If so, they will interrupt or deny the "You probably …" allegation or respond with only slightly concealed animosity, "Yes, I would be interested." To that the therapist does not applaud but merely says "Okay" and makes the assignment.

The client who is indifferent or easily bored needs to be awakened to the fact that new discoveries can add excitement to life. Being told this is true is not enough. Questions such as, "What interested you when you were a child? Are you still interested in it? If so, why, and if not, why not?" and "What has excited you to learn more about since then?" often lead clients to think about what gives meaning to their lives and how to find more meaning and, consequently, experience less boredom. The options of returning to school at any age, developing a new hobby, joining an interesting organization, or becoming a volunteer for a worthy cause are only a few situations that may eliminate indifference and boredom.

Reluctant clients who despair about being able to do homework that will contribute to their happiness may indeed feel hopeless and despairing. This may be linked to childhood or because of a current situation such as the loss of a job, loss of a partner, the loss of physical health, or loss of a life dream. As despair sometimes masks clinical depression, the client may need medical attention.

Whereas the loss of a job, a partner, or one's health may need to be faced as current reality, the loss of the dreams that clients have can be reworked and new achievable ones designed. I believe it is never too late to be happy. When clients are *willing* to make a list of their past and present positive achievements, when they are *willing* to evaluate the list instead of giving in to archaic feelings of inadequacy, or rebelliousness or boredom, when they are *willing* to set goals and make plans to achieve them, they deserve approval. Whether the approval is verbal or nonverbal, it must be authentic. After all, they've done new homework. Thus, reluctant clients can become confident and able to conquer problems with new courage and hope.

What Do I Want?

Therapist: Jesper Juul, MA

Affiliation: Marriage and Family Counselor; Former Executive Director, Kempler Institute of Scandinavia—Center for Family and Postgraduate Education, Denmark; Private Practice, Denmark. He is now affiliated with Family-Lab International, an organization dedicated to spreading his ideas and theories.

Major works:

Juul, J. (2000). *Your competent child—Toward new family values.* New York: Farrar, Strauss, & Giroux.

Your Competent Child (originally published in 1995 in Danish) has become an international best seller (eight countries). Jesper Juul is a world-renowned speaker, trainer, and supervisor.

Population for whom the technique is appropriate: Individuals, couples, and families
Cautionary notes: None

About 35 years ago when I began my training as a family therapist I overheard one of our teachers asking a female client, "What do you want?" What a clever question, I thought to myself, I must remember that one! I forgot it 5 minutes later, and 5 years passed before it came back to the conscious part of my mind. I had a 2-month vacation coming, and my wife and son were going to work and school. It seemed the perfect time to practice *answering* this important question. And there I was—every morning alone in a comfortable garden chair—paper and pencil on the table and by simply asking myself, "What do you want today, Jesper?" my mind went blank! After a few days of practice, I managed to write a short list of four or five things that I wanted and secretly patted myself on the back.

When I reviewed the list a few hours later, it became clear that I had answers to what my wife would like me to do, what would make her happy if I did it, what my son would expect from me coming home from school, what needed to be done anyway …

and so my overcooperative and corrupted mind went on and on for many days, until I finally managed to come up with one small thing that I wanted to do for my life that day. I was embarrassed and humbled by the experience.

Working, as I do, mainly with couples and families in crises or simply frustrated by their inability to be as valuable to each other as they would like to be, I very often give the adults this question as homework: What do you want?

Why as homework? There are two reasons for this. Many people in this fast-moving and service-oriented world would benefit immensely from solitary contemplation to (maybe!) discover what they want—not just "right now"—what they *really* want for themselves and from the people closest to them. When couples seek counseling or therapy, at least one of them is experiencing frustration, a mixture of emotions, ideas, and thoughts that makes most of us focus on what we are *not* getting. The assumption that these are also the "things" we want is far from always being true.

To be beneficial, the question must be asked by the therapist in a kind, profoundly interested way—more as an invitation than an assignment. After 35 years I'm still saddened by the fact that most clients are hearing this invitation for the first time in their life. The sadness also is inspired by the fact that I was 25 before anybody asked me and even older before I felt that I (too) had the right to answer it.

Often clients feel unable to find the "right" answers to this question, but that is not so important for the moment. We learn important facts and secrets about ourselves and the people dearest to us by examining all the answers, just as our wisdom increases when we ask the other person for what we want and realize that he or she is unable or even unwilling to provide us with it.

Over the past 3 decades, marriage and love relationships between adults have changed from being (also) a social necessity to becoming an emotional or existential choice or both. The adjoining concept, "Stay if it gives you what you want and leave if it doesn't," is somehow contradictory to the nature of love, although it is very much in tune with the attitude of our consumer societies in the wealthy parts of the world. Focus tends to be on fun, pleasure, and leisure, and it often makes us think that the other person (store, agency, company) should give us what we want. In the family, often we must depend on ourselves to get what we want, and this assignment often is very helpful when we strive to improve our relationships. It can bring people closer to the reality of their own beings, and—old fashioned or not—that is still a prerequisite for durable and rewarding contacts with others.

This basic question leads to two new questions:

- From whom/with whom can I get what I want?
- How can he or she help me get what I want and vice versa?

The therapist can help raise these important questions and assist in formulation and negotiations, but, as we often see, the most important therapy takes place between sessions.

On Becoming a Therapist: Helping Clients Try "My Own Therapy"

Therapist: Nikolaos Kazantzis, PhD

Affiliation: School of Psychological Science, La Trobe University, Australia

Major works:

Kazantzis, N., Deane, F. P., Ronan, K. R., & L'Abate, L. (Eds.). (2005). *Using homework assignments in cognitive behavioral therapy.* New York: Routledge.

Kazantzis, N., & L'Abate, L. (Eds.). (2007). *Handbook of homework assignments in psychotherapy: Research, practice, and prevention.* New York: Springer.

Kazantzis, N., Reinecke, M. A., & Freeman, A. (Eds.). (2010). *Cognitive and behavior theories in clinical practice.* New York: Guilford Press.

Population for whom the technique is appropriate: People of all ages

Cautionary notes: None

After a certain high level of technical skill is achieved, science and art tend to coalesce in esthetics, plasticity, and form. The greatest scientists are always artists as well.

—Albert Einstein

The manner with which the therapist discusses between-session therapeutic tasks, or "homework," will ultimately determine whether a client chooses to engage with them. The therapist ideally facilitates a therapeutic environment of collaboration and empiricism. In other words, the therapist aims to engage the client in a therapeutic alliance of sharing the work of identifying ideas (hypotheses) based on client experience ("data") and considering strategies to be tested (experimentation). In taking such an approach, there can be a true spirit of learning through homework and opportunities for new discoveries and insight.

Therapists are advised to carefully consider their approach for integrating homework into sessions. Many clients perceive homework as an evaluation of their personal value, their ability, or as an indication of the likely outcome of their therapy. Some clients feel challenged by the task in terms of the emotions it raises or the apparent inconsistency between the task and their current coping strategies. Others have strong memories of significant figures in their lives when being asked to try a homework task.

Our scientific advances have helped us to establish psychotherapy as an effective way of helping our clients, but our science has yet to answer questions about how to practically carry out psychotherapy. Regarding the process of integrating homework, we are only beginning to reach the point where we have empirical evidence to guide our in-session discussion or selection of different homework tasks. The reader is encouraged to review the aforementioned major works for guidance on these elements.

This homework assignment I call "My Own Therapy" serves to extend the shared work in selecting, planning, and reviewing homework beyond the end of therapy. In this activity, the therapist asks the client to set aside about an hour (or the usual length of the session) for the client to conduct his or her own therapy session. If the therapist has socialized the client to the notion that therapy is about "helping a client to become their own therapist," clients often respond well to this task.

In using this homework in individual and group therapy contexts, I have been surprised by the diversity of ways in which clients have elected to use it. In terms of process, clients who have given the most positive feedback have set themselves an agenda, reviewed their previous week's homework, settled on an agenda (usually comprising some rereading or reflection of therapeutic skills or their application), and arrived at some "new" homework for themselves. What clients choose for their own agendas and homework speaks volumes about what has been helpful during the course of their sessions.

The task requires that the client have a degree of personal responsibility for change and a relatively stable emotional state. For these reasons, I have reserved its use for the latter stages of therapy when sessions begin to space out fortnightly or monthly. I have found that this homework softens the termination process.

The task is also excellent as a vehicle for relapse prevention and maintenance.

Although this is a favorite homework assignment, I do not use it will all clients all the time. I find it helpful to spend the main portion of one session collaboratively discussing with a client how their "own therapy session" might proceed, and usually I incorporate imagery to enable clients to rehearse starting with the task. When used in this way, imagery is particularly useful as an opportunity to seek client feedback about the emotions, thoughts (including images and memories), and physiology that are triggered by the task. By projecting into the future about the likely experiential obstacles, the therapist can assist clients to consider their options in the present.

There are no specific forms for this homework assignment. I generally encourage my clients in individual sessions to keep their own session notes and keep these notes in a safe place. Group therapy clients are provided with a workbook. Fostering client self-sufficiency includes enabling clients to decide upon the shape and form of the note keeping for their own therapy sessions.

Acknowledgments: This homework assignment is consistent with many of the tenets of Dr. Aaron T. Beck's cognitive therapy, and I am indebted for the training I received from Dr. Aaron T. Beck, Dr. Judith S. Beck, and Dr. Leslie Sokol. I also acknowledge Dr. Christine A. Padesky for suggesting the idea for this homework assignment during a cognitive therapy–training workshop. My mentor, Dr. Frank M. Dattilio, and my La Trobe colleagues, Dr. Susan Paxton and Dr. Eleanor Wertheim, have also been inspirations for this writing.

The "J" and "A" Rocks: Homework Assignment for Handling Jealousy, Anger, and Impulsive Responses

Therapists: Bradford Keeney, PhD, Kristi Lawson, PhD candidate, and Melissa Roose, MS

Affiliation: Bradford Keeney, PhD, is Professor and Hanna Spyker Eminent Scholars Chair in Education, University of Louisiana; Kristi Lawson is a doctoral student at the University of Louisiana and a therapist at the Center for Children and Families, Monroe, Louisiana; Melissa Roose is a therapist at the Center for Children and Families, Monroe, Louisiana.

Major works:

Erickson, B. A., & Keeney, B. (2006). *Milton H. Erickson, M.D.: An American healer.* Philadelphia: Ringing Rocks Press.

Keeney, B. (2009). *The creative therapist: The art of awakening a session.* New York: Routledge.

Keeney, B., Lawson, K., & Roose, M. (in press). *Innovations in creative therapy.* Portland, OR: ICT Press.

Population for whom the technique is appropriate: People of all ages; clients who have difficulties handling either anger or jealousy.
Cautionary notes: None

This technique is meant to interrupt potentially disruptive emotions and thoughts before they are carried out in problematic actions and to transform them into a positive experience. We used this assignment with a client whose mother sought help because her son was getting angry, emotionally shutting down, and refusing to finish his work in school. He actually enjoyed going to school and was in the second-grade honors class. After further exploration of the situation, it seemed apparent that other students were picking on him because they were jealous that he was a good student and did well in school. We asked his mother to try an experiment with him as a way to help him explore recognizing when he was becoming angry. We suggested that she find a rock on which she would write the letter "J" for "jealous" and instruct her son to carry it in his pocket so that he could rub it or hold it to remind himself that even though his classmates were jealous, he should wait to respond to them until he enjoyed completing his schoolwork. Before we left, the mother picked out a rock from their backyard and wrote a "J" on it, using a red marker. She said that she would explain the exercise to her son when he returned home from school.

The following week, the mother reported that her son had been suspended from school for 3 days during the previous week for "flipping the bird" at a girl who had done it to him first. The mother said that she asked her son if he had used his "J" rock. He told her that he did but still flipped her off because she did it first. We proposed that he might need another rock—one for each pocket—which would have occupied both hands, keeping him from using either one of them to "flip the bird." The mother said that she would write an "A" for "anger" on the second rock. We also suggested that the client make a bed for his rocks so that they would have somewhere to "rest" and be ready for action each day at school.

After several weeks of following this assignment, the client began completing his schoolwork and became one of the best-behaved students in his class, according to his teacher. His grades improved and he was back on honor roll. When the family moved, the client packed the rocks and took them with him. He reported that he lost one but found a new one to use. The mother decided that she would make different rocks for each of her children because she had been so encouraged by her youngest son's improvements.

We encourage telling your clients the story of how these rocks helped a second grader not be distracted from enjoying his success at school. Go on to say that there is no need to let others steal their happiness and victories by sidetracking their emotions. Gather a collection of small rocks and smooth stones for your office so that clients may choose one for their particular needs. There are many letters, names, metaphors, and symbols that can be drawn on them, depending upon the situation you are addressing. They can be used, as illustrated previously, for sidetracking sequences of problematic interaction or carried as a means of empowering someone to draw upon a special resource. Or you might have a generic diagnostic rock that simply has a question mark on it: "?" Loan this to a client who is trying to find "the answer," or "the meaning," or "the solution" to their challenges and difficulties. Have them carry it with them and rub it whenever they catch themselves brooding over their life situation. Tell them that this exercise will charge their whole being into being better equipped to have a new kind of focus. Then have them place the rock under their pillow before sleeping. Tell them that if the rock is sufficiently charged, they just might get lucky and have a dream that helps them move forward with their life.

When there is any kind of improvement in their therapy, consider giving them an R&R rock. Tell them this is a special "Rock & Roll" stone. Its purpose is to remind them that sometimes all they need is a good rock in order to roll with life. Make them promise to show the rock to anyone who they think could use a lift, whether it be a friend, family member, or colleague. If they are able to get enough people to carry their own rocks, announce that they might someday become a member of your Rock and Roll Hall of Fame. We invite you to use all kinds and shapes of rocks to move your metaphors and action in a creative therapeutic direction. But please don't tell anyone that your therapy has anything to do with getting stoned! It is more about handling rocky situations in a resourceful and pleasing way.

Unthinkable Home-Work*

Therapist: Walter Kempler, MD

Affiliation: Family Psychiatrist; Founder and Director, Kempler Institute USA, Costa Mesa, California; Cofounder of the Kempler Institute of Scandinavia

Major works:

Kempler, W. (1973). *Principles of Gestalt family therapy.* Costa Mesa, CA: Kempler Institute.

Kempler, W. (1981). *Experiential psychotherapy with families.* New York: Brunner/Mazel.

Dr. Kempler is one of the leading figures in Gestalt therapy as well as the family therapy movement.

Population for whom the technique is appropriate: There are no restrictions regarding the populace, at large. Appropriateness has more to do with the suitability of the therapist and the therapist's orientation than the recipient's. This approach is possible for all therapists who resonate with the notion that durable change is more likely to occur when motivated by our natural inclinations for integrity within and harmony with others than from intellectual coercion.

Cautionary notes: Don't try what you don't believe in.

Although I treasure the memory of the rare teachers who knew that my enthusiasm was the key to my learning and doing home-work, I can't say I ever liked home-work. Basically, I still believe that coercion is a temptation worth resisting. However, early in my practice occasionally I suggested activities that people could experiment with or practice between sessions. I had been programmed to give home-work and unwittingly used home-work for my patients to improve my sense of value as a healer.

More than 60 years later I now see that destiny has intervened.

Home-work is a tactical title for one way of generating, sustaining, or reinforcing progress between interviews. As far as I am concerned, an unforgettable experience in the therapist's office does

---

* Editor's Note: Dr. Kempler prefers hyphenated spelling of home-work.

what home-work hopes to achieve. Durable impact is the underlying objective: impact that brings change, change that endures.

Bypassing the individual's or family's vote is the essential difference between what is well known as home-work and the impacting experiences that can occur within the session itself. From a theoretical perspective, thoughtful, conscious, recommended action is omitted in favor of psychological spontaneity. We don't have to practice rubbing a bruise. The bruise elicits the rub. We don't have to be trained to laugh at a good joke. The joke builds in the response. When working up to speed, what is needed happens without having it suggested or assigned as a postscript.

An example from my files follows.

A couple came from a distant city for 3 days to save their 20-some-year-old marriage. The wife comfortably and articulately introduced herself as a religious person seeking a genial life with her husband in a difficult marriage. When asked for something specific, she became hesitant, passed the baton to her husband, who, in turn, answered slowly and thoughtfully with, "I know she has been unhappy with me for a long time. I don't understand what I am doing wrong." From the soft, hesitant way he spoke, I wondered if he was a shy farmer. Spontaneously, the wife tersely replied, "How can you say that you don't understand: I've told you again and again."

As we narrowed down the details, the wife drew an imaginary half circle around herself and between her and her husband, and said clearly, among other things, "I need space for myself in which I am not always being interrupted."

I first thought of suggesting that he ask her for an appointment, but instead—and this is where unthinkable home-work begins—I turned to her husband and translated what I "understood."

"What your wife is trying to tell you and what you have difficulty understanding is that you are her husband in name only. Actually, you are her neighbor."

He looked blank and she looked surprised. I continued. "You see, your wife is so modest, she draws a rather small circle around herself. Actually, from what I am hearing, you do not understand that she is talking about the house. It only appears to be a skirt she is talking about, but it goes well beyond that. She is talking about her home. Of course, she would have been nicer about it if you had actually been the neighbor. My guess is that she would even talk nicer about it to the dog, if you have one. But since you haven't realized what I am telling you, you keep coming back to her as if you really belonged there. That is what is so frustrating for her."

Both were silent. I knew which one would answer, but I didn't know what she would say. I stared out into space and waited.

When the wife spoke, she accurately repeated and disqualified all that I had said in reference to her, adding, "I am not a bad person."

Gold. Pure gold. And, more than I expected so soon.

I appreciated what she had recalled from what I had said and firmly added that I did *not* say she was "a bad person." I continued: "I wonder where you got that idea? I would venture that your husband would never say that about you, either. I didn't hear your husband say anything like that here."

For the first time, her husband spontaneously spoke up. Emphatically, he said to her, "I never thought *that* about you."

After several minutes, she looked at me and said, "I don't understand."

Thinking to myself, "the shoe is now on the correct foot" (or, as one might also formulate it, "now the unthinkable home-work is installed"), I replied: "Yes, I know. We will stop here for today."

The next morning they returned. She came in tears. Her husband was solicitous, silent, and looked worried. I didn't have long to wait. Invited to share her thoughts, she told of her lifelong cover-up; she had buried a badly bruised child under a shrine of religious service. To me, her tears were a child's joy of coming home.

Her husband's unsolicited parting remark was something about our time together being an answer to his years of prayer. We didn't use the third day.

Coping Chain

Therapist: Melissa T. Korenblat-Hanin, MSW, ACSW

Affiliation: Licensed Clinical Social Worker in St. Louis, Missouri, with more than 20 years of experience working with clients diagnosed with asthma

Major work:

Korenblat-Hanin, M., & Moffett, M. (1993). *The asthma adventure book.* Rochester, NY: Fisons.

Population for whom the technique is appropriate: Children ages 5 to 12, in individual, group, or family therapy, who are coping with a chronic disease, low self-esteem, or personal or family change

Cautionary notes: Involve parent or guardian because children must be supervised when using scissors and stapler.

In today's world, being a child is not easy. Children have unique fears, concerns, and worries. The intensity of feelings, fears, and worries accelerates during times of uncertainty (or painful and traumatic situations or events). The anxiety that results can be debilitating and can overwhelm children, thus contributing to physical and emotional illness. Promoting wellness by creating innovative, fun, and therapeutic activities that can be used by adults, parents, youth, and children to improve coping mechanisms and quality of life is of paramount importance. Children must develop skills to communicate and cope with their feelings and their surrounding environment. The process of communicating one's feelings can be especially challenging for children who have not mastered the art of verbal communication.

Activity Objective

This activity allows children to identify and explore the numerous feelings they have (about their families, divorce, changes, or chronic disease) as well as to identify specific interventions or strategies they could utilize to express or handle their thoughts or feelings or both. The activity promotes wellness while allowing the children to create a collection of coping skills. The "coping chain" activity serves to acknowledge a child's feelings, fears, worries, or all of these while helping to facilitate expression and exploration. It assists children with mastering the process of externalizing their experiences and feelings. For the therapist it can increase awareness of the psychosocial issues children are struggling with, as well as serve as a tool for assessing coping skills. The ultimate goal is for the children to develop many coping strategies to successfully manage their feelings, fears, thoughts, or struggles. The act of interlocking the coping techniques and feelings symbolizes the strength created when a variety of coping mechanisms are woven together.

Instructions

The child is given different-colored construction paper to take home, and the following explanation is given.

1. Cut construction paper into strips (wide enough to write or draw on).
2. Each day write on a strip of paper something that happened and a feeling or thought that was experienced. (Younger children can draw their feelings, or the parent and child can work together.)
3. Identify one or two ways to express the thought or feeling and write them on a strip of paper.

   For example: *Feeling:* anger and sadness. (Kids made fun of me at school.)

   Coping ideas: Draw a picture of my anger, talk to my Mom about my sadness, talk with my teacher about how I felt at school.
4. The ends of the first strip are connected in a ring shape, either stapled or taped. The subsequent strips are put through the preceding ring, forming a paper chain.
5. The final chain can be brought into the counseling session and shared. Then they can be displayed in the child's room.

   This activity highlights the fundamental importance of developing healthy and safe coping mechanisms.

Psychotherapy Consists of Homework Assignments: Less Talk and More Interaction—A Radical Iconoclastic Conviction

Therapist: Luciano L'Abate, PhD, ABEPP

Affiliation: Professor Emeritus of Psychology, Georgia State University, Atlanta, Georgia.

Major works:

Kazantzis, N., & L'Abate, L. (Eds.). (2007). *Handbook of homework assignments in psychotherapy: Research, practice, and prevention.* New York: Springer.

L'Abate, L. (Ed.). (2007). *Low-cost approaches to promote physical and mental health: Theory, research, and practice.* New York: Springer-Science.

L'Abate, L. (Ed.). (2008). *Toward a science of clinical psychology: Laboratory evaluations and interventions.* New York: Nova Science.

Population for whom the technique is appropriate: Anybody who is willing and able to complete forms before seeing the professional for the first session. If they are unable to perform this task, it is questionable whether they can be helped psychologically and other, possibly medical, approaches may be more appropriate.

Cautionary notes: In diverting from established counseling and psychotherapy practices that rely almost exclusively on face-to-face talk, and starting to work with participants through programmed distance writing (PDW), it would be ethically and professionally proper to use an informed consent form (ICF) to be signed by participants before introducing PDW interventions. A copy of such an ICF is available in L'Abate (2010).

The counseling and psychotherapy communities are now at a difficult crossroad in their evolution. They have to choose whether to (a) stay the same and embrace the status quo or change and move forward to keep up with societal, technological, and cultural changes that have occurred in the past generation; (b) remain in the past century or move on to this one, where many more additions and alternatives to face-to-face (F2F) talk-based (TB) approaches are available to mental health professionals as well as to people in need of help; (c) limit the impact of psychological interventions using outdated and outmoded models or enlarge that impact with new alternatives and technologies that are springing up every day (L'Abate & Bliwise, 2009); and, last, but not least, (d) choose whether to practice as artists/charlatans/phonies or as professional/scientists. I am making this choice a dichotomous one on purpose: You practice either as an artist/charlatan or as a professional/scientist. I am not going to waste my time debating shades of gray between these two choices. Make your choice and pay your price. I have made mine as shown by what I am writing here.

After 42 years of experience in clinical, prevention, and psychotherapy practices and research (L'Abate, L'Abate, & Maino, 2005), I have become convinced that the best use of my time and possible expertise is to assign as much written homework assignments (HWAs) as possible to willing, able and disabled participants, and limit my interventions to as few F2F TB contacts as possible, in order for me to (a) evaluate, with an exhaustive, systematic assessment, the nature and proximal and distal contexts of the reason for the referring concern, problem, question, or symptom; (b) not rely on my unique, magical intuition, idiosyncratic creativity, variable mood, wonderful personality, foreign accent, terrific sense of humor, and capricious wits and whims; (c) assign specific homework that matches as much as possible the reason for referral; (d) control and evaluate completed HWAs either in F2F talk or at a distance online through writing; (e) give specific feedback for each completed homework assignment (L'Abate, 2010) either F2F or online (L'Abate, 2008a, 2008b); (f) assign new homework as necessary that is consistent with the original evaluation and the process of previous HWAs; and (g) evaluate short- and long-term outcomes, both immediately after termination and at least 3 months after termination, if not longer: the longer after termination the better.

To accomplish most if not all the foregoing functions, for the past quarter of a century, I have put all my chips (energy, interest, name, reputation, and time) on the line, creating and developing and, when possible, evaluating structured, *programmed distance writing* (PDW), called *workbooks* in the past and *interactive practice exercises* in the present (L'Abate, 1986, 1992, 2001, 2002, 2004a, 2004b, 2010). Why did I do that?

Because I would argue that PDW allows us professionals to (a) repeat our interventions ad infinitum, providing a way to evaluate our interventions that are cumulatively and comparatively helpful or unhelpful within our own practice and among practices of similarly practicing colleagues; (b) change from a nonrepeatable medium of communication and perhaps healing, such as F2F talk, to perhaps a more efficient and possibly more cost-effective, different medium of communication and healing that is completely replicable, such as PDW; (c) link evaluation with interventions in ways that are difficult to replicate with F2F TB contacts; (d) avoid expensive F2F TB practices in the use of our energy for professional time; and (e) put the responsibility for change squarely on the hands and shoulders of participants, dedicating our time to as many participants as possible who need our help, including inmates and juveniles in jails and penitentiaries who do not have available help of any kind (L'Abate, 2010).

I will try to expand and explain why I am taking such a drastic, if not extreme and radical, position, a position that I hope will go against the status quo of current counseling and psychotherapeutic practices that rely almost exclusively on F2F TB contacts. This conviction is based on the following experiential and empirical grounds. I would argue that a great deal of F2F TB contacts are inefficient and costly. More than a decade ago (L'Abate, 1999), I challenged and questioned five sacred cows of psychological interventions that have been overlooked if not ignored, as far as I know, by the counseling and psychotherapy communities. Strangely enough, thus far, I have not been excommunicated by either community as yet. Therefore, I may as well summarize what those sacred cows are and see whether I will succeed in being drummed out of this profession for good for my iconoclastic conviction.

Sacred Cow No. 1. Talk improves behavior even though (a) talk is cheap and expensive at the same time; anybody can talk ad infinitum, but professional time is expensive because it is limited;

(b) talk is inefficient when you consider what and how much participants remember after they leave a therapist's office, just as how many remember afterward sermons preached in church; (c) talk is uncontrollable and, therefore, it takes a research grant and special expertise to record it, analyze it, and code it; furthermore (d) because of the inadequacy in controlling it, talk is a not replicable behavior, making it difficult to find the relationship between prescriptive evaluation at the outset of therapy with the process of what has occurred throughout the process and length of the intervention. Part of the mystique about talk is due to its uncritical acceptance as the sole medium of communication and healing without any consideration about alternative, and perhaps more effective, methods to help physically and emotionally disabled people (L'Abate, 2008b).

Sacred Cow No. 2. Seeing a professional F2F improves behavior even though by now we know that we can help people at a distance without ever seeing them, as in the case of PDW (L'Abate, 1992, 2001, 2002, 2004a, 2004b) and computer-assisted interventions on the Internet (Harwood & L'Abate, 2010) and Pennebaker's (2001) expressive writing (Lepore & Smyth, 2002). However, to make sure that we match what we preach, especially when working at a distance from participants, a thorough, systematic, objective evaluation and a signed ICF must be paramount in counseling and psychotherapy (L'Abate, 2008a, 2008b, 2010).

Sacred Cow No. 3. The professional's talk and personality improve the therapeutic alliance as the cornerstone of the participant–professional relationship even though thousands of alliances are occurring every day on the Internet where there is no F2F TB contact between two or more parties. In no way am I denying the importance of a therapeutic alliance and especially of a written contract between professionals and participants; rather, I am denying that that alliance and a written contract have to be based on F2F talk to occur. These requirements can occur at a distance, without ever seeing our participants, just as well as, and perhaps more efficiently than, in F2F talk.

Sacred Cow No. 4. The more family members involved, the better the intervention will be, in spite of the fact that most research shows that outcomes between individual and family therapy are comparable (Szapocznik & Prado, 2007). Through PDW and the Internet, the number of people we can help is irrelevant. We can help as many people as we can who want and need our help as long as they work for change, relying on the best possible HWAs we can administer to them.

Sacred Cow No. 5. The more sessions the better: The longer I see participants the more adequate I am as a therapist, and I can prove it at any party where my colleagues and I congregate to share "war stories." It does not matter how many sessions it takes to help somebody. It does matter whether we help them or not. Therefore, we need to evaluate and monitor process and outcome from the very outset, throughout the process to its very end and thereafter.

Furthermore, I would argue that in the not-too-distant future a great deal, if not the majority, of psychological treatments will occur online. Involving participants in the process of change puts the responsibility squarely on their shoulders and not on the shoulders of therapists. However, under these conditions, the functions of therapists using PDW and HWAs are to evaluate at the beginning of psychotherapy, evaluate throughout the whole process, evaluate at termination, and evaluate some time after termination.

Why evaluate and why should evaluation be objective and systematic? There are at least three reasons for requiring such an evaluation: (1) to create a baseline functioning to serve as an assessment of whether short- and long-term improvement has occurred after an intervention; (2) to guarantee that evaluation will occur on a pre-post-intervention and follow-up; and (3) to charge the complete evaluation fee from the outset and in between the first three sessions labeled as therapy (L'Abate et al., 2005), as should be explained in full in an ICF administered even before a potential participant enters the professional's office for the first time. Additionally, I would make an objective evaluation mandatory for licensed psychotherapists on ethical, professional, and scientific grounds.

This recommendation is not too far off considering recent results about the negative effects on family functioning from psychosocial treatments (Szapocznik & Prado, 2007). As Szapocznik and Prado argued: "Whereas medical products are required to be tested for safety with respect to vulnerable organ systems, psychosocial treatments are not required to be tested for safety with respect to vulnerable social systems such as the family" (p. 468). Aren't human beings more important than material objects or medical products? Shouldn't we offer them the best possible service based on evaluation rather than on the subjective and very likely faulty impressions of an artist/charlatan?

Therefore, my conviction leads me to support continuous evaluation of the following grounds: ethical, professional, and scientific.

Ethical Grounds

Here is where we need to differentiate clearly between artists/ charlatans/phonies and full-fledged professionals/scientists. Artists and charlatans are so convinced about their inherent personal qualities and verbal skills that no evaluation of any kind is necessary, except perhaps a subjective interview of questionable professional and scientific value, and of their clinical judgment and superior intuition of absolutely no value. Immediacy is the hallmark of the artist and the charlatan, entering right away into a therapeutic action with a minimum of evaluation and a maximum of self-assurance and conceit. In this way, it is practically impossible to demonstrate any improvement or outcome, but as long as one can make a good living at it, why question it?

Professional Grounds

The difference between artists/charlatans and professionals/scientists lies in how long it takes to evaluate a referral problem. For instance, after 10 years of traditional practice (L'Abate et al., 2005), we decided to dedicate the first three sessions to evaluation *as a reciprocal process between professionals and participants* ("We need you to evaluate us to see whether we can be helpful to you."). Participants should be empowered to evaluate us throughout the whole three-session so-called evaluative relationship before entering into a therapeutic contract, because that evaluation occurs whether we like it or not. The best way to assure their trust in us is to assure potential participants of their right to evaluate us as much as we evaluate them reciprocally. The cost of the pre-post-evaluation and follow-up should be included in the three evaluation sessions, by charging 33% over the usual fee for the first three sessions to assure that the whole process of pre-, post-, and follow-up evaluation is paid from the beginning. In this way, potential participants know from the very beginning, as should be explained in the ICF, that they are in professional hands and not in an artist or charlatan's hands. As Detweiler-Bedell and Whisman (2005) found, treatment outcomes are associated with specific therapist behaviors (i.e., setting concrete goals and discussing barriers to completing the homework), characteristics of the homework task (i.e., written reminders of the homework), and client involvement in the discussion.

Participants should be able to evaluate the competence of therapists by how well they are being evaluated, because, after all, we therapists are being evaluated by participants as well. The more they are evaluated the more participants will be able to trust the professional, knowing that she or he is not an artist or a charlatan. During the 15 years that we followed this approach (L'Abate et al., 2005), no single individual, couple, or family objected to this approach or turned us down. They allowed us to evaluate them through a signed ICF during the three so-called evaluation sessions, answering questionnaires or rating sheet before the first F2F TB session, in between sessions, after termination, and months after termination. Furthermore, the number of sessions for those participants (individuals, couples, and families) who completed HWAs was significantly higher than the number of sessions for participants did not receive HWAs. Consequently, counselors or therapists do not need to fear losing business. Evaluation might prolong business.

If evaluation is as important as I am convinced it is, especially when it deals with HWAs and PDW, then it should occur sequentially in steps, or hurdles: (1) before seeing the therapist; (2) between sessions while seeing the therapist, either F2F or at a distance during the first three sessions; (3) after termination; and (4) some time thereafter.

Scientific Grounds

To understand the nature and severity of the reason for referral, evaluation must be objective and systematic, using a battery of quick and dirty but reliable and valid individually and relationally oriented tests. For this purpose, my collaborators and I (L'Abate, Cusinato, Maino, Colesso, & Scilletta, 2010) created and validated an inexpensive battery of theory-derived, relational, self-report, paper-and-pencil tests that are relatively easy to administer, score, and interpret, including a still-experimental, structured, self-administered interview with weights to evaluate the level of functionality (L'Abate, 1992) and an ecologically oriented rating checklist to evaluate the same level of functioning (Harwood & L'Abate, 2010; L'Abate, 2008a, 2008b).

Linking Evaluation With Intervention: Prescriptive Evaluation

The need to evaluate continuously and consistently and link evaluation with treatment can be obtained through *prescriptive evaluation* by converting our passively inert paper-and-pencil, self-report questionnaires or tests into dynamic and interactive workbooks or practice exercises. Any single-item test or factor list of symptoms such as those in the *DSM-IV* or single-dimension instruments such as the Beck Depression Inventory, or the Content Scales of the Minnesota Multiphasic Personality Inventory can be converted to a workbook or interactive practice exercise through a very simple transformation that allows matching any concern, problem, reason for referral, or symptom into a series of written, sequential HWAs, including interactive practice exercises (L'Abate, 1986, 1992, 2010).

This transformation occurs through four easy-to-follow steps: (1) asking participants to define (in writing, of course) each term of a list, and (2) give two examples from the definition, a nomothetic task; (3) rank-order the items according to how important those items are to them, an idiographic task; and (4) administering standard forms for each item that requires participants to expand and give all the possible information on the particular item. For instance, if "Crying" is ranked first on the list, a general standard form would ask severity, duration, origin, personal and relational outcomes for crying (L'Abate, 2010). The next assignments would follow the same individual rank-order given initially by each participant. This is one way to match treatment with evaluation in ways that would be difficult, if not impossible, to follow verbally but that can be accomplished through PDW (L'Abate, 2008a, 2008b).

What about the objective and systematic evaluation itself? As already noted, before seeing the professional, the individual participant's (a) historical background could be obtained through an experimental structured interview (L'Abate, 1992) with weights that allow to discriminate between functional and dysfunctional adjustment; (b) present functioning could be obtained through an experimental ecological checklist that allows to report current functioning (Harwood & L'Abate, 2010; L'Abate, 2008a, 2008b); (c) a standard overall measurement of depression as assessed by the thermometer of mental health, and that is the Beck Depression Inventory or equivalent test; and (d) a copy of the ICF to be signed by participants only by the third evaluation session, when during this session, participants and the professional will discuss whether treatment should be started or whether another preventive or therapeutic avenue seems the most appropriate course of action for each particular case.

Consequently, when setting a time for the first session over the phone, potential participants should be asked to come to the appointment at least 1 hour earlier to complete forms necessary for an evaluation of the referral problem or question. Seeing the professional is contingent on completing this information. Other tests can be administered from the first to the second session so that they can be scored by the final, third evaluation session.

Because the professional will not have time to score these forms before seeing the participant(s) for the first evaluation session, the professional might give a superficial glance at them but reassure participants that these questionnaires or tests will be scored appropriately from the first to the second sessions of the evaluation. Detailed suggestions on how to conduct this process of evaluation have been given in L'Abate (2008a). From this process, participants need to bring the signed ICF by the third session, if they want to continue the therapeutic process. If written HWAs are assigned at the end of the third session, they should match the referring question or any variation that may have arisen during the first three-session evaluation period. As a whole, a tentative termination date may be given at this time, requiring no more than six more HWAs.

Conclusion

I am aware of the dangers of the foregoing conviction, but I believe that any intervention without a before and after evaluation and follow-up is essentially unprofessional. Anything short of these three steps could be considered unethical because participants need to have a structure under which they can operate and be reassured by the fact that the therapist has a specific plan and course of action particularly tailor-made for them and for no one else, within guidelines for continuous and thorough evaluation of process and outcome through systematic HWAs. The veterinarian does it with my cat, so why should we not do it with human beings?

References

Detweiler-Bedell, J. B., & Whisman, M. A. (2005). A lesson in assigning homework: Therapist, client, and task characteristics in cognitive therapy for depression. *Professional Psychology: Research and Practice, 36,* 219–223.

Harwood, T. M., & L'Abate, L. (2010). *Self-help in mental health: A critical evaluation.* New York: Springer-Science.

L'Abate, L. (1986). *Systematic family therapy.* New York: Brunner/Mazel.

L'Abate, L. (1992). *Programmed writing: A self-administered approach for interventions with individuals, couples, and families.* Pacific Grove, CA: Brooks/Cole.

L'Abate, L. (1999). Taking the bull by the horns: Beyond talk in psychological interventions. *The Family Journal: Counseling and Psychotherapy with Couples and Families, 7,* 206–220.

L'Abate, L. (2001). Distance writing and computer-assisted interventions in the delivery of mental health services. In L. L'Abate (Ed.), *Distance writing and computer-assisted interventions in psychiatry and mental health* (pp. 215-226). Westport, CT: Ablex.

L'Abate, L. (2002). *Beyond psychotherapy: Programmed writing and structured computer-assisted interventions.* Westport, CT: Ablex.

L'Abate, L. (2004a). *A guide to self-help mental health workbooks for clinicians and researchers.* Binghamton, NY: Haworth Press.

L'Abate, L. (Ed.). (2004b). *Using workbooks in prevention, psychotherapy, and rehabilitation: A resource for clinicians and researchers.* Binghamton, NY: Haworth Press.

L'Abate, L. (2008a). Proposal for including distance writing in couple therapy. *Journal of Couple & Relationship Therapy, 7,* 337–362.

L'Abate, L. (2008b). Working at a distance from participants: Writing and nonverbal media. In L. L'Abate (Ed.), *Toward a science of clinical psychology: Laboratory evaluations and interventions* (pp. 355–383). New York: Nova Science.

L'Abate, L. (2010). *Sourcebook of interactive practice exercises in mental health.* New York: Springer-Science.

L'Abate, L, Cusinato, M., Maino, E., Colesso, W., & Scilletta, C. (2010). *Relational competence theory: Research and mental health applications.* New York: Springer-Science.

L'Abate, L. & De Giacomo, P. (2003). *Improving intimate relationships: Integration of theoretical models with preventions and psychotherapy applications.* Westport, CT: Praeger.

L'Abate, L., L'Abate, B. L., & Maino, E. (2005). A review of 25 years of part-time professional practice: Workbooks and length of psychotherapy. *American Journal of Family Therapy, 33,* 19–31.

Lepore, S. J., & Smyth, J. M. (Eds.). (2002). *The writing cure: How expressive writing promotes health and emotional well-being.* Washington, DC: American Psychological Association.

Pennebaker, J. W. (2001). Explorations into health benefits of disclosure: Inhibitory, cognitive, and social processes. In L. L'Abate (Ed.), *Distance writing and computer-assisted interventions in psychiatry and mental health* (pp. 157–167). Westport, CT: Ablex.

Szapocznik, J., & Prado, G. (2007). Negative effects of family functioning from pro-social treatment: A recommendation for expanded safety monitoring. *Journal of Family Psychology, 21,* 468–478.

Being the Qualitatively Whole New Person in the Real World

Therapist: Alvin R. Mahrer, PhD

Affiliation: Clinical Psychologist; University of Ottawa, Canada; Private Practice; www.almahrer.com

Major works:

Mahrer, A. R. (1989). *Dream work in psychotherapy and self-change.* New York: Norton.

Mahrer, A. R. (2003). *The complete guide to experiential psychotherapy.* Boulder, CO: Bull Publishing.

Author of 17 books and over 300 publications. Dr. Mahrer pioneered experiential psychotherapy.

Population for whom the technique is appropriate: Persons who are dedicated to having experiential sessions by themselves; persons who have sessions with an experiential teacher-therapist

Cautionary notes: In preparation for the person to carry out the homework successfully and well, the person should first have carried out the experiential session successfully and well.

Homework Comes From Sessions Where the Person Works With a Therapist-Teacher or With Oneself

Homework is arrived at and used in virtually every session. However, the experiential therapist functions mainly as a teacher who shows the person what to do and how to do it. Homework also is arrived at and used in virtually every session when the sessions are by and with oneself.

In Each Session, Figuring Out What the Homework Will Be Starts by Discovering a Deeper Potentiality Inside the Person

Each session opens by searching down inside the person to discover a deeper inner quality, some deeper potentiality for experiencing inside the person. This almost always is hidden from the person, not a part of who and what the person is ordinarily. In this session, for this person, the deeper potential may be that she can become a qualitatively new person who is able to experience a newfound sense of delightful control, being in charge, being on top of things. The homework is a way for this person to actually live and be as this whole new person.

During the Session, Get Ready for the Homework by Literally Being the Qualitatively New Person

The person is to undergo a radical, qualitatively transformational shift into being a whole new person who is filled with happiness, joy, and excitement in undergoing the newfound experiencing of being in absolute control, in charge, on top of things.

Welcome, love, cherish the newly discovered deeper potentiality for experiencing. First the person is to welcome, to love, to cherish this newly discovered potentiality that has been sealed off, hidden, kept deep inside her.

Literally become the qualitatively new person who is this deeper potentiality for experiencing in contexts of playful unreality. The person is then to undergo a radical transformation into being a whole new person who is the live embodiment of experiencing and being in absolute control, totally in charge, fully on top of things. The person is to be this whole new person in scenes and situations from the recent and remote past, and to do so in a context of sheer playfulness, outlandishness, silliness, joyfulness, free of reality constraints, in safety-providing fantasy and merriment.

Toward the End of the Session, Prepare to Carry out the Postsession Homework

As the qualitatively whole new person, she moves from being this whole new person in the context of recent and past scenes, and into the context of postsession scenes from the next few days or so.

Be the qualitatively new person in imagined postsession scenes that are wild, unrealistic, zany, silly, unthinkable. To sample what it is like to be the qualitatively whole new person in the postsession world, the person deliberately looks for imminent scenes that are wild, unrealistic, zany, silly, unthinkable. In these forthcoming scenes, she experiences, tries out, and undergoes what it is like to be this whole new person who is the full living out of absolute control, being totally in charge, on top of things.

This person is loud, uncontained, silly, happy, vibrant, explosive as this whole new person in imminent scenes of banishing commercials as she watches television, commanding her manager to apologize to her in front of the entire department, forcing supercilious waiters to bend to her absolute control, and, beginning this evening, eradicating every disgusting little habit of the fellow with whom she lives.

Rehearse and refine being the qualitatively whole new person in more appropriately realistic imminent scenes. Now move into finding more appropriately fitting and realistic scenes in which the whole new person would be ready and eager to live and be, to get a genuine taste of being in absolute control. As this whole new person, she selects an imminent scene in which ordinarily she would assume the role of being the one who is to make all the arrangements for trips, vacations, visits to friends, and her partner fulfills the companion role of the nagging critic, the displeased complainer about her arrangements.

She rehearses changing the roles, abdicates being the one who is forever to blame, and lays down new rules for how preparations are to be done. After a series of in-session trials, refinements, and rehearsals, she arrives at a wonderful sense of enlivened control, being in charge, on top, as she dictates how every shred of preparation is to be done together, as assigned by her, as they prepare for the week-long camping trip with three couples. Laying down the new laws goes through a final refinement and rehearsal, and it is judged as right, solid, pleasant.

The final act is a ready and eager commitment to carrying out this homework with her partner. Tonight.

The Session Is Preparation for the Homework; True Change Occurs in Actually Being the Qualitatively New Person in Doing the Homework

A session is successful and effective if it leads to the person doing the homework. The homework is successful and effective if the person is actually the qualitatively new person in carrying out the homework assignment.

The next day, she was truly being the qualitatively new person who sat her partner down, who reveled in the solid new sense of control, in charge, on top of things as this whole new person laid down complete new rules for how they were going to spend the day preparing together for the week-long camping trip. Doing this and being this way was fun, felt right, and seemed to free both of them from their painful old roles. Indeed, so successful was the homework that they canceled the camping trip with the three couples and decided instead to spend the day, and maybe the whole week, enjoying their new selves, together, at home.

Feelings Inside Out: The Paper Plate Activity

Therapists: Jean Marnocha, MSW, and Beth Haasl, BS

Affiliation: Jean Marnocha is an Independent Clinical Social Worker and Beth Haasl is a Grief Counselor. Both have done extensive work in the area of grief counseling and bereavement with children's groups in Green Bay, Wisconsin.

Major work:
Haasl, B., & Marnocha, J. (1999). *Bereavement support group program for children.* New York: Taylor & Francis.
(Editor's note: This work is available in a "Leader Manual" for use with children ages 5 to 15 and a "Participant Workbook" for use with children ages 7 through 15.)

Population for whom the technique is appropriate: Children of any age who are grieving a death loss

Cautionary notes: When giving the homework assignment, the child must be in a safe environment with a trusted adult.

During the grief experience children may have feelings that they have difficulty expressing externally and may cover up grief feelings in different social situations. The following activity can be beneficial in assisting children to recognize and respond to their grief feelings.

A. Have the children use paper plates and markers and ask them to draw pictures of their face on one side of the plates showing how they feel in various situations. On the other side of the plates, ask the children to draw a face depicting how they feel inside during those same situations. The counselor can suggest situations, such as being at home with their family, at school, playing with a friend, alone at bedtime, or at a party.

B. Have the child bring his or her plate and share it at the next counseling session.

C. Point out the following:
   1. Sometimes we appear to feel differently on the outside than we feel on the inside.

   2. Feelings of grief are always a part of us even though we can participate in normal activities.
   3. It is normal to sometimes feel differently inside than what we show others.
D. This can lead to a discussion of feelings such as, "How can we express these feelings appropriately? What can we do to deal with these feelings?"

Taming the PIT Monsters

Therapist: Maxie C. Maultsby, Jr., MD

Affiliation: Professor of Psychiatry, Department of Psychiatry, College of Medicine, Howard University, Washington, D.C.; certified by and Fellow of the American Board of Psychiatry

Major works:

Maultsby, M. C. (1979). *The rational behavioral alcoholic-relapse prevention treatment method.* Lexington, KY: Rational Self-Help Books.

Maultsby, M. C. (1984). *Rational behavior therapy.* Englewood Cliffs, NJ: Prentice Hall. (Now available also in Polish)

Maultsby, M. C. (1986). *Coping better ... Anytime, anywhere.* New York: Simon & Schuster.

Dr. Maultsby formulated and research tested the comprehensive, therapeutic, cognitive-behavioral methods of rational behavior therapy (RBT) and rational self-counseling (RSC). His research and professional focus mainly have been on the emotional and physical behavioral problems of normal people; he is one of the rare, internationally recognized experts on medically proven, emotional and behavioral self-help concepts and techniques for normal people. He has been referred to as the normal people's psychiatrist.

Population for whom the technique is appropriate: Underachieving or emotionally and spiritually distressed normal teenagers and adults

Cautionary notes: None

Taming the PIT monsters* is a highly effective way to help appropriate new clients immediately get and stay motivated for rapid therapeutic change. "Appropriate clients" means people whose brains are healthy, that is, free of detectable malfunctions, either

---

* PIT monster is a psychoemotional construct in RBT and RSC, derived from human medical research on the psychosomatic learning theory of normal human behavior. The P stands for the adjective personal, the IT monster refers to any belief or external event that the concerned person gets upset about. PIT monster really means your personal, generic IT monster.

naturally so or with prescribed medication. In RBT or RSC the term *PIT monster* is the name of any personal belief that unsuspectedly has these three characteristics: (1) More often than its owners want it to, the personal belief unexpectedly causes its believers to have confusing, negative emotional feelings; (2) in their emotional confusion, PIT monster believers accuse their associated external events or people of causing their negative emotional feelings; (3) then, both illogically and inappropriately, PIT monster believers demand that their accused external events or people either stop, or be stopped from, causing the negative emotional feelings the PIT monsters believers' own belief is causing.

Universally Common but Unsuspected PIT Monsters

There are several types of PIT monsters, but limited space allows me to discuss only one. It, however, is the "mother of all PIT monsters"; yet, it consists of just eight little, innocent sounding words: *"It upsets me and I can't help it,"* meaning "I can't keep my miserably upsetting feelings from occurring. For that reason, the first two steps in RBT and RSC* are (1) to help clients most quickly discover that unsuspected PIT monster, and (2) to help them tame or eliminate the monster.

Think of PIT monsters as being unsuspected psychoemotional pollutants. They are analogous to one of the unsuspected, but potentially harmful, air pollutants that you are now breathing. But, unless you have an allergy, you don't notice any of them. If the concentration of any one of them increases enough, however, it will make you sick or even kill you.

PIT monsters are usually modern versions of beliefs, once held by ancient, absolute rulers of Western world societies, prior to the age of scientific thought. At that time, voicing ideas that were contrary to those of the rulers resulted in death or severe punishment.

On the other hand, Mother Nature's scientific laws of ideally healthy emotional self-management have existed and often

---

* The most comprehensive scientific references for both are in the section "Major works" at the beginning of this homework entry.

have been described for as long as healthy people have existed. Unfortunately though, medically valid, general descriptions of the natural, neuropsychophysiological laws relating to the "It upsets me" PIT monster probably did not appear until about 110 years ago. More than 50 years ago, the psychosomatic, medical research of W. J. Grace and D. T. Graham (1952) and D. T. Graham, J. A. Stern, and G. Winokur (1958) revealed the following evidence: *It (the external world of people and events) doesn't directly cause any normal people's emotions: To the contrary, normal people directly cause their own emotional feelings with their attitudes and beliefs about It, the external world of people and events.*

Normal people empirically prove that medical fact themselves every day. How? EASILY! Think of any specific daily life event that is observed by these normal people: Person A has a positive attitude about such events, person B has a negative attitude about such events, and person C has an indifferent attitude about such events. The emotional feelings that each normal person has in response to that event will be caused solely by the individual's existing attitudes about such events, and NOT by the event. The event itself will have done nothing more than exist.

But that's not all. The following objective event will further highlight the innocence of it—the event. What if the aforementioned three people were falsely informed, by credible sources, that the previous event had occurred? Then those normal people would still have the same emotional feelings about that news that they would have had if they personally had observed such an objectively real event. Obviously, therefore, it is naive at best and unfair at worse to ever accuse any "him, her, them, or it" of ever doing any emotional thing to you or to anyone else.

Faced with those compelling medical facts, the next fact seems at best ironic: Today's physicians are the best trained of the health professionals in Mother Nature's human neuropsychophysiological laws of ideally healthy emotional self-management. Yet today virtually all students in medicine, psychology, and other health professions are still almost exclusively taught these more than 2,000-year-old, medically disproved, Aristotelian variations on the "mother of all PIT monsters": Anger is caused by undeserved slights, fear is caused by the perception of danger, and shame is caused by deeds that bring disgrace or dishonor. "Undeserved slights," "perception of," "deeds that bring"—all of those phrases exist ONLY in the beliefs of the observers. Yet they are based on the easily disprovable, but almost universally believed, assumption that normal people's emotional feelings are directly caused by external events, that is, he, she, they, or it.

At this point, believers in Aristotle's PIT monster emotional myth usually ask: If the belief that "It upsets me," or can upset me is wrong, how, Dr. Maultsby, do you explain that so many brilliant people since Aristotle continue to believe and react logically to it? The most accurate response is: EASILY. But it is even easier to let the following historical facts speak for themselves.

For nearly 2 decades (343–324 B.C.), Aristotle (384–322 B.C.) was the most favored and therefore unchallenged savant of the tyrannical Greek King Alexander the Great. Aristotle's Greece still has the reputation of being the source of noteworthy Western world knowledge. So, with the death threat backing of Alexander the Great, all of Aristotle's correct and incorrect ideas were overtly accepted immediately as if they were divine revelations. And remember, science and scientific thought only came into being about 2,000 years after Aristotle's death. When normal people are coerced into teaching and reacting logically to unchallenged ideas for hundreds of years, those ideas become as automatically accepted as were the ideas that the earth was flat and that the sun revolved around the earth.

Aristotle was at the zenith of his intellectual influence when he proclaimed the still universally popular but medically invalid and absurd belief that "The heart, not the brain," as many then and prior to Aristotle held, "is the center of sensation and of the soul's motor impulses" (Gillispie, 1970). Aristotle based his proclamation on his personal observations of the heart action of developing chicken embryos. Then it seems, he used his then famous syllogistic method of logic and reasoning in the following way: The heart action in chick embryos changes when they are externally stimulated. The heart action in people changes when they are externally stimulated and they get specific emotional feelings about the stimuli. Therefore, external stimuli cause people's emotional feelings.

No, I do not have any proof that Aristotle ever described that syllogism. But I am unaware of Aristotle ever saying anything about the brain that proved to be medically valid. And I know of no other more credible logic for his still-popular, emotional proclamations than his then-famous syllogistic system of logic. In any event, the core meaning of Aristotle's well-documented claims about anger, fear, and shame (Gillispie, 1970) has been equally well proven to be medically incorrect. Only magical thinking can justify beliefs such as "It" (external world events and other people) "upsets me" (i.e., other normal people), "makes me feel mad, glad, sad, and so on, and I can't help it."

Like all scientifically based cognitive-behavioral approaches to therapy and counseling, RBT and RSC are based on these well-proven medical facts: "It," that is, an external event or nonphysical contact with another person, "does not do any specific emotional thing to any normal person," that is, one possessing a healthy brain. Instead, normal people do every emotional thing to themselves with their existing attitudes about "It."

In RBT and RSC, attitudes label the neurologically created and stored behavior-eliciting messages represented by people's strongest personal beliefs. With that valid, neuropsychophysiological knowledge, it becomes easy to help appropriate clients quickly take these two ideal therapeutic actions. The first is to see clearly how they alone create, maintain, and eliminate their own emotional feelings. The second is to help them discover that fact right away. That frees them to quickly learn how to tame to their satisfaction, or even eliminate, their various, unsuspected versions of the Aristotelian "It upsets me and I can't help it" types of PIT monsters. Next is the generic way I help appropriate clients do that as well as train my professional RBT and RSC trainees to also do that with their clients.

In my first formal therapy session with appropriate clients, I give them a real-life, self-discovery example of how healthy human emotions really work. One of my favorite such self-discovery examples is the burglar example. I ask clients, "Vividly and sincerely imagine that you awaken at 2 a.m. in response to a noise in your kitchen. Your first belief is 'My God! A burglar is in my kitchen.' If you are like most normal people, you instantly will feel an agonizing fear. You also will immediately start doing what you believe is best to do in such situations. But, before you dial 911 or get your gun, and so on, suppose that your roommate says, 'That is no burglar; that is just the rattling of the wind in our Venetian blinds. I forgot to close the window after I let out the odor of your burned roast.' Then your roommate smilingly continues, 'Besides, don't you remember? You personally had all of our windows and doors covered with iron bars that are so close that even a baby burglar could not get in without first waking up the whole apartment building. So go on back to sleep while I go and close that darn window.'"

Now, if you believe your roommate, in the "hot second" that it would take your healthy brain to process those facts, what will happen to your fear? Almost all of my clients know and admit that it will have disappeared. And, I always agree: That is one universally popular way of looking at such events. But in RBT we want clients to learn the best, that means the ideally healthy, way to understand their emotions. So let's take an in-depth look at that medically proven way of understanding normal human emotions (Maultsby, 1984).

The healthiest proven medical understanding is this: Your fear will be gone only because you will have stopped creating and maintaining it. That is why it is incorrect, inappropriate, and unfair to accuse the innocent noise, or any external "It" or people, of causing your emotional feelings. If the noise had caused your fear, like broken glass would cause pain in your foot, then this could not and would not have happened. You could not have calmed down while the noise continued. It's only because you would have believed your roommate that you immediately would have calmed down and would have stayed calm, even though the noise would have continued until someone closed the window. Of course, here's another free-will option you would have had: You could have calmly said, "Don't bother to close it; some of that smell may still be there to remind me of my stupid debacle. I'll just use my earplugs and ignore the noise, so go on back to sleep."

By then, my typical 30- to 45-minute session would be about over. So, I tell my client, "The session is about over and I don't want to give you sensory overload. I just want you to remember these four most important therapeutic insights: (1) You, not the noise, but you alone, will have caused your fear with your fearful attitudes about such noise. (2) The only reason your fear disappeared is because you will have changed your fearful attitudes and beliefs about the noise. (3) At that same time, you instantly will have eliminated as well as disproved the mother of all PIT monsters. (4) Fortunately, all normal human emotions work in analogous ways. Otherwise, no one could help you without impairing your healthy brain with powerful drugs or neurosurgery."

Now as you, the reader, have probably guessed, there is much more to quickly helping clients solve their emotional problems than just identifying the "mother of all PIT monsters." Also, I admonish clients: "Expect to soon forget most of the medical details that I have just given you. That will be a perfectly normal reaction at this stage of your emotional reeducation. Granted, those well-proven medical facts are easy to demonstrate, and they control normal people from their births until they die. But those facts are in conflict with personal beliefs that you have held for as long as you can remember. Such personal beliefs don't instantly lose their old emotional power just because you have heard contrary facts. Such new facts don't usually become easy to recall accurately until you have objectively rethought them at least 3 times. Also, here are two other medical facts that may keep you from clearly remembering the medical fact that I described, before you objectively rethink them for the third time.

"Healthy human brains do not care about facts; healthy brains genetically are programmed to create only the emotional reactions that are most logical for people's strongest, existing beliefs about the facts that they are focused on at the moment. The second medical fact is this: Healthy human brains genetically are programmed to make all facts that conflict with an existing personal belief feel wrong at first. So, I am sure that some of what I have said feels a bit wrong to you right now. That is perfectly a normal reaction. It could not have been otherwise; unless before now, you already knew and have been controlling your emotions in light of the facts I have just described. If that is not the case, some wrong feelings by you now are virtually avoidable, but that's true only at first.

After enough practice thinking about and correctly acting out the medical facts that I described, expect this to happen. Any 'wrong feeling' you may have now will begin to 'feel right' to you."

The RBT name for those initially unavoidable "wrong feelings" is cognitive-emotive dissonances (CED). The almost universally understood example of CED is the wrong feelings Americans get when they drive in England. Correct English driving is the opposite of correct American driving. So, even though those Americans intellectually know that the correct way to drive in England is on the left side of the road, driving the correct way feels totally wrong to them at first. Only after enough practice does correct English driving, or any new learning that conflicts with existing beliefs, begin to feel right. Therapeutic emotional reeducation (which is all any effective talk therapy or counseling is) is analogous to English driving reeducation for people who have first learned to drive as Americans drive.

With those objective facts in mind, the second step in the most rapid therapeutic progress becomes obvious: It's for the therapist or counselor to quickly help clients get past their CED for their new therapeutic learning. Assisting clients in this way gives me the opportunity to emphasize this important fact. I tell them: "Genuine therapeutic learning normally does not begin until you give yourself a third sincere exposure to the relevant therapeutic facts, which at first feel wrong to you. That's because about the only thing normal people can learn to do well with just one or two exposures or trials is naively create personal problems.

"As I explained in your intake session, I routinely tape-record my first few therapy sessions. That's because they contain many vital, natural, and therefore, empirical, emotional facts and insights that most clients either haven't discovered or they have forgotten. Yet clients need to be applying them every day. But, cognitive-emotive dissonance can easily prevent clients from remembering most of my first description of those vital emotional facts and insights. To prevent such limited remembering and therefore slow, initial therapeutic progress, I give my clients the therapeutic homework assignment to listen alone at home, at least three times, to the tape of each taped session, before their following session. I shall therefore, lend you the tape of this session and I now give you the homework assignment to listen to it at least three times before your next session with me.

"As you listen to the tape, make written notes about anything you don't understand, that you don't believe and especially, any statements that don't feel right to you. Your notes will be the first things that we shall discuss in your next session. Also, remember that this tape is of your therapy session. No other person is to listen to it. And be sure to give it back to me at your next session; it's an important part of my records of your therapy."

Postscript

This short essay could not accurately give you a realistic feel for the relaxed, naturally pleasant ambience that is typical of RBT or RSC sessions. Also unavoidably missing were these two important experiences: (1) an accurate view of the reassuring, yet thought-eliciting Socratic style of therapist–client interactions, which many of my trainees and I prefer; and (2) the chance for you to "hear" typical client responses to the psychoemotionally instructive nature of the interactions in RBT and RSC. However, in my listed books, interested readers will find many detailed case examples that clearly reveal both of those unavoidable omissions.

References

Gillispie, C. C. (Ed.). (1970). *Dictionary of scientific biographies* (Vol. 11, pp. 249, 262). New York: Scribner & Son.

Grace, W. J., & Graham, D. T. (1952). Relationship of specific attitudes and emotions to certain bodily diseases. *Psychosomatic Medicine, 14,* 243–251.

Graham, D. T., Stern, J. A., & Winokur, G. (1958). Experimental investigation of the specificity of attitude hypothesis in psychosomatic disease. *Psychosomatic Medicine, 20,* 446–457.

Maultsby, M. C. (1984). *Rational behavior therapy.* Englewood Cliffs, NJ: Prentice Hall.

Eavesdropping to Enhance Social Skills

Therapist: Clifton Mitchell, PhD

Affiliation: Professor of Counseling, East Tennessee State University; Professional Mental Health Trainer; Licensed Psychologist (Tennessee); Mind Management Seminars, specializing in teaching techniques for managing resistance therapy and in legal and ethical issues training

Major work:

Mitchell, C. W. (2007). *Effective techniques for dealing with highly resistant clients* (2nd ed.). Johnson City, TN: Author.

Population for whom the technique is appropriate: Adults and adolescents

Cautionary notes: This technique is appropriate for normal functioning individuals who have inappropriate conceptions of other's or their own social skills. I would use caution in suggesting it to clients whose demeanor and skills were not such that they can eavesdrop and still remain socially appropriate.

Many clients come to therapy because they are delayed in some area of their development. One of the most common areas of developmental delay is in social skills. This lack of social skills is often central to client problems and, thus, becomes an essential factor in overcoming problems and moving forward in life.

Sometimes social skills are lacking because there have been no appropriate role models in clients' lives. Sometimes the opportunity to practice good social skills has not been provided or has been avoided because of a fear of failure. You may also find that various levels of trauma have occurred with regard to social situations, which have resulted in stifled development. In addition, other trauma may have occurred that has left the client so internally devastated that social situations are avoided and, thus, social skills are delayed.

Regardless of the reason, the result is often an unrealistic perspective of what constitutes appropriate, healthy social skills. Many times clients have exaggerated views of how poor their social skills are and, concomitantly, exaggerated views as to how much better others' social skills are than theirs. In more psychological terms, clients create cognitive distortions regarding social skills. These distortions fuel the fear often encountered as clients attempt to "catch up" with their peers. One of the therapist's tasks is to find ways to dispel these cognitive distortions and create realistic views of what constitutes suitable social skills. Along the way, it is also nice to have some models of typical social behaviors from which to build an understanding in clients' minds of what is realistic. I stumbled upon the eavesdropping homework assignment in an effort to do just this.

When encountering clients struggling with social skills issues, I often suggest that they do not make any attempts to change their social skills immediately. Instead, I give them the assignment to deliberately eavesdrop on other's conversations during the week and report back to me with their findings. We often discuss when and in what settings this can be accomplished and the need for discretion. Sometimes they just sit and listen to others, and sometimes they are instructed to stand with others they know and acutely observe the conversation. The instruction to "acutely observe" or "observe in detail" or "intently observe" or, depending on the personality of the client, "scientifically observe" is a crucial part of the assignment. They are to consciously, deliberately eavesdrop and report back to me. I offer no suggestions as to what they will discover, only that I am anxious to learn of their observations.

I once did this with a college student who had joined a fraternity in an attempt to improve his social skills, particularly with women. He was devastated by his perceived lack of skills in talking with women. His perceptions of his ability to converse with the opposite sex had virtually paralyzed him, and he had an extreme fear of attending upcoming social events. Further, he was convinced that his fraternity brothers were much more adept and clever at conversing with women than he. Thus, he was given the assignment to spend the week eavesdropping on his fraternity brothers' conversations. Upon reporting back, he was astounded at how mundane and juvenile his fraternity brothers' conversations were.

I can still hear him proclaiming to me, "They're not saying any-thing! They're just talking a bunch of garbage!" Needless to say, his perceptions shifted immensely, and he moved on to doing his own conversing. Thus, the cognitive distortions were refuted by the client in an empirically based manner and without the thera-pist having to do any refuting of the client's internal logic.

If the client were to report that he or she experienced others as hav-ing superior social skills, the exercise would simply be framed as an excellent place to start studying what is missing in his or her reper-toire. A detailed examination of what was observed would be under-taken initially. During the process of exploring this information, an assessment of which communication skills needed to be developed first would be made, and models to emulate could be noted. The client could then be sent out to apply what was learned. You may discover that more study of others is necessary. In such instances, the exercise could be repeated with particular emphasis on the study of facial expressions, the use of compliments, body language, social cues, opening phrases, and so on. Of course, other techniques, such as role plays, could then be integrated into the sessions.

There are a number of benefits to this assignment. First, as the cognitive theorists would expound, it empirically validates or invalidates perceptions. Assignments that empirically validate perceptions are a crucial part of cognitive therapy approaches. Such assignments answer the question, "Is it true?" Second, the assignment invariably shifts perceptions regardless of the out-come. The disruption of current patterns is always beneficial in promoting change. Building from almost any perception shift, good therapists can move toward new behaviors. Third, the assign-ment makes use of readily available models in the real world. This is different from role play in the therapist's office that may appear unrealistic to clients. Finally, the assignment provides much to talk about and build from in the therapeutic conversation, regard-less of the information gleaned. The beauty of the assignment is that it is not given with any specific purpose in mind; therefore, whatever emerges from the client's observations can be used as a therapeutic tool. Because of the open-ended outcome that can be framed by the therapist in any manner deemed helpful, this assignment has a high success rate.

The Life Imprint

Therapist: Robert A. Neimeyer, PhD

Affiliation: Professor, Department of Psychology, University of Memphis

Major works:

Neimeyer, R. A. (Ed.). (2001). *Meaning reconstruction and the experience of loss.* Washington, DC: American Psychological Association.

Neimeyer, R. A. (2002). *Lessons of loss: A guide to coping.* Memphis, TN: Center for the Study of Loss and Transition.

Neimeyer, R. A. (2009). *Constructivist psychotherapy.* New York: Routledge.

Author of 22 books and over 300 book chapters and journal articles; see http://web.mac.com/neimeyer

Population for whom the technique is appropriate: Adolescents and adults who are processing an experience of loss or transition, particularly the bereaved

Cautionary notes: Special care should be taken when clients have lost a negative or ambivalently regarded figure, such as an abusive or neglectful parent; in such cases more time should be spent processing the conflicted feeling the life imprint can engender.

In a sense, we are all "pastiche personalities," reflecting bits and pieces of the many people whose characteristics and values we have unconsciously assimilated into our own sense of identity. This "inheritance" transcends genetics, as we can be powerfully or subtly shaped not only by parents, but also by mentors, friends, siblings, or even children we have loved and lost. These life imprints are not always positive; at times, we can trace our self-criticism, distrust, fears, and emotional distance to once influential relationships that are now with us only internally. In therapy with the bereaved, whether in an individual or group context, I often innovate upon Vickio's (1999) *life imprint* concept and extend it into a therapeutic assignment, which can be undertaken as homework or used as an exercise in group therapy or workshop settings. This involves encouraging clients to reflect upon someone they have loved and lost, and privately to trace his or her imprint on their lives at any of the following levels that apply, writing a phrase, sentence or (in homework applications where more time is available) paragraph about each. Then, at the client's discretion, I invite them to discuss their observations with one or two partners in the context of group work, or with me in the context of individual therapy. The basic framework for reflecting on this follows.

> The person whose imprint I want to trace is _____
> This person has had the following impact on:
>> My mannerisms or gestures:
>> My ways of speaking and communicating:
>> My work and pastime activities:
>> My feelings about myself and others:
>> My basic personality:
>> My values and beliefs:
> The imprints I would most like to affirm and develop are:
> The imprints I would most like to relinquish or change are:

I include the latter two prompts in recognition that life imprints are sometimes ambivalent, so that even a loved figure (e.g., a devoted mother) may exemplify some traits (e.g., a tendency toward martyrdom) that the client would prefer to let go of in his or her own life. In cases of extremely conflicted relationships, for example, with a critical and rejecting father, the client might discover a "negative imprint" that has powerfully shaped his or her life by modeling "what *not* to be." But like a photographic negative, such imprints are no less influential and important for being reverse models for the client's later construction of self.

Usually clients find this a very affirming exercise, one that strengthens their sense of a continuing bond to their deceased loved one, while also conveying that this person continues to live on, in a significant sense, through the client's own life. Moreover, the subsequent sharing phase, especially in a group work setting, commonly leads to a sense of affirmation and joy as clients tell stories of the loved one's life and impact on them to responsive others. However, even when the imprint revealed is negative, this can usefully focus discussion on what might be done to relinquish it, often in the form of a healing ritual.

Variations on the basic life imprint include having the client note his or her mood in a word or two or a phrase following the reflective writing portion of the assignment, and then again following the social sharing. This commonly reveals a shift from a sense of grief to celebration, although many individual variations are possible, which might suggest whether further journaling or guided disclosure would be more therapeutic for a given person. Likewise, I have found the life imprint to be strong medicine to administer when the client is actively losing a loved one to debilitating illness, when it can shift attention usefully from a preoccupation with managing the disease to appreciating the life legacy of the ill or dying person. Finally, some clients have innovated further on the method by using it as an "interview" structure to document the imprint of their loved one on mutually known others, which greatly extends and validates the deceased person's impact on the world. Honoring the life and legacy of the lost seems to mitigate grief, in the great majority of cases, and helps focus the client on life purposes and activities that continue to connect their lives with those who have gone before.

Reference

Vickio, C. (1999). Together in spirit: Keeping our relationships alive when loved ones die. *Death Studies, 23*, 161–175.

Favorite Counseling Assigned Tasks: The Basics

Therapist: Richard C. Nelson, PhD

Affiliation: Professor Emeritus, Counseling and Development, Purdue University, Lafayette, Indiana.

Major works:

Nelson, R. C. (1990). *Choice awareness: A systematic, eclectic counseling theory.* Minneapolis, MN: Educational Media Corporation.

Nelson, R. C. (1992). *On the CREST: Growing through effective choices.* Minneapolis, MN: Educational Media Corporation.

Nelson, R. C., Dandeneau, C. J., & Schrader, M. K. (1994). *Working with adolescents: Building effective communication and choice-making skills.* Minneapolis, MN: Educational Media Corporation.

Population for whom the technique is appropriate: All clients, particularly students

Cautionary notes: None

In my work as a school counselor educator, I often made the point that the tremendous potential that exists in the time between counseling sessions too often is overlooked or wasted. It is my conviction that anytime a counselor expects to see a client again, he or she ought to give what I prefer to call an *assigned task,* since many school-age clients have a negative attitude about *homework.* Actually, the same two points tend to be relevant for clients of any age and with any type of concern: All clients need tasks between sessions that encourage continued growth, and many may not respond well to the word *homework* but may be more than willing to take on *assigned tasks* they see as relevant.

Any homework assignment or assigned task needs to fit the situation, and many suitable assignments are both inherent in, and basic to the situation. For example, clients can make observations that may give them insight into their situation, offer compliments daily to Mom or Dad or another key person in hopes of changing the direction of a relationship, or initiate with a different pattern of behavior. Choice awareness theory (Nelson, 1990) suggests that clients of all ages continuously are making choices, and they may be able to create a more positive environment for themselves through assigned tasks that help them implement more positive patterns of choices.

Here are four examples of tailored assigned tasks.

Count to 10 and Observe

Paul, a middle-school student who had been threatened with expulsion if he got into one more fight—and was really afraid of the punishment his parents would hand out if that happened—agreed to two basic assigned tasks. First, he was to count to 10 whenever he felt like fighting, and, second, he was to make a written observation, to note the day and time when the feeling occurred, plus what was happening and who was present. By the time Paul came to the next counseling interview he realized that one of his buddies, Jerry, a much smaller classmate, had been present each time he had been tempted to fight. He noticed that Jerry tended to manipulate the situation so that Paul was always defending Jerry. Based on his observations, Paul told Jerry he was not going to be manipulated into fighting for him anymore.

Tallies as Observations

Denise, an 11-year-old, who complained to the counselor, "I cry all the time," was asked to tally the number of times she cried, note what was happening, and who was present (Nelson, 1990, pp. 313–316). She came into the next interview all smiles. Contrary to her expectation, she had only cried six times in the interval, rather than "all the time," and after some discussion she realized that three of those times she had something worthwhile to cry about.

Complimenting

Rudy told his counselor that his mother was always "on my frame about something—anything." He was dubious as to the value of the suggestion, but he accepted the assigned task of finding one thing to compliment about his mother or her actions each day in the week until the counselor saw him again. He knew he would have the opportunity to compliment his mother's cooking, so he practiced that, and he decided he could say something positive about the washing and ironing she did for him. Rudy learned that his compliments brought smiles from his mother, although she was skeptical when he began complimenting her. On the second day his mother asked him, "Why are you buttering me up, and when am I going to learn what you want or what you've done wrong?" At that point Rudy realized how seldom he said anything positive, and he began to change his ways on his own.

Initiating

Laura, a middle-school student who once had a very positive relationship with her father, was devastated when he began to be accusatory about her behavior with boys her age (Nelson, 1990, pp. 142–143). She rejected a variety of possible suggestions, but then she agreed to approach her father first and to initiate the interactions at least once each afternoon until the next counseling interview. She was delighted with the success of her efforts.

The first day she initiated contact by suggesting she and her dad play a game of checkers, an activity previously they had enjoyed together; her father agreed, they played several games, and he criticized many of her moves, but she was delighted that the topic of boys didn't enter the conversation. On the second day she knew her father was upstairs dressing for a church meeting, so she waited for him and initiated the conversation by telling him how nice he looked; once again, her initiation directed the conversation in a positive channel. Pleased with those results, on the third day she did what she had told me she would "never, never, never, never, never," be able to do. She said, "Dad, we used to have a really good relationship, and we haven't been getting along very well lately. We need to talk." The talk led to hugs and tears, and although no long-lasting miracle resulted, Laura learned a really powerful lesson. If she waited for her father to initiate interaction, the first move and the outcome were often negative, but if she initiated, she could at least control the first direction of the interaction.

The Choice Awareness View

Choice awareness theory (Nelson, 1990) suggests that clients of all ages need to be empowered to make positive choices in their lives and to implement more positive choices in their everyday, moment-to-moment interactions with others. Well-chosen, relevant, basic assigned tasks or homework assignments that may only take a few moments each day can serve as model choices for clients of all ages. Through positive words and actions, people who may otherwise feel powerless often can slow the course of a downward-spiraling relationship, and, with continued effort, may turn the spiral in a positive direction.

Reference

Nelson, R. C. (1990). *Choice awareness: A systematic, eclectic counseling theory.* Minneapolis, MN: Educational Media Corporation.

Variety Is the Spice of Life: A Developmental and Diagnostic Approach to Choosing Homework Assignments

Therapist: Edward Neukrug, EdD

Affiliation: Chair, Department of Educational Leadership and Counseling and Professor of Counseling and Human Services, Old Dominion University, Norfolk, Virginia; Licensed Professional Counselor and Psychologist, Norfolk, Virginia

Major works:

Neukrug, E. S. (2002). *The world of the counselor: An introduction to the counseling profession.* Pacific Grove, CA: Brooks/Cole.

Neukrug, E. S. (2007). *Theory, practice and trends in human services: An overview of an emerging profession.* Pacific Grove, CA: Brooks/Cole.

Researcher of constructive development and its relationship to education of the helping professional, Dr. Neukrug is the author of dozens of articles and other publications.

Population for whom the technique is appropriate: Clients of all ages

Cautionary notes: The counselor should use clinical discretion when applying these principles.

When I was asked to provide a favorite homework assignment for the book, I was stymied. I thought and thought and could not focus on one homework assignment that I would use consistently. Then I quickly realized how silly it was to think that I would continually use one homework assignment. Isn't each client unique? Isn't the manner in which I work with each client particularly suited for that client? I soon understood that the homework assignments I have given over the years always have been tailored to the needs of the clients. However, after further reflection I also understood that there is some order to this madness, for in developing my homework assignments I take into account a number of things. Let me delineate some of these items.

1. *Develop a safe relationship.* Homework assignments must challenge clients to change. However, if the client is willing to take the risk involved in following through on a good homework assignment, it must be presented within a supportive relationship. How does one build a supportive relationship? I generally do it through empathy and understanding. But it can be done in many ways, depending on your own style. You might be "friends" with the client, as Glasser attempts to do; you might "join" with the client or family, as Minuchin likes to do; or you might attempt to bond with the client through storytelling, as some constructivists might do. Whatever your approach, you must build a safe relationship if your homework assignment is going to work.

2. *Assess client developmental level.* In developing homework assignments, it is critical that one is aware of the developmental level of the client. In general, it is worth noting that such models present stages of development that are orderly, sequential, painful yet growth producing, continuous throughout one's lifespan, and a natural and potentially positive part of our existence. Today, there are many kinds of developmental theories, all of which can be helpful to us in creating homework assignments. For instance, we can examine a client's cognitive development, faith development, career development, lifespan development, and interpersonal development, to name just a few. Being able to match the developmental level of the client with the homework assignment is crucial to successfully meeting treatment goals.

3. *Perform clinical assessment.* It is important when working with clients that the clinician make an accurate clinical assessment. Increasingly, it has been shown that clients within certain diagnostic categories respond best to specific techniques as reported in the literature. For instance, it has been shown that phobics work best in a cognitive-behavioral approach, whereas individuals going

through a period of bereavement after the death of a loved one would do best to have an empathetic, understanding counselor. Because the homework assignment is based, to some degree, on the presenting problem and the resulting diagnostic classification of the client, making an accurate clinical assessment is crucial.

4. *Introduce variety.* Clinicians must have a wide range of knowledge of different approaches to counseling if they are going to have a "bag of tricks" to present to their clients. Knowing just a few potential homework assignments limits the counselor's ability to accurately match homework assignment with client developmental level and client diagnosis.

5. *Employ creativity.* A good counselor can vary the way homework assignments are given and create new homework assignments based on his or her knowledge of different theories and on knowledge about the client.

6. *Maintain commitment.* Any homework assignment worth its weight must be given with a sense of commitment on the part of the counselor and be received at least somewhat positively by the client. Although some clients might argue about the worthiness of a specific homework assignment, this might be because the assignment is right on target; that is, it challenges the client just enough so that the client is a little wary and anxious about following through on it.

7. *Provide follow-through.* A good homework assignment challenges the client, and thus some resistance can be expected with many clients. It is important to quietly challenge your client to follow through on the homework assignment, especially if it seems that the assignment is on target.

8. *Remember humility.* It is important to distinguish whether the resistance is in response to a good (i.e., challenging) homework assignment, a poorly chosen homework assignment, or poor timing of the homework assignment (e.g., given too early in treatment). In the latter case, the counselor must be willing to admit his or her failings and move on by either massaging the original homework assignment, coming up with a new homework assignment, or totally giving up on the idea.

Let me give an example of how the previous steps can be used with a client: Jillian, a 40-year-old female, who has been living with her current partner for 4 years, presents with mild to moderate depression. She relates this depression to the fact that she recently was passed over for a promotion and to a failing relationship in which she describes her partner as verbally abusive. She describes herself as a recovering alcoholic who stopped drinking 2 years ago and states that she now regularly attends Alcoholics Anonymous. She reports a history of physical abuse in past relationships but denies physical abuse currently. She is a very successful executive in a major computer company and presents herself as assertive and in charge of her life. She relates well and her affect seems appropriate.

Now, using the steps noted previously, this is how I proceed with Jillian:

1. *Develop a safe relationship.* Using empathy and spending a few sessions to explore the relationship in more depth, I quickly realized that Jillian's history is much more involved than she presented initially. Her family of origin was chaotic and her father was verbally abusive with her mother. Drinking to drunkenness was common in her family. Her initial assertive presentation is one that she presents at work, but there is a sheepish, shy, and self-doubting person behind this façade. She also shows fearfulness and doubts about the future.

2. *Assess client developmental level.* Using a number of developmental schemes, I realize that Jillian has an easy time thinking in abstract ways (Piaget's formal-operational stage; Piaget, 1954), sees her identity based on others (Kegan's interpersonal stage; Kegan 1982), has struggled most of her adult life with issues of intimacy (Erikson, 1963, 1968, 1998), and is unsure of whether she wants to make a shift in her current job (Super's establishment stage; Super, 1957, 1976, 1996).

3. *Perform clinical assessment.* Although my initial assessment of Jillian resulted in a diagnosis of adjustment reaction with moderate depression, after developing a deeper

relationship with the client I now assess her as having a diagnosis of dysthymic disorder as well as alcohol abuse in full remission.

4. *Introduce variety.* Based on my assessment of Jillian, a number of homework assignments can be examined now. These can vary tremendously but should focus on my developmental and clinical assessment of her. Thus, I am likely to develop homework that has to do with Jillian's understanding of her dependency issues, her feelings of low self-esteem, her feelings of isolation in the world, her alcohol addiction, and her current immobilization in her career path. The use of medication as an adjunct to therapy would be considered in this case, and a referral to a psychiatrist would be appropriate (this could be considered another homework assignment for Jillian).

5. *Employ creativity.* Because Jillian is comfortable with postformal thinking, the types of homework assignments I give to her are limited only by my lack of creativity.

6. *Maintain commitment.* Through my work with Jillian, I show her, and indeed will even tell her, that I am committed to helping her work through her issues. I am "on her side" and willing to do my homework to find creative ways of working with her.

7. *Provide follow-through.* When Jillian does not follow through on some homework assignments that I believe are "on target," I challenge her and gently nudge her to "try again."

8. *Remember humility.* Although I will prod Jillian to follow through on some homework assignments, I am also willing to admit when a homework assignment is inappropriate or clearly not on target. I am willing to say, "Let's give up this idea and try something else."

Summary

The use of targeted homework assignments for clients based on a developmental and clinical assessment model can greatly help clients reach their therapeutic goals. Such homework assignments need to be given with a base of support, should be timely, should gently prod clients toward new understandings about themselves, should be given humbly (knowing that they may need to be changed or reworked), and should offer a creative outlet for the counselor in helping the client meet his or her goals.

References

Erikson, E. H. (1963). *Childhood and society* (2nd ed.). New York: Norton.

Erikson, E. H. (1968). *Identity: Youth and crisis.* New York: Norton.

Erikson, E. H. (with Erikson, J. M.). (1998). *The life cycle completed.* New York: Norton.

Kegan, R. (1982). *The evolving self.* Cambridge, MA: Harvard University Press.

Piaget, J. (1954). *The construction of reality in the child.* New York: Basic Books.

Super, D. E. (1957). *The psychology of careers.* New York: Harper & Row.

Super, D. E. (1976). *Career education and the meaning of work.* Washington, DC: Office of Career Education.

Super, D. E. (1996). Career and life development. In D. Brown, L. Brooks, & Associates (Eds.), *Career choice and development* (3rd ed.). San Francisco: Jossey-Bass.

Creating a New Family Play

Therapist: Fred Newman, PhD

Affiliation: Director of Training, East Side Institute for Social Therapy; Artistic Director, Castillo Theatre, New York

Major works:

Newman, F., & Holzman, L. (1993). *Lev Vygotsky: Revolutionary scientist.* London: Routledge.
Newman, F., & Holzman, L. (1997). *The end of knowing: A new developmental way of learning.* London: Routledge.
Newman, F., & Holzman, L. (2006). *Unscientific psychology: A cultural-performatory approach to understanding human life.* Bloomington, IN: iUniverse.

Dr. Newman is the author of several other books and dozens of journal articles.

Population for whom the technique is appropriate: Families, "traditional" and otherwise (including parents and adult children and siblings who may not reside in the same household, former spouses who share custody of their children, unmarried couples, and same-sex partners)

Cautionary notes: Social therapy, a cultural-performatory approach to human development, is effective with children, adolescents, and adults regardless of their presenting problem; social, emotional, cognitive, or all of these abilities; or the type and severity of any previous diagnosis (including addiction and psychosis). Although the following discussion concerns a family in which the teenage daughter was diagnosed with anorexia, "creating a new family play" has shown itself to be effective with all sorts of families in a variety of situations.

Similar to many families, Norman and Marilyn Petrie and their teenage daughter Nancy were in the terribly painful and frustrating situation of being estranged from one another despite their mutual love and concern. When they came to see me they seemed like actors in a bad play, compelled to act out roles that they knew only too well—"guilt-stricken mother," "angry father," "problem child." Stuck in those roles, complete with familiar lines, gestures, emotions, and assumptions (about right versus wrong, truth versus lies, reality versus "imagination," and so on), it was all but impossible to change how they were reacting to one another.

Under my direction, they created a new family play that enabled them to go beyond their limited, and limiting, roles. In other words, they *performed* their way out of the emotional box they were in by being other than who they were (as defined by the old script), thereby opening up the possibility of seeing themselves and one other differently.

When the Petries first came to see me, it was after a difficult year in which 16-year-old Nancy, increasingly preoccupied with her weight, had virtually stopped eating and spent most of her time engaged in strenuous physical exercise that left her visibly exhausted. A few months earlier, after she had suffered several fainting spells at school, Nancy was hospitalized for 2 weeks. The Petries' family physician diagnosed anorexia, discharging her with the warning that she was doing irreparable harm to her body and could be endangering her life. It was at his recommendation that Norman and Marilyn Petrie came to see me.

Since Nancy's hospitalization, according to Mrs. Petrie, their family life had degenerated into a "civil war," each mealtime a tense standoff between the two sides: she and her husband trying everything short of physical coercion to get their daughter to eat something versus Nancy, "just not hungry," demanding that they leave her alone. Mr. and Mrs. Petrie, bewildered and frightened by their daughter's behavior, were worried also about the impact of all this on the two younger children, 11-year-old twins.

So far, Nancy, who apparently had accompanied her parents to the session only at their insistence, had not spoken a word. I asked her how she felt about what was going on, and she replied: "My Mom and Dad used to fight with each other all the time, and now they're acting as if the only problem they have is me. Well, that's just not true. I love my parents, but I wish they would mind their own business."

"If you're starving yourself to death, damn it, that is our business!" Mr. Petrie interrupted, glaring at his daughter.

"We don't want you to ruin your health," Mrs. Petrie told Nancy. "We don't want you to die." Then, turning to me, she said tearfully: "I feel so terrible, Dr. Newman. It's as if we're living on different planets, and that we're speaking a language she can't even hear—much less understand. How do we get through to her? What are we going to do?"

I suggested that they could create a new family play, and spoke with them briefly about what I understood to be the relationship between performance and development.

Not surprisingly, the Petries were skeptical initially. "How can I be someone else when I'm me?" Mr. Petrie wanted to know. His wife nodded. "What good will it do to play a game of make-believe when we have this terrible real-life problem?" she asked me. "It sounds so phony—pretending that everything is fine when it's not. It's like changing the subject when you don't want to talk about something."

I pointed out that the roles they currently were playing were not particularly "natural" in the sense that they had been learned, or acquired, rather than being innate. Nor was the "angry father," in my opinion, necessarily the *real* Norman Petrie any more than the "guilt-stricken mother" was the *real* Marilyn Petrie or the "problem child" was *really* Nancy. The important difference between the family play the Petries were in and any new family play they might create together, I said, was that in performing/creating it they would have the opportunity to engage in the developmental activity of *choosing* who, and how, they wanted to be.

Nancy was more receptive to the idea of performing: "It sounds kind of weird," she said approvingly. "I'll do anything to change the subject. If this means that we can finally stop having these horrible, boring conversations—'Eat, Eat, Eat … You're so thin, you're so thin, you're so thin'—then, yes. What play should we do?"

I said I didn't know. The fascinating thing about performance is that *what* people perform—a troupe of circus clowns; their next-door neighbors; astronauts from different countries, or centuries, who run into each other on Mars; guests at a costume party—isn't all that important. *That* they perform shows them that they aren't doomed (astrologically, biologically, psychologically, or any other way) to be how they are; rather, they can make (not simply in the sense of selecting, but by creating) choices to be who they aren't. In other words, they can choose to grow, change, develop.

By the end of the session the Petries had all agreed, more or less conflictedly, that they would try to do the homework assignment.

When the three of them came back to see me the following week, I learned that on the way home they had decided that whenever they were together Mrs. Petrie and Nancy would be Venus and Serena Williams (the two newest superstars on the tennis scene at that time), and Mr. Petrie would be their father/coach, Richard Williams. The two younger Petrie children were delighted to be "cast" as the Williams sisters' trainers.

Here are some excerpts from the Petries' review of their family play after a 1-week "run."

Mrs. Petrie: I was so relieved that we were talking to each other again without fighting.
Nancy: My Dad used to play tennis when he was younger, and he took his role as Mr. Williams very seriously. He kept telling us how good we were, that we were the best. And he was tough at the same time, like a real coach. My Mom and I had fun acting like sisters. It was cool.
Mr. Petrie: It felt pretty silly at first, but then I kinda got into it. I read the sports section every day to see how the Williams girls were doing and what Richard Williams was saying about it. And then I tried to act accordingly. I have to admit that when I talked to my wife and my daughter not as ourselves, I started to see some of what's been going on a little differently. That surprised me.

Six months later, Nancy is eating and exercising (she plays tennis regularly) normally, and she is no longer underweight; the problem of her anorexia has disappeared. And Mr. and Mrs. Petrie, having learned that they can create a new marriage play for themselves, are no longer acting their old parts (the exhausted husband, who comes home after a long day at work to stare at the television with a virtual "Do Not Disturb" sign around his neck, and his resentful, sarcastic wife); they are discovering that there are no limits to being other than who they are, continuously.

Digging Out of the Hole: Self-Sabotage and the Problem Gambler

Therapist: Lia Nower, JD, PhD

Profession: Psychotherapist, Attorney, Social Worker

Affiliation: Associate Professor and Director, Center for Gambling Studies, Rutgers University

Major work:

Richard, D. C. S., Blaszczynski, A., & Nower, L. (in press). *The Wiley-Blackwell handbook of pathological gambling.* London: Wiley.

Population for whom the technique is appropriate: Most problem and pathological gamblers, particularly those in a current state of gambling-related crisis (e.g., relationship, job, financial, legal)

Cautionary notes: None

Description

This exercise consists of a series of three homework assignments, adapted from the author's treatment manual. Each completed homework assignment is processed in session with the counselor before the next homework is begun. Before assigning the first homework exercise, the counselor asks clients to describe their current crisis situation, including the nature and extent of the gambling-related problems, their associated feelings, and the thoughts about themselves that result. The counselor should also ask about other times clients have been in a similar crisis situation and what they did to "dig themselves out of the hole."

Homework 1

The client is asked to write answers to the following questions. Each response should be as cryptic or detailed as the client sees fit. Some answers will be long and descriptive, whereas others may consist of a timeline or a series of words. There are no right or wrong answers.

> What lesson did I learn the last time I dug myself out of a hole?
> What was most frightening about that experience?
> What was most exciting about that experience?
> Why do I need to do it again?
> What patterns do I recreate for myself over and over again?
> What do those patterns say about me?

In session: Client and counselor process the reasons that underlie the client's pattern of moving from crisis to resolution and then back again. The counselor assists the client in understanding the positive by-products of self-sabotage and the reasons why the client may be more comfortable with the process of digging out than with being out of the hole.

Homework 2

The client is assigned the second series of questions with the same instructions.

> What do I feel I need to prove to other people in my life?
> What do I feel I need to prove to myself?
> To whom do I most feel I need to prove myself?
> What would it mean to me to be successful? How would I
>   know I'm successful?
> What do I most resent about this?

In session: Client and counselor discuss motivations behind repeating dangerous patterns in order to solicit validation from self and others. Clients are encouraged to identify healthier ways to satisfy this need.

Homework 3

The client answers the last series of questions (same instructions).

> Looking back, what did you always want from your mother/
>   father that you didn't receive?

How did you react when you didn't receive it?
What did you get instead?
How have you tried to make up for this loss?

In session: These final questions mark the beginning of a transition from the gambling behavior to the motivations that drive the need to gamble pathologically. Processing these answers will lead the counselor to the next step in addressing the grief, loss, and/or inadequacy that fuel the need to gamble.

Reference

Nower, L. (2002). *Problem gambling treatment manual.* St. Louis: Author.

Challenging Body Comparisons: Building Positive Body Image

Therapist: Susan J. Paxton, PhD

Affiliation: School of Psychological Science, La Trobe University, Australia

Major works:

Paxton, S. J., & Hay, P. H. (Eds.). (2009). *Interventions for body image and eating disorders: Evidence and practice.* Sydney, Australia: IP Communications.

Paxton, S. J., McLean, S. A., Gollings, E. K., Faulkner, C., & Wertheim, E. H. (2007). Comparison of face-to-face and Internet interventions for body image and eating problems in adult women: An RCT. *International Journal of Eating Disorders, 40,* 692–704.

Richardson, S. M., & Paxton, S. J. (2010). An evaluation of a body image intervention based on risk factors for body dissatisfaction: A controlled study with adolescent girls. *International Journal of Eating Disorders, 43*(2), 112–122.

Population for whom the technique is appropriate: Females and males, of all ages, with body image problems

Cautionary notes: None

In the absence of both a physical and a social comparison, subjective evaluations of opinions and abilities are unstable.

—**Festinger**
(1954, p. 119)

Body image problems, or body dissatisfaction, in which the whole body or specific parts of the body become a source of negative emotions, anxiety, and disparagement and result in interference with role functioning, are frequently observed in both females and males (Eisenberg, Neumark-Sztainer, & Paxton, 2006). In the Western world, body dissatisfaction in females tends to be focused on perceptions of being overweight, whereas in males it tends to be focused on concerns about being insufficiently lean and muscular. Body dissatisfaction may be observed in the absence of other symptoms, but it is frequently observed in the presence of eating disorder symptoms (e.g., extreme weight loss behaviors and binge eating) and is also a key diagnostic criterion for anorexia and bulimia nervosa.

Numerous risk and maintenance factors have been identified for body dissatisfaction (Wertheim, Paxton, & Blaney, 2009). One risk factor for body dissatisfaction is the tendency to compare one's body with others: This is known as body comparison. This concept is derived from Festinger's (1954) social comparison theory in which Festinger postulated that individuals assess their own qualities by comparing themselves with other, preferably similar, people and that typically comparisons are made with others deemed above themselves on the relevant dimension: This is called an upward comparison. Upward comparisons, by their very nature, result in negative evaluations of the self.

This is certainly the case in the body image domain. Individuals who engage in frequent body comparisons are at greater risk of body dissatisfaction than individuals who do so to a lesser degree, regardless of body mass index. Not surprisingly, comparing oneself with celebrities, models, or one's slim best friend is likely to emphasize perceived inadequacies and contribute to the development or maintenance of body dissatisfaction. But conceptualized as a cognitive behavior, the nature and frequency of body comparisons can be challenged and changed. What would happen if a patient started comparing with others deemed below himself or herself, that is, to make downward comparisons?

Homework tasks designed to change body comparison behaviors appear valuable and have been used as part of successful body dissatisfaction interventions (e.g., Paxton, McLean, Gollings, Faulkner, & Wertheim, 2007). The aim of therapy for body comparisons is to reduce the frequency of body comparisons (especially upward comparisons), to select more realistic targets for comparison, and to alter the negative emotional impact of comparisons when made. The first step is to identify the nature of a patient's body comparisons for which a monitoring homework task is employed. Situations and targets of body comparisons are noted. In addition, the specific nature of comparisons and consequent cognitions, affect, and behaviors are recorded. The patient and therapist explore the record and normally will be able to identify that selective comparisons have been made on features with which the patient is not satisfied (ignoring features with which they are satisfied), and with unrealistic targets (e.g., with a different age group), resulting in negative self-evaluation and mood.

The second phase of the homework is a behavioral experiment in two parts (Paxton & McLean, 2009). First, the patient records thoughts and feelings after 10 of his or her usual comparisons. Next, the patient makes an additional 10 body comparisons, but this time is instructed to compare with 10 consecutive people of the same gender who pass by without being selective for the target. The patient then examines the consequences of both sets of comparisons. Normally, the patient will appreciate that in the latter sequence, their conclusions about their body are relatively positive and their mood is not as negative. Further, the patient learns that comparisons are within his or her control and that choices can be made about comparison targets and, consequently, upward or downward comparisons. Cognitive restructuring may be employed to challenge cognitions resulting from comparisons. Finally, a choice may be made whether to make body comparisons at all!

References

Eisenberg, M. E., Neumark-Sztainer, D., & Paxton, S. J. (2006). Five-year change in body satisfaction among adolescents. *Journal of Psychosomatic Research, 61*(4), 521–527.

Festinger, L. (1954). A theory of social comparison processes. *Human Relations,* 114–140.

Paxton, S. J., & McLean, S. (2009). Body image treatment. In C. Grilo & J. Mitchell (Eds.), *The treatment of eating disorders* (pp. 471–486). New York: Guilford Press.

Paxton, S. J., McLean, S. A., Gollings, E. K., Faulkner, C., & Wertheim, E. H. (2007). Comparison of face-to-face and Internet interventions for body image and eating problems in adult women: An RCT. *International Journal of Eating Disorders, 40*(8), 692–704.

Wertheim, E. H., Paxton, S. J., & Blaney, S. (2009). Body image in girls. In L. Smolak & J. K. Thompson (Eds.), *Body image, eating disorders and obesity in youth* (2nd ed., pp. 47–76). Washington, DC: American Psychological Association.

After-Hours Therapist

Therapist: Howard G. Rosenthal, EdD, NCC, CCMHC, MAC, LPC, Founding Human Services-Board Certified Practitioner

Affiliation: Program Coordinator and Professor of Human Services and Addictions Study, St. Louis Community College at Florissant Valley, Missouri

Major works:

Rosenthal, H. G. (2005). *Before you see your first client: 55 things counselors and human service providers need to know.* New York: Routledge.

Rosenthal, H. G. (2006). *Therapy's best: Practical advice and gems of wisdom from twenty accomplished counselors and therapists.* New York: Routledge.

Rosenthal, H. G. (2008). *Encyclopedia of Counseling: Master review and tutorial for the National Counselor Examination, state counseling exams, and the Counselor Preparation Comprehensive Examination* (3rd ed.). New York: Routledge.

Dr. Rosenthal is the author of a number of counseling books and is best known for his counselor licensing/certification and comprehensive exam preparation programs.

Population for whom technique is appropriate: Children, adolescents, or adults who have been in therapy for at least four or five sessions and like to write or have a creative imagination

Cautionary notes: None

Many people are adept at modeling behavior as well as anticipating what others will do or say. This ability—combined with this incredibly simple, yet unusually effective, strategy—allows clients to progress at a faster rate. That is to say, this technique actually permits the client to flourish as if he or she was receiving additional sessions. I think the reader will agree that in this golden age of limited session managed care treatment, this is no small accomplishment! The homework assignment can be prescribed to the client something like this:

> You seem to be a very perceptive person. For example, you generally seem to know what your boss will say to you at work or what your husband will assert when you get into an argument with him. Last session you remarked that your daughter would roll her eyes at you when you suggested that she ask her boyfriend about his family, and just moments ago I discovered you were correct.
>
> Therefore, it seems logical that since you have seen me for six sessions now you have a fairly good idea of what I am going to say and how I am going to say it. This week I would like you to keep a very special journal to help you cope with particularly stressful situations. If you encounter an incident that upsets you markedly, I want you to write it in your journal. Then I want you to begin a Dr. Rosenthal–client dialogue *as if you were right here in the office.* Write down precisely what you would say to me if I were with you at that moment for a session and then write down specifically (based on your experience with me during previous sessions) what I would most likely say to you. If you're not sure what I would express, just take an educated guess. If time permits, continue writing until the imaginary Dr. Rosenthal has helped you resolve the situation. Finally, bring the journal to our next session so we can examine your imaginary therapy consultation.

If a client is not an adept writer (or is a young child) a tape-recorded dialogue can be substituted for the written assignment. A client who has a vivid imagination could perform the assignment on a covert level and then report the essence of the imaginary therapeutic exchange.

In many instances, the mere act of creating the make-believe session is therapeutic for the client. To get maximum benefit from the assignment, however, the counselor should help the client analyze what the therapist said to him or her in order to teach the client to *think like a therapist.*

A final caveat is that the helper—yes, the helper—often can benefit from information gleaned from the fanciful sessions. If the client has you responding in a manner that is different from the way you've been responding during the course of treatment, you may well want to evaluate whether the client's imaginings could be superior to what you are doing! If, for example, the imaginary you as helper is much more directive on the tape or in the journal, you could indeed experiment with such behavior during your current and future sessions with the client. On the other hand, if the imaginary therapist is inappropriate, you might wish to say something like: "Now let's think about this. You know that I have never screamed obscenities at you. It seems you are still beating yourself mentally for …"

In my previous work in this book series, *Favorite Counseling and Therapy Techniques: 51 Therapists Share Their Most Creative Strategies,* Raymond Corsini (1998) shares an intervention technique he calls "Turning the Tables on the Client," which is the perfect follow-up to the strategy described herein. Corsini suggests a paradigm in which the client acts as if he or she is the therapist while the therapist plays the role of the client. I strongly suggest the reader peruse Corsini's description prior to implementing my methodology.

The bottom line on after-hours therapy is that the price is right, and as far as I know there isn't a managed care organization on the face of the planet that has figured out a way to make therapists secure approval units for imaginary sessions of this ilk … yet!

Reference

Corsini, R. J. (1998). Turning the tables on the client: Making the client the counselor. In H. G. Rosenthal (Ed.), *Favorite counseling and therapy techniques* (pp. 54–57). Philadelphia: Accelerated Development/Taylor & Francis.

Understanding and Coping With Transitions

Therapist: Nancy K. Schlossberg, EdD

Affiliation: President, TransitionWorks; Professor Emerita, University of Maryland, College Park

Major works:

Goodman, J., Schlossberg, N. K., Waters, E., & Anderson, M. L. (2006). *Counseling adults in transition*. New York: Springer.

Schlossberg, N. K. (2007). *Overwhelmed: Coping with life's ups and downs*. Lanham, MD: M. Evans.

Nancy K. Schlossberg, author of seven books, is a fellow in three divisions of the American Psychological Association and has served as president of the National Career Development Association, a Division of the American Counseling Association. She is also the coauthor of *The Transition Coping Questionnaire* and *The Transition Coping Guide.*

Population for whom the technique is appropriate: Normal adults facing transitions (e.g., returning students, managers in business and industry, residents in retirement homes, people whose jobs have been eliminated, retirees, workers being promoted)

Cautionary notes: This is a cognitive approach that helps people better understand and cope with their transitions. It is not a panacea and does not delve into some of the underlying psychological issues that interfere with people making transitions. It is used often in conjunction with therapy but is not replacement for therapy.

Adults in Transition

People often wonder why they coped easily with one transition but then found they did poorly with the next. For more than 40 years, I have conducted many studies of people in transition so that I might answer that question. I studied people moving, adult learners returning to school, men and women whose jobs were eliminated, clerical workers dealing with work–family balance, not getting promoted, not having a baby, not having the career or relationship dreamed about, and not being able to retire when expected.

These and other transitions can be categorized in the following way:

- *Anticipated transitions*: the major life events we usually expect to be part of adult life, such as marrying, becoming a parent, starting a first job, or retiring
- *Unanticipated transitions*: the often-disruptive events that occur unexpectedly, such as major surgery, a serious car accident or illness, a surprise promotion, or a factory closing
- *Nonevent transitions*: the expected events that fail to occur, such as not getting married or not being able to afford to retire

Transition Model

To better understand transitions, I developed a way of analyzing any transition. This model can help individuals make sense out of the transitions they are experiencing, because often there is confusion and mystery surrounding our reactions to change. The model has three major components.

Component 1: Transitions Change One's Roles, Relationships, Routines, and Assumptions

Everyone experiences transition, whether they are events or nonevents, anticipated or unanticipated. These transitions alter our lives—our roles, relationships, routines, and assumptions. The birth of a first child and taking early retirement appear to have little in common, but both change a person's life. Becoming a new parent adds a *role,* changes *relationships* with one's spouse or partner, clearly changes one's routines, and changes one's *assumptions* about self and life. The same is true when one retires. One's role as worker changes, as well as relationships with former coworkers, daily routines, and assumptions. It is not the transition per se that is critical, but how much it alters one's roles, relationships, routines, and assumptions.

Component 2: The Transition Process Takes Time

Transitions take time, and people's reactions to them change—for better or worse. At first, people think of nothing but being a new graduate, a new widow, a recent retiree. Then they begin to separate from the past and move toward the new role, for a while teetering between the two. I interviewed a man who retired 6 months ago from the public school system. He said his first month was very difficult, as he was so used to his routine, his relationships, and his professional identity. But now, 6 months later, he is very comfortable with his new set of activities. He is active in an exercise program, became a volunteer for the court system as a guardian ad litem, and is becoming active with the League of Women Voters.

The process of leaving one set of roles, relationships, routines, and assumptions and establishing a new set takes time. For some the process happens easily and quickly; for others it might take years. There are many people floundering, looking for the right niche, even after years. For example, it takes time to adjust to moving into any kind of retirement institution because many people define it as the "last move."

Component 3: The 4-S System for Coping With Transitions

Even though we recognize that coping with transitions takes time, we see that people differ in how they cope with what seems to be the same transition and often cope well with one transition but feel ineffective in the next. How then do we handle this journey, live through it, and learn from it?

By identifying the features common to all transition events and non-events, however dissimilar they appear, some of the mystery can be taken out of change. These features are the potential resources or deficits one brings to each transition, and it is important to remember that these resources or deficits change. They can be clustered into four major categories, what I call the *4 Ss: situation, self, supports, strategies.*

- *Situation:* This refers to the person's situation at the time of transition. Are there other stresses? For example, if one is promoted to a supervisory job at the same time that one's significant other becomes critically ill, coping with this job change becomes difficult.

- *Self:* This refers to the person's inner strength for coping with one's situation. Is the person optimistic, resilient, and able to deal with ambiguity? Clearly what one brings of oneself influences how one copes.
- *Supports:* The support one receives or that is available at the time of transition is critical to one's sense of well-being. If a new retiree, for example, moves to a new city knowing no one, with no supports, the adaptation might be slowed down.
- *Strategies:* There is no magic coping strategy. Rather, the person who uses lots of strategies flexibly will be better able to cope.

People have often asked, "Should we move to California when we retire?" There is no easy answer to that. However, one can look at one's 4 Ss and ask, is my situation good at this time? Do I bring a resilient self to the move? Do I have lots of coping strategies in my repertoire? Do I have enough support? If all Ss are positive, a move might be a good decision. However, if one's situation is problematic and one's supports are minimal, there might be a decision to delay the move until one builds supports in the new community and one's situation improves.

To restate: The transition model clarifies the transitions we are experiencing by identifying the following:

- The degree to which one's life has been altered (changes in roles, relationships, routines, assumptions)
- Where one is in the transition process (considering a change, beginning the change, 2 years after the change)
- The resources one can apply to making it a success (each of us approaches the transitions of retirement in a unique way, depending on the 4 Ss)

Application

To make the transition model real, you need to apply it. Take the following steps:

1. Select several people in the seemingly same transition.
2. Interview them using the description of the model as your guide.
   a. Identify the type of transition.
   b. Identify the degree to which it has altered their lives.
   c. Identify where they are in the transition process.
   d. Identify their resources or deficits, or both, for coping.
3. Each individual will have a different profile. For some their situation will be positive, supports negative, self negative, strategies negative. For others, the situation will be negative but self and strategies positive.
4. Select those resources that are deficits and work together with the client concerning ways to strengthen their resources. For example, if one person's support system is low because of a recent move to an unknown area, there are ways to figure out how to develop temporary support systems. Another person might be low on self. For that person, therapy might be recommended. In other words, the 4-S system enables you to identify where the deficits exist and then develop individual plans to help.

The goal is to illustrate that the same external transition is not the same for any two people. Hopefully, the transition model provides a structure for looking at any transition.

Bring in the Clowns

Therapist: Gary Schultheis, MA

Affiliation: Licensed Marriage and Family Therapist, Private Practice

Major works:

Schultheis, G. M. (1998). *Brief therapy homework assignments.* New York: Wiley.

Schultheis, G. M., O'Hanlon, B., & O'Hanlon, S. (1999). *Brief couples therapy homework assignments.* New York: Wiley.

Population for whom the technique is appropriate: Persons in marriage or other committed relationships

Cautionary notes: I don't introduce this exercise until I have developed a working relationship with a couple. I want to be confident that they won't be insulted by a humorous (but very serious) suggestion.

Although I do not use this intervention frequently, I have found that in the right situation it is quite effective and introduces a bit of humor to an otherwise bleak situation. It provides a way to intervene behaviorally that immediately breaks the problem pattern and virtually forces a change in the interaction.

I consider using this exercise when a couple tells me that they are unable to discuss their problems without ending up in an argument. Frequently they say their arguments follow a familiar pattern and are about "stupid things." They feel powerless to change this pattern and don't even know where to begin. I want to help them break their old pattern in a way that makes it impossible to continue as they have in the past. An advantage of this intervention is that it doesn't require them to learn a complex method for changing their communication, and it demonstrates to them that a pattern that they experienced as completely out of their control can be altered rather easily. Indirectly, it encourages them to begin to venture outside their familiar ways of thinking.

The first step is to get clear on the pattern that the couple wants to break. I like to have them describe step by step how the typical argument unfolds. I then ask them to define the moment in the process for each of them when they know that an argument is about to take place. This may be something that is said, an expression, a tone of voice, or an internal feeling. At this point I tell them that I have an unusual suggestion to make, and I pull two bulbous plastic red clown noses from my desk. I very seriously hand one to each of them with the instruction that at the point where one of them first feel that an argument is about to develop, he or she to say, "It's time to do our homework." They will each put on their nose and then proceed with their discussion.

Most couples find it virtually impossible to argue in their old way while dressed like clowns. Communication gets confused. On one hand they are saying "I'm serious" and on the other, "I'm clowning around." In the confusion, the old pattern can get lost. For some couples this is all that is needed. For others, it opens space for them to practice new skills that have been suggested by the therapist but may have been impossible for the clients to utilize previously.

One of the more attractive aspects of this exercise is that clients frequently don't have to actually carry through with it for it to be effective. Many times the thought of wearing the nose is enough to break the power of the spell that has stymied them.

Of course, this exercise can be altered in any number of ways to adapt to the particular situation. Who knows what you might come up with?

The Amazing Personal Note Technique

Therapist: Meg Selig, MAEd in Counseling

Affiliation: Adjunct Professor of Counseling, St. Louis Community College at Florissant Valley, St. Louis, Missouri
Major work:

Selig, M. (2009). *Changepower! 37 secrets to habit change success.* New York: Routledge.

Population for whom the technique is appropriate: Adults and college-age students and adolescents
Cautionary notes: Counselors should send notes or letters only when doing so would not violate the client's confidentiality. Ideally, where and how any correspondence is sent should be discussed when establishing the therapeutic contract. The incidents described here took place B.C.E. (Before Cell phones and E-mail). These personal electronic tools can solve many confidentiality problems. However, there are some risks to e-mail and cell phone communication, and counselors should alert clients to those risks.

Because I don't assign homework to clients, my favorite counseling homework assignment is the one I give myself: Write a concerned note when a personal counseling client or group counseling member starts to miss sessions. This task may sound prosaic, and it truly is less of a technique than a professional obligation. Nonetheless, writing a note led to one of my most magical and memorable counseling experiences.

Sooner or later every counselor must grapple with a client who fails to show up for appointments or group sessions or who cancels as often as he or she appears. Why is this happening? A caring note or letter may help clarify matters.

Via letter or note, the counselor can (a) describe the client's pattern of absences and ask whether the client wishes to terminate counseling; (b) outline the client's options, for example, to terminate now but return in the future, to see another counselor, or to come in for a last closure session; (c) briefly review the work that has been done; and (d) wish the client well regardless of the decision he or she makes. A note could include some or all of these items, depending on what is appropriate for a given client. Should the client decide to return to counseling, a caring letter assures the client that he or she is welcome back.

My experience with the amazing power of a note occurred when I was leading an assertiveness training class at the community college many years ago. During our first session, I started off with the usual introductions, asking each person to tell the group his or her first name and a way to remember it.

I kicked things off: "Hi. Feel free to call me Meg. When you think of the actress Meg Ryan, think of me." We proceeded around the circle. "I'm Ebony. My mom named me after the song 'Ebony and Ivory.'" "I'm David. You can remember my name by remembering King David in the Bible."

Finally we reached a sullen-faced, heavy-set, young African American woman. She hesitated dramatically as if she were deciding whether to cooperate or not. At last she said, "I'm Lovedee. You can remember that because I love de drugs." A few embarrassed titters of laughter rose up. None of us would forget that name, that's for sure.

Lovedee (a pseudonym, but an accurate representation of the student's actual name and comments) proved to be one of the most trying students I'd ever had. Whoever had recommended assertiveness training for her knew his oats. Lovedee blurted out aggressive comments to both me and the other students without regard to anyone's feelings or the guidelines that the group had established. When I used assertive phrases to rein her in, she responded with subversive mutterings, kept just low enough to be unintelligible. Sometimes she would spend the entire class sitting sphinx-like, arms folded over her chest, in a pose of defiance.

So I was relieved when Lovedee missed class one week. Then she missed again. If she had a third absence, she would fail the class. (At my college, students in psychoeducational groups earn a grade and one credit hour if they complete the class successfully.)

The cowardly part of me—the side of me that likes life to be easy—considered breaking my usual habit of note writing. After all, I rationalized, the assertiveness training class was as much a class as a counseling group, and teachers were under no obligation to write notes. But my professional side won out. Reminding myself that students like Lovedee were probably coping with more than I could imagine, I handwrote a note expressing my concern about Lovedee's absences, my hope that nothing was wrong, a reminder about the absence policy, and encouragement to complete the class successfully. Then I duly copied the note and put it in Lovedee's file, bracing myself for whatever would happen next.

As the next class session began, Lovedee walked in without her usual threatening swagger. In fact, she was dressed up in a suit and heels. One of the other students asked if she was going to a job interview.

"No," she replied, "Meg wrote me a very nice note and I'm dressing up to show her I appreciated it." She smiled at me—a genuine smile. I smiled back, relief and astonishment fueling my broad grin. It was a transformational moment. From that instant on, Lovedee became a cooperative and contributing member of the group. In fact, the following semester Lovedee surprised me by dropping into the classroom on the first day of the group to praise the assertiveness training method and to admonish the new students to listen and learn!

When I told this story to Hannah, a colleague in private practice, she relayed her own story about the amazing power of a caring note. A woman came to therapy to end an abusive relationship but dropped out after only a few months. Because the client's boyfriend lived with her, Hannah couldn't call to ask what was wrong. She settled on writing a note to her client's work address. Still, she heard nothing.

Years later Hannah ran into her former client. The client hugged her and told Hannah that she had eventually found the courage to end the abusive relationship. "It took me a long time to be ready," she said. "When I got discouraged, I would read over your lovely note. I still have it, in a special place in my top bureau drawer."

So, write that note! Apart from the satisfaction of knowing you've fulfilled your professional responsibility, you never know how much a caring note could mean to someone.

References

Fisher, C. B. (2009). *Decoding the ethics code: A practical guide for psychologists.* Thousand Oaks, CA: Sage.

Glidden-Tracey, C. (2005). *Counseling and therapy with clients who abuse alcohol or other drugs.* Mahwah, NJ: Erlbaum.

Anodyne Therapy: Relieving the Suicidal Patient's Psychache

Therapist: Edwin S. Shneidman, PhD, deceased

Affiliation: Licensed Clinical Psychologist (California); Professor of Thanatology Emeritus, University of California, Los Angeles; Founder, American Association of Suicidology

Major works:

Shneidman, E. S. (1985). *Definition of suicide.* New York: Wiley.

Shneidman, E. S. (1998). *The suicidal mind.* New York: Oxford University Press.

Shneidman, E. S. (2002). *Deaths of man.* Blue Ridge Summit, PA: Jason Aronson.

Sadly, Dr. Shneidman passed away on May 15, 2009 at the age of 91.

Deaths of Man was nominated for a National Book Award.

Population for whom the technique is appropriate: Primarily adolescents and adults but practically anyone

Cautionary notes: None

Homework Suggestions

Anodyne therapy is intended to reduce the patient's psychological pain by means of an emphasis on the patient's psychological needs. The basic syllogism goes something like this:

1. *Major premise.* We begin with the assertion (hypothesis) that the primary element in any suicide is mental pain, the pain of negative emotions—shame, guilt, loneliness, angst, envy, anger, bereavement, dysphoria, self-abnegation, hopelessness, and so on—an introspectively felt hurt in the mind, what I have called *psychache* (Shneidman, 1993). With this belief, other factors are secondary—male or female, Black or White, young or old, rural or urban,

rich or poor, high levels of cerebral spinal fluid chemicals or low levels, parents who were crazy or parents who were neurotic. All these issues are interesting and often are relevant background hum or even background music, but they are, nonetheless, background. Keep your eye on the bulls-eye: It is the high level of psychological pain that is paramount. No pain, no suicide; if it doesn't hurt, it doesn't count.

2. *Minor premise A:* In general, the *sources* of elevated psychache are thwarted or frustrated *psychological needs.* These psychological needs—from Henry A. Murray (1938)—include the needs for abasement, achievement, affiliation, aggression, autonomy, counteraction, defendance, deference, dominance, exhibition, harm avoidance, inviolacy, nurturance, order, play, rejection, sentience, shame avoidance, succorance, and understanding (see Figure 3.12). Everyone in the world can be rated (and assessed) in terms

---

Subject:_____ Sex:_____ Age:_____ Rater:_____ Date:_____

___**ABASEMENT.** The need to submit passively; to belittle oneself
___**ACHIEVEMENT.** To accomplish something difficult; to overcome
___**AFFILIATION.** To adhere to a friend or group; to affiliate
___**AGGRESSION.** To overcome opposition forcefully; to fight back
___**AUTONOMY.** To be independent and free; to shake off restraint
___**COUNTERACTION.** To make up for loss by restriving; to get even
___**DEFENDANCE.** To vindicate oneself against criticism or blame
___**DEFERENCE.** To admire and support, praise; to emulate a superior
___**DOMINANCE.** To control, influence, and direct others; to dominate
___**EXHIBITION.** To excite, fascinate, amuse, or entertain others
___**HARM-AVOIDANCE.** To avoid pain, injury, illness, and death
___**INVIOLACY.** To protect the self and one's psychological space
___**NURTURANCE.** To feed, help, console, and protect another; to nurture
___**ORDER.** To strive for organization and order among things and ideas
___**PLAY.** To act for fun; to seek pleasure for its own sake
___**REJECTION.** To exclude, banish, jilt, or expel another person
___**SENTIENCE.** To seek sensuous, creature-comfort experiences
___**SHAME AVOIDANCE.** To avoid humiliation and embarrassment
___**SUCCORANCE.** To be taken care of; to be loved and succored
___**UNDERSTANDING.** To know answers; to know the hows and whys
<u>100</u> Total rating

FIGURE 3.12 Need form. (Adapted from Murray, H. A. 1938. *Explorations in personality.* New York: Oxford University Press.)

of 100 points—a constant sum—distributed among these 20 needs. Two sets of needs can be distinguished: *modal* needs, the disposition of needs one ordinarily lives with, and *vital* needs, the needs that one would die for. That is what suicide revolves around. A basic aspect of the therapist's task is to understand the patient in terms of this template of blocked needs. There are many unnecessary deaths, but there is never a needless suicide.

3. *Minor premise B.* If the villain is psychological pain, then we need something that fights that pain. There is a word for that: *anodyne.* An anodyne is a substance that (or an agent or person who) assuages pain. Psychotherapy in general ought to be anodynic. But with a highly suicidal patient—a person with perturbation and, even more seriously, high lethality—the anodynic function of the therapist is vital.

   The most famous essay on anodynes is Thomas De Quincey's 19th-century *Confessions of an English Opium Eater* (1821/1986), a brilliant piece on the role of anodynes in alleviating suffering.

4. *Conclusion.* It follows that in dealing with a suicidal patient, the main task is to assess and address the patient's psychache that stems from unfulfilled psychological needs. The therapist should serve as an anodynic agent—to relieve the pain so that the patient's *raison d'être* for suicide is mollified and the need to end the inner suffering is no longer pressing. Lessen the pain and the motivation for suicide is decreased sufficiently to fall below the threshold for overt self-destructive action.

Anodyne-Therapy Homework

In anodyne therapy, the homework (office work)—almost by definition—is for the therapist, work done for the patient in the absence of the patient. It consists of continual (session-to-session) ratings of the patient's vital unfulfilled psychological needs, and then, during and between the therapy sessions, doing those things that are calculated specifically to address those unfulfilled needs. These might include comments and interventions tailor-made for that particular patient and, whenever possible, couched in the language of that patient's psychological needs.

I have found it extremely helpful to read certain extensive suicidal diaries, published and in the public domain and available from most university libraries—for example, *From a Darkened Room: The Inman Diary* (Aaron, 1996) or *The Burning Brand* (1961) the diary of Cesare Pavese, the Italian author—and to rate Inman and Pavese in terms of the psychological needs that I might, in fantasy, have used to help them if I had had the responsibility of seeing them in therapy as patients.

There is nothing in the anodyne therapy approach that interdicts straightforward action like hospitalization or prescribing appropriate medication or anything else if any of them seems therapeutically advisable, so long as the basic anodynic function is kept clearly in the therapist's mind. The two key recommended readings for this anodynic approach to suicidal patients are an edited volume by Leenaars (1999) and a book by Shneidman (2001).

References

Aaron, D. (Ed.) (1996). *From a darkened room: The Inman diary* (2 vols.). Cambridge, MA: Harvard University Press.

Allport G. (1942). *The use of personal documents as psychological science.* New York: Social Science Research Council.

De Quincey, T. (1986). *Confessions of an English opium eater.* London: Penguin Classics. (Original work published 1821)

Leenaars, A. (Ed.). (1999). *Lives and death: Selections from the works of Edwin S. Shneidman.* Philadelphia: Brunner/Mazel.

Murray, H. A. (1938). *Explorations in personality.* New York: Oxford University Press.

Murray, H. A. (1967). Dead to the world: The passions of Herman Melville. In E. Shneidman (Ed.), *Essays in self-destruction.* New York: Science House.

Pavese, C. (1961). *The burning brand* (E. A. Murch, Trans.). New York: Walker.

Shneidman, E. (1973). *Deaths of man.* New York: Quadrangle.

Shneidman, E. (1979). Risk writing: A special note about Cesare Pavese and Joseph Conrad. *Journal of the American Academy of Psychoanalysis, 7,* 575–592.

Shneidman, E. (1980). *Voices of death.* New York: Harper & Row.

Shneidman, E. (1985). *Definition of suicide.* New York: Wiley.

Shneidman, E. (1993). Suicide as psychache. *Journal of Nervous and Mental Disease, 181,* 147–149.

Shneidman, E. (1996). *The suicidal mind.* New York: Oxford University Press.

Shneidman, E. (1999). Psychological pain assessment scale. *Suicide and Life-Threatening Behavior, 29,* 287–294.

Shneidman, E. S. (2001). *Comprehending suicide: Landmarks in 20th-century suicidology.* Washington, DC: American Psychological Association Books.

Using Hip-Hop in Family Therapy to Build "Rap"port

Therapist: Catherine Ford Sori, PhD

Affiliation: Licensed Marriage and Family Therapist; Clinical Member, AAMFT; Member, American Counseling Association, Association for Play Therapy; Associate Professor, Division of Psychology & Counseling, Governors State University, University Park, Illinois; Associate Faculty, Chicago Center for Family Health, an Affiliate of The University of Chicago

Major works:

Sori, C. F. (2006). *Engaging children in family therapy: Creative approaches to integrating theory and research in clinical practice.* New York: Routledge.

Sori, C. F., & Hecker, L. L. (2008). *The therapist's notebook: Vol. 3. Homework, handouts, and activities for use in psychotherapy.* New York: Routledge.

Sori, C. F., Hecker, L. L., & Associates (2003). *The therapist's notebook for children and adolescents: Homework, handouts, and activities for use in psychotherapy.* New York: Haworth Press. (Currently being translated into Hebrew)

Also authored or coauthored 3 other books, over 50 book chapters, and numerous journal articles, many on children in family therapy.

Population for whom the technique is appropriate: Families in family sessions who have adolescents and/or children; children or adolescents in individual therapy

Cautionary notes: In recent years some forms of rap and hip-hop have gotten a bad "rap" (pun intended!) with some parents, so therapists should clarify that these therapeutic approaches are attempts to "redeem" rap and use it in positive ways.

This homework assignment describes various ways to incorporate hip-hop into family therapy sessions to engage, assess, and treat children, adolescents, and adult family members. Hip-hop fits under the meta-theory of family play therapy (see Dermer, Olund, & Sori, 2006), wherein the language of play is often the preferred method of communication for children but is also easily understood by adults. Playful techniques are useful in engaging clients and helping them be more active participants in the therapy process. Hip-hop is a culturally relevant activity that fits with many family therapy theories, including structural, experiential, solution focus, or narrative.

Introduction to Using Hip-Hop

For the past few decades the phenomena of hip-hop has gone from something seen in the ghettos of African American communities to being part of the mainstream American culture. It is enjoyed by children, adolescents, and young adults from all races and ethnicities. Hip-hop is the voice of the youth culture, and those who work with this population will benefit from having some familiarity with hip-hop and what it represents.

Although there are several elements to hip-hop (see Sori, 2008), this homework assignment focuses on rap, beat-box, and street dancing, or movements. Rap is the rhythmic and often rapid recitation of lyrics with a particular message. Often alliteration is used, and the stanzas may or may not rhyme. Rap is accompanied by the beat-box, or rhythmic sounds kids in the street made using whatever materials were available, such as their mouths (Smith & Jackson, 2005). Simple hip-hop moves are encouraged, as they energize participants and observers and make the interventions feel more authentic.

Rationale

There is much research on the effects of music on the brain and there are entire fields of both music and dance therapy. Tootle (2003) encourages all family therapists to recognize the benefits of music and movement in family therapy. However, little has been written about using hip-hop therapeutically with young people and families. Hip-hop is a sure-fire way to engage silent, sullen adolescents, to bring all family members together in playful activities that breathe life into sessions, and to join with families by recognizing young people's expertise with hip-hop and with their own stories (see Sori, 2008).

Materials

Toy plastic microphones are readily available at discount and novelty stores or on the Internet, and can be purchased for a few dollars apiece. Small percussion play instruments are an option, but often people use their mouths, fingers, hands, or feet for the beatbox rhythmic accompaniment. Giving families videotapes, audio recordings, or CDs of the hip-hops can encourage participation and punctuate change.

Instructions

Hip-hop can be used as homework assignments for clients in several ways. Early in therapy family members might be asked to each write *individual raps* about themselves, their likes, dislikes, relationships, struggles, or view of the problem. These can be unique ways for clients to "introduce" themselves and can provide insight into each person's "story." After each person writes his or her own verse, the family can combine them all and practice together as a family. At their next session they all can be invited to perform together for the therapist.

After they finish and the applause and high-fives die down, the therapist can discuss both the process and content (see Gil & Sobol, 2000) of each person's rap. Process observations might include noticing the family's level of enjoyment and how they performed together. Clinicians can inquire about how it was to write their individual raps, how they worked to put it all together, what practice sessions were like, and how it was for them to perform together. Therapists might ask individuals if they had any help or advice from anyone, or who had the easiest/hardest time doing the homework. Content discussions can focus on what clients said about themselves and how others react to those statements. Be sure that all family members have the opportunity to share their reactions.

Hip-hop can also be assigned as a *family project homework assignment* that they all create together. While acknowledging that young people may have a lot of expertise in hip-hop, I usually put the parent(s) in charge of orchestrating (no pun intended!) this activity. The assignment is for them to collaboratively write a rap about their family. This can be an introduction of them as a family, descriptions of each family member, or they could rap about their view of the problem and how their strengths will help them solve it. Later in therapy the instructions might be to write a hip-hop that tells the story of how they are they are working together to overcome the problem that brought them to therapy, detailing the progress made to date. If the therapist used a narrative approach and externalized the problem, the rap might describe how the family is working to defeat the influence of the externalized problem; it could describe how the family will be when the problem is eliminated. Solution-focused raps might highlight what will be different when the miracle has occurred or the problem is reduced in size. Whatever the content, the family should work collaboratively on the assignment. After they perform, the therapist can process both the content of the rap and the process for the family as described earlier.

Here's an excerpt from a family rap done at the termination session of a family consisting of a single mother and her three adolescents. This was the second rap they had written as homework and performed for the co-counselors. The first example was performed by the 15-year-old daughter:

> Hey, hey we're the Hamilton family; we are a set of four and
> As we bust out with our rhyme, you'll be begging us for more!
> We've had a few struggles, now we're feeling kinda fine!
> Had to get ourselves together, so we won't do any time!

The other children performed their raps, and mom concluded with this:

> Now you see who we are, who we know you wanna love
> But we owe all of our greatness to the Father up above!

Hip-Hop as a Therapeutic Letter

One of my favorite ways to incorporate hip-hop in therapy is for the therapist and team, if available, to write a therapeutic letter (e.g., Pare & Rombach, 2003) in a rap that summarizes the client's progress and strengths. To be convincing and effective using this approach, it is important for therapists to be in touch with their own playfulness (Sori & Sprenkle, 2004). Families are intrigued and excited when told their professional therapist is going to rap for them, especially if they have written and performed one or more hip-hops for the therapist. It levels the playing field.

Before performing for clients, I usually take a one-down position and comment that because the young people have much more expertise than I do on hip-hop, mine won't be nearly as good as theirs. I often include a simple chorus that is repeated about every four lines, and halfway through I signal for the family to join in the chorus. They almost always spontaneously begin keeping the beat and participate without hesitation, sometimes jumping to their feet and participating without any invitation!

If the therapist has an observation team available, they can assist in writing the therapeutic rap and in performing it for the family. Everyone should be comfortable with the lyrics, the movements, and rhythmic accompaniments the team decides to use. It is important to practice a few times before the session so everyone is fairly confident and stays on beat. At the end, be sure to give each family member a written copy of the therapeutic letter rap that they can take home.

Afterward the family is invited to share their reactions to the therapist's rap, to look over the words and see what seems to fit them, what suggestions they may have for improving it, or what they might like to change. This is a time to further solidify positive changes noted in the rap. The family can even be invited to help write "revisions" of the rap as homework and perform it for the therapist and team the following week.

Puppet Hip-Hop Therapeutic Letters

One way to expand this activity is to incorporate puppets for each family member into the rap. These could be puppets the family has used in a family puppet interview (Gil, 1994; Irwin & Malloy, 1975), those the team had used in a puppet reflecting team (Sori, 2011), and/or puppets selected by the therapist and team to metaphorically represent family members, the externalized problem, their strengths, and so on. Puppets enrich this activity even more by introducing an added visual element that increases the dramatic impact and elicits an even greater positive, playful response from clients.

In the case of the aforementioned Hamilton family, following their family hip-hop the co-counselors and team performed a therapeutic letter rap written to emphasize the positive qualities of the family, and to punctuate all the changes that had occurred. We incorporated some of the puppets the family had used in an earlier session during a family puppet interview (Gil, 1994; Irwin & Malloy, 1975) and added an additional wise owl with glasses puppet for Timothy, who had been the identified patient. The team used toy microphones, movement, and beat-box sounds in addition to holding up the puppets at appropriate times. There was a verse for each person, and one about the Hamiltons as a family. Here are some excerpts to illustrate. The first is about the mother, and the second is for Timothy, who had been expelled from school but was now doing well, since his mom was spending more positive time with him. The final lines highlight the family's overall progress and strengths.

(Chorus, which was repeated twice after each verse)
Hey, hey, hey, the Hamilton rap! Everybody stomp, snap, and clap!

Maryann, what a mom! She loves her kids and they think she the bomb!
She's so strong, keeps her kids from doin' wrong,
Knows how to rap and she really blows a song!

Timothy, Timothy—he's so smart and he has a big heart.
His really cool glasses make him look GQ! He is so cool in his new school!
He got a plan to succeed, and he will, indeed!

He now asks for what he needs; Mom responds and he's so pleased!
In the puppet show they were in the know; they got civility, creativity!

They took the notion to use the lotion,* and humor for them
  is like a potion!
They said, what the heck, let's connect! They a tight-knit
  group like alphabet soup.
They so funny like they rolled in honey,
If funny were money every day would be sunny!
Hey, Hey, Hey the Hamilton Rap! Everybody stomp, snap,
  and clap!

As soon as we started, both mom and the oldest teen pulled out their cell phones to record us. After a few lines they all spontaneously jumped to their feet, started moving to the beat, and joined us enthusiastically on the choruses. As we ended, they cheered and high-fived us. Later they all discussed how amazed they were that the team captured them and all their work in a few verses. They all loved the raps—both doing them together and watching the team. Mom said how disgruntled she was at first to come to therapy but how much they all enjoyed it and, after the first session, looked forward every week to coming back. As the session was ending and they were preparing to leave, each with a copy of their "therapeutic letter rap" in hand, Timothy emphatically proclaimed that this had "indeed been the transformation of the Hamilton family!"

One-Therapist Therapeutic Letter Raps

Because many clinicians outside of training settings don't have the option of including a team, the use of hip-hop as a therapeutic letter can be adapted in several ways for use by solo therapists. Therapists can simply write the therapeutic letter rap and perform it by himself or herself, with the family as the audience. This takes a bit of courage and playfulness but should be performed with confidence and flair, so practice in front of a mirror is recommended. A recording of some background rhythm or hip-hop instrumental music (perhaps from a karaoke recording) helps provide a good foundation and can help cover any slips!

---

* The therapists in this case had integrated some Theraplay (Munns, 2003) techniques into family sessions in order to promote touch and attachment and increase enjoyment among the family members. The lotioning of each other's hands was a Theraplay activity that really resonated with this family.

Although this may at first seem a bit intimidating to some, if you can abandon yourself a bit to the process and trust your own creativity, both you and your clients will feel energized and see positive results. I have found that if people exaggerate their enthusiasm, body movements, hand motions, and punctuate certain words they are better able to let go of their inhibitions, which frees them to enjoy the process. And if the therapists enjoy themselves, so will the clients!

Alternatively, family members can be engaged to be participant/observers. The therapist can assign each family member a role in providing back-up (e.g., beat-boxing using their mouths, hands, feet, etc., and/or hip-hop movements) for the therapist's performance. The family could also be invited to perform the chorus while the therapist does the verses, in the manner of a 21st-century Greek chorus!

Sometimes it is helpful to use only the young people as participant/observers, perhaps to better join with them or to showcase their special talents and expertise. Therapists might meet with the children alone to prepare and practice so they can perform for the rest of the family in the next session. Young hip-hop experts can even be asked to contribute ideas or participate in writing parts of the therapeutic letter rap, or may be invited to expand or revise it as a homework assignment. Whichever approach is used, the activity can be processed in the manner described earlier.

Conclusion

Hip-hop is especially effective in family therapy with children or adolescents because it is culturally relevant; and because it is both written and performed, it makes a stronger impact on clients. The message is more memorable because this technique goes beyond talk therapy to involve music and movement, involving more of the senses. Hip-hop encourages creativity, increases family fun and a sense of connectedness, and goes beyond "boring" talk therapy. Clients will look forward to coming to sessions and be more engaged in the process! So just remember that

When you're stuck and don't know what to do
With that "resistant," mute kid, who's just a lookin' at you,

Ya can't just sit back! Ya gotta meet him where he's at!
So get up on your feet, start a movin' to the beat! ...
Clinician's Rap ... Uh! ... Kid's Rap ... Uh! (Sori, 2008)

Acknowledgments: A special thanks to the co-counselors for the Hamilton (not their real name) family, Pamela Harrison and Kim Pronitis, and all the team members for their hard and creative work with this family.

References

Dermer, S., Olund, D., & Sori, C. F. (2006). Integrating play in family therapy theories. In C. F. Sori (Ed.), *Engaging children in family therapy: Creative approaches to integrating theory and research in clinical practice* (pp. 37–65). New York: Routledge.

Gil, E. (1994). *Play in family therapy.* New York: Guilford Press.

Gil, E., & Sobol, B. (2000). Engaging families in therapeutic play. In C. E. Bailey (Ed.), *Children in therapy: Using the family as a resource* (pp. 341–382). New York: Norton.

Irwin, E. C., & Malloy, E. S. (1975). Family puppet interviews. *Family Process, 14,* 170–191.

Munns, E. (2003). Theraplay: Attachment-enhancing play therapy. In C. Schaefer (Ed.), *Foundations in play therapy* (pp. 156–175). New York: Wiley.

Pare, D., & Rombach, M. (2003). Therapeutic letters to young persons. In C. F. Sori & L. L. Hecker (Eds.), *The therapist's notebook for children and adolescents: Homework, handouts, and activities for use in psychotherapy* (pp. 199–203). New York: Haworth Press.

Smith, E., & Jackson, P. (2005). *The hip-hop church: Connecting with the movement shaping our culture.* Downers Grove, IL: InterVarsity Press.

Sori, C. F. (2008). "Kids-rap:" Using hip-hop to promote and punctuate change. In C. F. Sori & L. L. Hecker (Eds.), *The therapist's notebook: Vol. 3. More homework, handouts, and activities for use in psychotherapy.* New York: Routledge.

Sori, C. F. (2011). Puppet reflecting teams in family therapy. In H. G. Rosenthal (Ed.), *Favorite counseling and therapy techniques* (2nd ed.). New York: Routledge.

Sori, C. F., & Sprenkle, D. (2004). Training family therapists to work with children and families: A modified Delphi study. *Journal of Marital and Family Therapy, 30*(4), 113–129.

Tootle, A. E. (2003). Neuroscience applications in marital and family therapy. *The Family Journal: Counseling and Therapy for Couples and Families, 11*(2), 185–190.

Switch and Snap Techniques: Breaking Negative Habits and Reducing Distress

Therapist: Len Sperry, MD, PhD

Affiliation: Professor of Mental Health Counseling, Florida Atlantic University; Clinical Professor of Psychiatry and Behavioral Medicine, Medical College of Wisconsin

Major works:

Sperry, L. (2006). *Cognitive behavior therapy of* DSM-IV-TR *personality disorders* (2nd ed.). New York: Routledge.

Sperry, L. (2008). *Treatment of chronic medical conditions: Cognitive-behavioral therapy strategies and integrative treatment protocols.* Washington, DC: American Psychological Association.

Sperry, L. (2010). *Highly effective therapy: Developing essential clinical competencies in counseling and psychotherapy.* New York: Routledge.

Population for whom the technique is appropriate: Clients in an outpatient setting experiencing negative habits or distressing thoughts or feelings

Cautionary notes: While research shows habit reversal can be effective with tic and Tourette's syndrome, considerable training is necessary for these applications.

Switch Technique

A particularly effective technique for helping my clients to reduce or eliminate a negative habit or other targeted behavior is habit reversal training. Originally developed by Azrin and Nunn (1973), habit reversal training has been applied to motor and vocal tics, nail biting, thumb/finger sucking, hair pulling or twirling, skin picking, and lip, mouth, tongue, or cheek biting and teeth grinding. It has been found effective for treating behaviors across age groups (i.e., children, adolescents, and adults), genders, and ethnicities (Miltenberger, Fuqua, & Woods, 1998).

The basic change mechanism of this technique is switching or substitution. So, instead of attempting to break or stop a negative habit, habit reversal training focuses on substituting it with a better or incompatible one. For example, if a client is trying to control impulsive eating or snacking while she watches TV, she can be helped to take up a hobby that requires the use of her hands such as cross-stitching. Because one cannot snack and cross-stitch at the same time, the negative habit will gradually extinguish. A client who is trying to break the caffeine habit can be helped to switch drinking hot water or herbal tea in place of drinking coffee. Or, a client who engages in compulsive hair pulling (called trichotillomania) can be encouraged to pinch the skin on her wrist instead of pulling out or twirling her hair. Because these and other habits are comforting to us, it is nearly impossible to directly break or remove them completely, because the subsequent feeling of loss or emptiness leads to repeating and reinforcing them. To overcome a negative habit, the substitute behavior should be able to prevent the negative habit from reoccurring, it should not be distracting to others, and it should be a behavior that the client can do for at least 3 minutes while carrying on normal activities.

Snapping Technique

When clients report that they feel "zoned out" and seek to break that spell by experiencing pain, they can be taught to quickly ground themselves. A dialectic behavior therapy (DBT) technique to replace the need to feel pain or be self-punitive is to exchange a self-injurious behavior for a painful but harmless behavior.

The basic change mechanism of this technique is distraction. A very simple and effective distraction technique is to hold a piece of ice in one's hand until it has melted entirely. This can be quite uncomfortable and painful while being safe. Because clients do not always have access to ice, there is an inexpensive and ready alternative: a wide rubber band that can be worn on the wrist. The directions are to snap the rubber band against the wrist until the client feels distracted by the stinging sensation and then calmer. This DBT technique was proposed by Linehan (1993) for individuals with borderline personality disorder to "snap themselves back" to reality from feelings of intense void and emptiness.

However, I have found that this snapping technique has much broader applications, including distressful feelings or obsessive thoughts. Snapping a rubber band on the wrist at the first awareness of an anxious or depressing feeling or an obsessive thought can quickly bring relief, as the client's attention to the feeling or thought is distracted by the stinging sensation.

Both of these techniques can be easily and quickly discussed and demonstrated in the therapy session and practiced by the client between sessions. Clients like and favor these techniques because they often experience successful outcomes—quickly— with their use.

References

Azrin, N. H., & Nunn, R. G. (1973). Habit reversal: A method of eliminating nervous habits and tics. *Behaviour Research and Therapy, 11*, 619–628.

Linehan, M. (1993). *Cognitive-behavioral treatment of borderline personality disorder.* New York: Guilford Press.

Miltenberger, R. G., Fuqua, R. W., & Woods, D. W. (1998). Applying behavior analysis to clinical problems: Review and analysis of habit reversal. *Journal of Applied Behavior Analysis, 31*, 447–469.

Opening Up: The NNS (Notice–Name–Support) Approach to Emotions

Therapist: Robert Taibbi, MSW, LCSW

Affiliation: Licensed Clinical Social Worker with over 45 years experience

Major works:

Taibbi, R. (1995). *Clinical supervision: A four stage process of growth and discovery.* Milwaukee, WI: Families International.

Taibbi, R. (1996). *Sitting on the edge: Pragmatism and possibilities in family therapy.* New York: Guilford Press.

Taibbi, R. (2007). *Doing family therapy: Craft and creativity in clinical practice* (2nd ed.). New York: Guilford Press.

Author of more than 100 journal and magazine articles in areas of supervision, clinical practice, and family life

Population for whom the technique is appropriate: Parents and adults concerned about their partners, adolescents, or children who have difficulty expressing their feelings to others, or who have explosive anger

Cautionary notes: None

The Problem

Parents and partners often come into therapy complaining that their partners or children, unlike them, never talk about their feelings. They're quiet, they say; they only talk about the positive, never the negative; or they hold everything in and then periodically, out of the blue, explode over something minor. Partners feel that opportunities for intimacy are missed in their relationship; they're frustrated that problems often fester and rarely get solved. Parents say they don't know what's going on inside their children, or they worry that their children will grow up without the communication skills they need to succeed in adult relationships.

Usually any efforts that the talkers have made to get their partners or children to speak up have only made matters worse. Fed up and frustrated, they will periodically openly complain or start to badger the nontalker with questions. The medium becomes the message, and what the partners or children hear is criticism, causing them to shut down even more. This prompts the talkers to push even harder, stirring up more resistance and more pushing until someone gives up, explodes, or walks out.

The Problems Beneath the Problem

If we think of silence as the nontalkers' solution, what is the problem? A few obvious possibilities come to mind: Many nontalkers have learned that it is not acceptable or safe to say how you feel: Others will ignore, make fun of, or get angry with you; saying how you feel can lead to conflict that stirs too much anxiety. Others honestly believe that they have nothing to say because they have never learned how to detect the lower levels of their own emotional volume and range. It is only when their emotions have reached explosively high levels and usually are beyond their control that they truly are aware of them. Finally, some adults and many young children don't talk about how they feel because they lack the words to label and describe them. Because they can't, they don't.

The Goals

Given these underlying issues, it's easy to see how talkers can help by enabling the nontalkers to feel safe and supported rather than anxious or threatened; by helping them notice their emotions at lower, more subtle levels; and by offering them the vocabulary they need to label their feelings.

The Solution: The NNS (Notice–Name–Support) Homework Assignment

This homework assignment focuses upon this conversational relationship between the talkers and nontalkers. Nontalkers are encouraged to change their behavior by helping the talkers change theirs.

The assignment is introduced by telling talker-clients that there is much they can do to help their partner or child learn new skills. Their job is not to somehow *make* the others talk (which they often erroneously believe), but rather to make it as comfortable as possible for them to do so. Slow and steady wins the race in this case, and it may take some time for the nontalker to feel safe to talk, to recognize his or her own emotions or find the words to communicate them. The parent or partner is advised to be patient and should be encouraged to follow these three steps as often as possible throughout the coming weeks.

Step 1: Notice the Feeling

Talkers need to be alert to those times, both big and small, at home when they sense that the nontalker is feeling something—sad, nervous, proud, angry, whatever—but isn't saying so. Usually talkers can tell easily by the expression on the other's face, the slump of his or her shoulders, the clenched fist, the sigh. Making a list of the other's common nonverbal cues in the counseling session can help the talker to be more aware of them at home.

Step 2: Name the Emotion

Once an emotional reaction is suspected, talkers are tempted to immediately comment about it to the other person. Bad idea. Instead, they should simply make a mental note of the other's reaction, then wait for some quiet moment to approach the partner or child. Why? Because the problem of talking about feelings is separate from the problem of generating the feelings. The situation needs to pass and the talker needs to have distance from it to be able to speak calmly, empathically, gently. Only with this tone of voice will the nontalker be able to listen. Any residual or unintentional harshness in the talker's voice will cause the other to withdraw.

Once they decide to approach the other, they should then say something like this: "You know, before when you were talking about _____ (your boss, your friend, what Harry said, etc.), it seemed to me that you might have been feeling a bit _____ (sad, angry, frustrated, disappointed, and so on). I wonder if you were."

Clients can change the words to fit their own personality; what is most important is the tone. Role playing and practicing their responses in the counseling session can be valuable.

Regardless of the good job the talkers may do at home, they need to expect the nontalker to deny any emotion: "No, I'm fine" or "No, I wasn't upset" is a typical response. That's fine. Simply by bringing up the topic, by providing gentle encouragement and feedback, by labeling the feeling, the talker is plowing new ground in the relationship and inviting the other to make changes. Now it only must be done over and over again.

Step 3: Support

Finally, the talker needs to be instructed in support. If the nontalker ever begins to say *anything,* absolutely anything, about how he or she feels, it is essential that the other person shut up and remain calm. Whatever pull there may be to argue back, rush in with advice, or to get very excited must be resisted. The goal at this pivotal moment is to simply keep the other talking, not steer the conversation or take it over. Be quiet and listen is the rule. After the other person stops, just quietly thank him or her for talking. Like the other steps, this one also can be practiced in the session.

Again, this is an ongoing assignment and generally is part of a larger counseling process. Because both talker and nontalker alike are learning new communication patterns, learning to move against his or her own grain, the talker-client may need help to stay on track. With perseverance, however, the old well-worn dysfunctional patterns of communication will lose some of their power, making room for new, more open, and healthier ones.

Strength and Resource Support Map

Therapist: Susan Steiger Tebb, PhD

Profession: Educator; Licensed Social Worker

Affiliation: Dean of the School of Social Service, Saint Louis University School of Social Service, St. Louis, Missouri

Major works:

Schmitz, C., & Tebb, S. (1999). *The unity and diversity of single parent families: Practice from the strengths perspective.* Milwaukee, WI: Families International.

Tebb, S. (1995). *Coping successfully: Cognitive strategies for older caregivers.* New York: Garland.

Author and coauthor of more than 25 professional articles and book chapters in the area of family caregiving and social work education

Population for whom the technique is appropriate: Family caregivers providing daily care to a family member with a chronic condition, such as dementia

Cautionary notes: None

Family is crucial in helping older persons maintain independent functioning. Most older people prefer to ask their spouse or children or both for assistance rather than friends or formal support systems, such as paid caregivers (Tebb, 1995). Eighty percent of older people needing some type of daily care live with family (Stone, Cafferata, & Sangl, 1987). The presence or absence of a family as a source of care is an important factor in delaying, and possibly preventing, institutionalization of the person (Colerick & George, 1986; Strawbridge, 1991). But this type of care takes its toll on family members and they are in need of both internal and external supports, strengths, and resources. Strengths are defined as inner supports such as strong faith, skills, humor, and self-respect, and resources are those external supports such as family, health care agencies, friends, and opportunities to which a person has access. Family members who care for elderly relatives frequently ignore their own needs. This self-sacrifice is harmful, particularly when sustained over long periods of time. This exercise helps to point out what resources and strengths are needed and where they might be cultivated while caring for a family member.

Support is needed by all of us. Support is defined as any physical, mental, social, or spiritual component that helps get us through various experiences in our lives. Support in the context of care providing often is found from two different sources: internal (strengths) and external (resources). External support can be both formal and informal support. Formal support is that which is received from social service agencies, hospitals, churches, and community agencies, and informal support is family, friends, and neighbors. A study on family care found that fewer than half of the caregivers receive any help from informal or formal supports or both (Tennstedt, Crawford, & McKinlay, 1993). Supports, both internal and external, are seen as buffers against life stresses, thus contributing to one's well-being.

Formal community supports provide many of the needed skills that family and friends cannot provide the care receiver, such as nursing, counseling, and medical skills. Often formal supports are tapped to obtain specialized knowledge and resources, for example, financial assistance or transportation. At other times formal supports are used to provide routine activities of living, such as housecleaning, bathing, and home maintenance (Springer & Brubaker, 1984). Using a formal support service this way, the caregiver has more time to give to herself or himself and to her or his care receiver.

A caregiver may not be able to rely on the informal supports that she or he has had in the past. At a time when the caregiver is feeling pressured and needing to conserve energy, she or he must expend energy locating new informal supports. The caregiver must learn ways to cope that not only promote the support of strengths, well-being, and self-control but also encourage locating and using resources.

What are your strengths? What are your resources? Mapping is a simple paper-and-pencil activity that has been developed to look at the strengths and resources available to you (see Figure 3.13). You as caregiver are within the large circle in the map's center. Within the large circle, put your strengths, your inner supports. Now, in the smaller circle marked "current household," put the people with

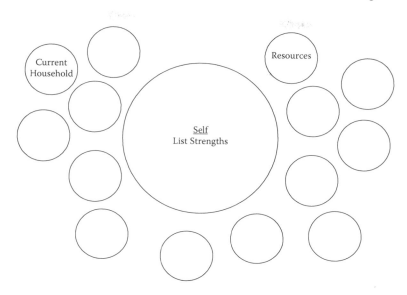

FIGURE 3.13 Strength and resource support map. (Adapted from Hartman, A. 1978. Diagrammatic assessment of family relationships. *Social Casework: Journal of Contemporary Social Work*, **59(8), 465–476.)**

whom you are living. It is common practice within this circle to draw circles to portray females and squares for males. In each of the drawn circles or squares, add the person's age. After drawing the current household members, use the other circles to represent the different resources and contacts that you have outside your current family unit. Some of the most common contacts and resources are health care, work, extended family, church, friends, recreation, and so on. Drawing lines between the large, self circle and the other circles depicts the relationships between you and these resources. A solid line represents a major relationship and a dotted line signifies a tenuous one. Broken lines or jagged lines across the main line are used to indicate a stressful connection. You also can indicate the direction of the person who is giving to a certain relationship by using arrows along the main line. Lines also can be drawn from the current household to an outside resource if all are involved or just from one member in the living unit to a resource if only that member is involved. Mapping enables one to view the various relationships of supports—both inner and outer—that you as a family caregiver must use to help establish well-being in your life (Hartman, 1978).

Mabel, when first seen by me in a caregiver support unit of a hospital, was caring for her husband, who had been diagnosed with Alzheimer's disease. For the past 18 months, he was needing progressively more and more supervision and care. When I met Mabel, she appeared extremely tired, listless, and had no sparkle in her eyes, but she claimed to be managing her husband's care very well and said she was very happy. As we talked, I realized Mabel only left the house to bring her husband to the hospital for his appointments. I gave the Strength and Resource Support Map to Mabel and asked her to look at it and think about how she might fill it in, and together we would look at it when I made a home visit the next week.

When I arrived at her home, Mabel had completed the smaller circles with the resources she had, and together we filled in the inner circle with her strengths. I discovered that Mabel missed a quilting group in which she had been active for many years but discontinued because of her husband's illness. I also learned that Mabel was not attending her church and missed this contact. Another area that Mabel had not been able to attend to was a regular exercise program that her doctor had recommended for her high blood pressure. Using the map and what it highlighted as Mabel's strengths and resources, we established a plan to begin to tap her support system for help in her caregiving. I gave her an assignment for the following week: She was to involve at least one friend or family member in the care of her husband. During the week, Mabel approached her minister who announced in church that Mabel needed someone to sit with Frank so she could attend the services. Several members began to take turns sitting with him in an empty church classroom during the Sunday morning service.

Our next assignment was to do one thing for herself, to strengthen her inner supports; for example, take a walk or exercise, meditate, take a leisurely bath, read for pleasure, go out to eat, or visit friends. Mabel took this assignment on and hired a neighborhood teen to sit with her husband every evening for half an hour to an hour while she began a regular program of daily walking.

The next assignment was much harder for Mabel. She was to locate one community/formal service that would give her help in caring for her husband. After much hesitation and thought,

Mabel agreed to use a local respite service so that she could again attend quilting classes. After a month of using both her reclaimed and newly developed strengths and resources, Mabel looked happier and was caring for herself as much as she was caring for her husband.

The use of this map provides an overview for both you, the clinician, and the caregiver of the relationships or supports, both nurturing and nonnurturing, that are available to the client. Mapping points out resources and lack of resources and strengths and lack of strengths and their relationships to each other and to your client.

References

Colerick, E. J., & George, L. K. (1986). Predictors of institutionalization among caregivers of patients with Alzheimer's disease. *Journal of the American Geriatrics Society, 34,* 403–498.

Hartman, A. (1978). Diagrammatic assessment of family relationships. *Social Casework: Journal of Contemporary Social Work, 59*(8), 465–476.

Springer, D., & Brubaker, T. H. (1984). *Family caregivers and dependent elderly.* Beverly Hills, CA: Sage

Stone, R., Cafferata, G. L., & Sangl, J. (1987). Caregivers of the frail elderly: A national profile. *The Gerontologist, 27*(5), 616–626.

Strawbridge, W. J. (1991). The effects of social factors on adult children caring for older parents. *Dissertation Abstracts International, 52,* 1094A.

Tebb, S. (1995). *Coping successfully.* New York: Garland.

Tennstedt, S. L., Crawford, S. L., & McKinlay, J. B. (1993). Is family care on the decline? A longitudinal investigation of formal long-term care services for informal care. *Milbank Quarterly, 71*(4), 601–624.

Healthful Behavior Diary

Therapist: Donald I. Templer, PhD, FPPR, BCFE

Affiliation: California School of Professional Psychology, Fresno

Major works:

Lonetto, R., & Templer, D. I. (1986). *Death anxiety.* New York: Hemisphere.

Templer, D. I., Hartlage, L. C., & Cannon, W. G. (Eds.). (1992). *Preventable brain damage: Brain vulnerability and brain health.* New York: Springer.

Templer, D. I., Spencer, D. A., & Hartlage, L. C. (1993). *Biosocial psychopathology: Epidemiological perspectives.* New York: Springer.

Author of several other books and more than 20 book chapters and 200 journal articles

Population for whom the technique is appropriate: Patients with anxiety, stress, adjustment, self-esteem, and self-confidence problems; persons wanting improvement in health, physical condition, and appearance

Cautionary notes: May not be appropriate for highly opposi-tional or psychotic persons. Persons who plan major exercise or dietary changes should consult with their physicians.

The patient recording of physical or psychological health behavior has four purposes. One is to assess the strengths and weaknesses of the patient's health behavior profile. The second is to establish baselines from which changes can be determined. The third is to reap the benefits of the patient's improved knowledge of himself or herself and associated mastery of the patient's composite life situation. The fourth purpose is to facilitate the therapist's perspective so that optimal information, advice, and reinforcement can be given to the patient. Praise should be given not only for desirable behavior but also for a reduction of maladaptive behavior, for example, smoking a pack of cigarettes rather than two packs of cigarettes per day.

The typical recording is in the following realms: food, alcohol, tobacco, prescribed psychotropic drugs, other prescribed drugs, over-the-counter and "health food" store drugs, exercise, and sleep. All of these categories are not relevant for all patients, and for some patients additional domains should be recorded.

The type and amount of food consumed and the time of consumption should be recorded. For some patients, more refined variables such as calories, fat, cholesterol, and protein are recorded. The patient should weigh himself or herself once a week. Quantity and time should be recorded for alcohol, tobacco, and therapeutic drug use. Illicit drug use also should be recorded, but many illicit drug users have such an undisciplined lifestyle that they would not be receptive to and compliant with a healthful living diary. For undesirable behaviors, circumstances preceding and contributing to setbacks should be recorded. For cardiovascular and endurance exercises, the speed and distance or duration should be recorded. For resistance exercise, the number of pounds, sets, and repetitions should be recorded.

The healthful living diary is congruent with increasing research evidence showing that physical and psychological health are closely intertwined and that what one ingests has considerable impact on how one feels and functions. Heavy alcohol consumption is one of the more common causes of depression. There are tremendous individual differences with respect to caffeine. Some persons feel better, work better, and sleep better if they consume 20 cups of coffee per day. For other persons one cup of coffee can produce appreciable anxiety and sleep difficulty. Many people are not aware of the fact that caffeine is contained in a number of different noncola soft drinks and over-the-counter medications. Exercise can be helpful for anxiety, sleep difficulty, depression, anger, and disruptive behavior, in addition to improving physical appearance, physical health, and self-esteem. Often there is a vicious cycle in which anxiety and depression cause sleep difficulty and sleep difficulty causes more anxiety and depression. Improved sexual functioning also commonly is associated with a healthier lifestyle.

A major cause of ineffectiveness in psychotropic drug and other drug treatment is noncompliance or insufficient compliance. Some patients believe, in spite of apparently clear instructions from their physicians and pharmacists, that antidepressant drugs should be taken on an as-needed basis or that if they are not effective in a few days they should be discontinued. Many people erroneously believe that if a substance is "natural," over-the-counter, or bought in a health food store, it cannot be harmful. The majority of health foods, herbal remedies, and substances sold to bodybuilders have not been subjected to well-controlled research to determine efficacy and safety. The recording of ingesting these substances in the context of other healthful living recording may provide the patient some indication of their effects if his or her physician is unable to provide a definitive opinion. The healthful behavior diary is designed jointly by the patient and therapist, jointly modified by the patient and therapist, and maintained and modified by the patient after the therapist is no longer needed.

Maximizing Human Potential With the Psychoeducational Life Skill Intervention Model

Therapist: Rosemary A. Thompson, EdD, NCC, LPC

Affiliation: Licensed Professional Counselor; Supervisor of Guidance and Counseling for Chesapeake Public Schools in Chesapeake, Virginia; Adjunct Professor, Department of Educational Leadership and Counseling, Old Dominion University, Norfolk, Virginia

Major works:

Thompson, R. A. (1992). *School counseling renewal: Strategies for the twenty-first century.* Muncie, IN: Accelerated Development.

Thompson, R. A. (2003). *Counseling techniques: Improving relationships with others, ourselves, our families, and our environment.* New York: Routledge.

Thompson, R. A. (2006). *Nurturing future generations: Promoting resilience in children and adolescents through social, emotional, and cognitive skills.* New York: Routledge.

Population for whom the technique is appropriate: Children, youth, and adults who have social, emotional, and cognitive skills deficits

Cautionary notes: None

Psychoeductional Life Skill Intervention Model

Youth and adults across the nation increasingly are manifesting serious social, emotional, and cognitive deficits. The indicators of *emotional deficits* manifest themselves in increased incidents of violence, suicide, and homicides. *Social deficits* manifest themselves with poor peer relations and an inability to resolve conflicts and to manage anger. *Cognitive deficits* place youth and adults at a disadvantage academically and reduce their career options, making them more vulnerable to criminal influences because they do not have the marketable skills to compete in a global economy.

The skills repertoire of youth and adults can be enhanced using a psychoeducational life skills intervention model. Teaching a life skill group session follows a five-step learning model: instructing (teaching), modeling (showing), role-playing (practicing), providing feedback (reinforcing), and employing "ownwork" (applying the skill outside the group setting). Modeling, providing feedback, role-playing, instructing, and employing situation logs and ownwork assignments reinforce desired behavior. The term *ownwork* is used rather than homework to reinforce one's own responsibility for changing behavior. The term *homework* often is associated with isolated drudgery. The psychoeducational life skill intervention model is a more comprehensive and systematic approach to the remediation and enhancement of interpersonal and intrapersonal effectiveness. It is practiced in a group setting and involves a combination of cognitive and experiential components.

This comprehensive skill delivery system emphasizes a psychoeducational life skill promotion and enhancement model in which (a) help is provided by a counselor, teacher, or therapist; (b) a client's difficulties are seen as gaps in knowledge or experiences rather than maladaptive behavior or deficits; and (c) the client is active in the design of his or her life skill development and management plan. An experiential group approach rather than a didactic one-on-one approach has been demonstrated as the most successful way to diminish self-defeating behavior, particularly among youth. The instructional psychoeducational intervention techniques are derived from social learning theory. Social skills are acquired primarily through learning (i.e., by observing, modeling, rehearsing, and providing feedback) and are maximized through social reinforcement (i.e., positive responses from one's social environment). Essentially, social, emotional, and cognitive skill deficits can be remedied through direct instruction and modeling. Behavioral rehearsal and coaching reinforce learning. Clients need these prerequisite skills to defeat dysfunctional behaviors and enhance their resiliency during stressful events.

Psychoeducational Life Skill Intervention Process

The psychoeducational group leader assumes the role of director, teacher, model, evaluator, encourager, motivator, facilitator, and protector. Role playing within the psychoeducational life skill intervention model provides opportunities (a) to try out, rehearse, and use new learning in a safe setting; (b) to discover how comfortable new behaviors can become; (c) to assess which alternative actions work best; and (d) to practice and repractice new learning by reality testing. Essentially, intellectual insight alone is not sufficient to change self-defeating behavior, nor can an isolated didactic dialogue between client and therapist serve to integrate new social, emotional, or cognitive skills into the client's behavioral repertoire. Role playing is a fundamental force of self-development and interpersonal learning.

Six-Step Process to the Psychoeducational Life Skill Intervention Model

Steps are outlined according to what the group leader should say and do to help youth integrate social, emotional, and cognitive skills into their behavioral repertoire. Training sessions are a series of action–reaction sequences in which effective skill behaviors are first rehearsed (role play) and then critiqued (feedback). Groups should be small (6–10 members, with gender and races mixed) and should cover one skill in one or two sessions. Every member of the group role-plays the given skill correctly at least once. Role playing is intended to serve as behavioral rehearsal or practice for future use of the skill. Further, a hypothetical future situation rather than a reenactment of the past event should be selected for role playing.

Step 1: Present an Overview of the Social, Emotional, or Cognitive Skill

This is considered the instructional portion of the process. An instructional vignette (5–10 minutes) is presented to teach the social, emotional, or cognitive skill. Introduction to the benefits of the skill in enhancing relationships, as well as the pitfalls for not learning the skill, is presented. Figures 3.14 and 3.15

We all have the right:

- To decide how to lead our lives.
- To express thoughts, actions, and feelings.
- To have our own values, beliefs, opinions, and emotions.
- To tell others how we wish to be treated.
- To say, "I don't know, I don't understand."
- To ask for information or help.
- To have thoughts, feelings, and rights respected.
- To be listened to, heard, and taken seriously.
- To ask for what we want.
- To make mistakes.
- To ask for more information.
- To say "no" without feeling guilty.
- To make a decision to participate or not to participate.
- To be assertive without regrets.

FIGURE 3.14   Social literacy skill: Understanding your assertive rights.

Very often, people who are aggressive do not have within their interpersonal reper-toire the ability to express themselves assertively. There are essentially six attributes that are specific to assertiveness:

1. *Self-awareness:* a developed knowledge of your goals, aspirations, inter-personal and intrapersonal behavior and the reasons for them. An ability to realize where changes are needed and believe in your rights.
2. *Self-acceptance:* Self-awareness acknowledges your own particular strengths and weakness.
3. *Honesty:* Congruency between verbal and nonverbal thoughts, feelings, actions, and intentions.
4. *Empathy:* Sensitivity and acceptance of your feelings, behavior, and actions, that is, to be able to walk in the other person's shoes.
5. *Responsibility:* Assuming ownership for thoughts, feelings, actions, needs, goals, and expectations.
6. *Equality:* Accepting another person as equal with a willingness to negoti-ate with their needs, wants, or desires.

FIGURE 3.15   Social literacy skill: Components of assertiveness.

contain suggested instructional overviews for the social skill of assertiveness.

The process continues:

- Next, ask a question to help the members define the skill on their own. Use language such as: "Who can define *asser-*

tiveness? What does being *assertive* mean to you? How is assertiveness different from aggressiveness?"

- Make a statement about what will follow the modeling of the skill: "After we see the examples of the skill, we will talk about how you can use the skill."
- Distribute skill cards and ask a member to read the behavioral steps aloud. A skill card is the social, emotional, or cognitive skill that the leader is working on with the group, for example, "anger management," "assertiveness," or "critical thinking."
- Ask members to follow each step as the skill is modeled.

Step 2: Model the Behavior Following the Steps Listed on a Flipchart or Chalkboard

Moving into the experiential component, the leader models for the group members what he or she considers to be appropriate mastery of the skill. This enables group members to visualize the process. The model can be a live demonstration or simulation media presentation. Identify and discuss the steps shown in Figure 3.16. Ask for feedback to correct any misperceptions. Encourage others to be clear, direct, and specific in their feedback to you: "Am I being clear?" "How do you perceive the situation?" "What do you want to do about this?"

Step 3: Invite Discussion of the Skill That Is Modeled

- "Did any of the situations you observed remind you of times that you had to use the skill?"
- Encourage a dialogue about skill usage and barriers to implementation among group members.

Step 4: Organize a Role Play Between Two Group Members

- Designate one member as the behavior-rehearsing member (i.e., the individual who will be working on integrating a specific social, emotional, or cognitive skill). Go over guidelines for role playing (see Figure 3.17).

Lack of assertiveness is one reason why conflicts occur in relationships. To foster understanding and cooperation rather than resentment and resistance:

1. Be direct. Deliver your message directly to the person with whom you are in conflict (not to a second party; that is, avoid the *"he said," "she said"* trap).
2. Take ownership of your message. Explain that your message comes from your point of view. Use personalized "I statements" such as "I don't agree with you" rather than "You're wrong."
3. State what you want, think, and feel as specifically as possible. Preface statements with:
   "I have a need."
   "I want to ..."
   "Would you consider ..."
   "I have a different opinion. I think that ..."
   "I don't want you to ..."
   "I have mixed reactions, for these reasons ..."

Step 1: "When you ..." (Concretely describe the other person's behavior.)
Step 2: "The effects are ..." (Describe objectively how the other person's actions have affected you.)
Step 3: "I feel ..." (Accurately describe your feelings.)
Step 4: "I prefer ..." (Suggest what you would like to see happen.)

For example:

Step 1: "When you are late picking me up for school in the morning ..."
Step 2: "I am always late for first bell and I always get detention."
Step 3: "I feel hurt and angry at you."
Step 4: "I am hoping that we could make plans so that I don't have to be late anymore."

FIGURE 3.16   Social literacy skill: Assertiveness.

1. Role playing will give a perspective on your own behavior.
2. It is a tool to bring a specific skill and its consequences into focus.
3. By rehearsing a new skill you will be able to feel some of the same reactions that will be present when you use the behavior outside our group in a real setting.
4. Role playing is intended to give you experience in practicing skills and in discussing and identifying effective and ineffective behavior.
5. Practice will enhance your confidence, and you will be able to feel more comfortable in real-life settings.
6. The more real the role playing is, the more it leads to deeper emotional involvement that will increase what you learn.
7. Real-life situations make it possible for you to try ways of handling situations without suffering any serious consequences if the methods fail.

FIGURE 3.17   Guidelines for role playing.

- Ask the behavior-rehearsing member to choose a partner—someone in the group who reminds him or her of the person with whom they would most likely use the skill. For example, ask the behavior-rehearsing member, "Which member of the group reminds you of that person in some way?" or "Which member of the group would you feel most comfortable doing the role playing with?" If no one is identified, ask someone to volunteer to rehearse the skill with the behavior-rehearsing member.
- Set the stage for the role play, including setting, props, and furniture if necessary. Ask questions such as, "Where will you be talking?" "What will be the time of day?" "What will you be doing?"
- Review with the behavior-rehearsing member what should be said and done during the role play, such as "What will be the first step of the skill?" "What will you do if your partner does _____?"
- Provide final instructions to the behavior-rehearsing member and the partner. To the behavior-rehearsing member: "Try to follow the steps as best you can." To the partner: "Try to play the part as best you can by concentrating on what you think you would do when the practicing member follows the steps."
- Direct the remaining members of the group to be observers of the process. Their role is to provide feedback to the behavior-rehearsing member and the partner after the exercise.
- The role play begins. One group member can stand at the chalkboard or flipchart to point out each step for the role-playing team.
- Coach and prompt role players when needed.

Step 5: Elicit Feedback From Group Members and Processes After the Exercise Has Been Completed

Generous praise should be mixed with constructive suggestions. Avoid blame and criticism. The focus should be on how to improve. Suggestions should be achievable with practice. The social literacy skill of giving constructive feedback that is an

1. Ask permission. Ask the person if he or she would like some feedback. (If no, wait for a more appropriate time; if yes, proceed.)
2. Say something positive to the person before you deliver the sensitive information.
3. Describe the behavior.
4. Focus on behavior the person can change, not on the person's personality.
5. Be specific and verifiable about the behavior. (Have other people complained?)
6. Include some suggestion for improvement.
7. Go slowly. True behavior change occurs over time.

FIGURE 3.18   Giving constructive feedback.

integrated part of every psychoeducational life skill intervention model is shown in Figure 3.18.

Important considerations for the feedback process:

- Instruct the behavior-rehearsing member to wait until everyone's comments have been heard.
- Ask the partner to process his or her role, feelings, and reactions to the behavior-rehearsing member. Instruct observers to report on how well the behavioral steps were followed; give specific likes and dislikes; and comment on the role of the behavior-rehearsing member and the partner.
- Process group comments with the behavior-rehearsing member. Ask the behavior-rehearsing member to respond to how well he or she did in following the behavioral steps of the skill. For example, "On a scale from 1 to 10, how satisfied were you with following the steps?"

Step 6: Encourage Follow-Through and Transfer of Learning to Other Social, Emotional, or Cognitive Settings

This is a critical component. Participants need to transfer newly developed life skills to personally relevant life situations. Assign the behavior-rehearsing member ownwork to practice and apply the skill in real life. Ask group members to look for situations relevant to the skill they might role-play during the next group meeting.

- Ask the behavior-rehearsing member how, when, and with whom he or she might attempt the behavioral steps prior to the next group meeting.
- Assign an "ownwork report" to get a written commitment from the behavior-rehearsing member to try out the new skill and report back to the group at the next group meeting. Discuss how and where the skill will be used. Set a specific goal to use the skill outside the group. Tell the behavior-rehearsing member: "Your social skills ownwork is an assignment that has been taught. You need to practice the social skill 5 times with other people, or peers. Write (a) a description of what happened, when it happened, and where it happened; (b) what you said and did; and (c) what the other person said and did."

Ownwork is assigned to enhance the work of the session and to keep the behavior-rehearsing member aware of the life skill he or she wishes to enhance. The ultimate goal is to practice new behaviors in a variety of natural settings. Ownwork puts the onus of responsibility for change on the behavior-rehearsing member, that is, doing his or her ownwork to resolve the problem. The following examples are appropriate ownwork assignments:

- *Experiential/behavioral assignments* are assignments for specific actions between sessions. For example, a behavioral assignment for lack of assertiveness may be to instruct the behavior-rehearsing member to say "no" to unreasonable requests from others.
- *Interpersonal assignments* are assignments to enhance perceived communication difficulties by writing down unpleasant dialogues with others, which can be reviewed during the next session to show how someone inadvertently triggers rejection, criticism, and hostilities in others.
- *Thinking assignments* are assignments such as making a list of things that are helpful to think about and to practice thinking these new thoughts throughout the day. For example, a person with low self-esteem can be instructed to spend time thinking about accomplishments of which he or she is most proud.

- *Writing assignments* are assignments such as writing in a journal or diary that can help participants develop an outlet for their feelings while away from the sessions. For example, a participant could keep a diary that lists for each day the frequency of new behaviors that are practiced.
- *Solution-focused assignments* are assignments that actively seek solutions to problems identified in the sessions. For example, a member might seek a resolution to an interpersonal problem by negotiating or resolving a conflict with another person.

Simulated Example for Social Literacy Skill: Maintaining Impulse Control

Instruction

Question: How would you define impulse control?

Impulse control is learning to stop and look at the consequences of your actions before you commit yourself to something. It is the ability to stop and think about who else is going to be affected by your actions and what the consequences will be. Is it worth it?

Simulation

Shelly is constantly overcommitting herself by being impulsive. She has a problem saying no and working within the boundaries that are comfortable for her. When she is asked to do something, she will say yes even if she does not have the time or resources to complete the task. Shelly was looking at the course catalogue for the fall and saw a class that looked interesting, so she signed up for it. She was already taking 15 graduate hours and working 20 hours per week. She is feeling extremely stressed because of her overload of classes and she is not sure if she will get her assignments completed on time. How can we help?

Signs of Loss of Control

1. Acting impulsively consumes lots of your energy and resources.
2. You feel driven and think of nothing else.
3. You feel like the decision is the only possible answer, and you let it take over all rational thinking.

Control Strategies

1. Ask yourself who else is going to be affected by this behavior.
2. Ask yourself how they are going to be affected by what you do.
3. Delay the action. Give yourself some time to think through the decision so that you can see the consequences and alternatives. Remember, choice is important.
4. Find a way to buy time, so you can think about your actions.
5. Think of past situations from which you had to extricate yourself because you had been too impulsive.

Modeling

Self-Help Strategies

1. Reward yourself each time you stop and think through a situation instead of acting impulsively.
2. Keep a journal and record your feelings about decisions you make and if you make them impulsively.
3. Write yourself a bill of rights and read it when you get ready to make decisions.

Reminders for Yourself

1. Having a choice is critical. It allows you freedom to act or not to act. It puts you in charge of yourself.
2. If you always do what you've done, you will always get what you have gotten in the past.

Consequences of Acting Impulsively

1. The consequences of acting impulsively are confusion, self-loathing, and feeling out of control.
2. The results of acting impulsively are spending a tremendous amount of time trying to resolve conflicts, mend relationships, or balance time and money.

Role Play

Shelly: Hey, Beth, I just saw this great course in the fall catalogue. I think I will take it.

Beth: Shelly, how many hours of classes are you already taking?

Shelly: Fifteen, but this course sounds interesting, and I really want to take it.

Beth: Shelly, I realize you really want to take it and it sounds interesting, but is it something that you can handle right now with work and school?

Shelly: It will mean more homework and being up late at night, but I really think I can do it.

Beth: Shelly, remember last semester how stressed you were during finals? Do you want that again?

Shelly: No, but Beth you don't understand. I really want to take this class.

Beth: Look at your "plus versus minus" ratio. How is it going to benefit you and how is it going to impact your family?

Shelly: It's going to help me with general knowledge but not toward my degree. I hadn't thought about my family.

Beth: Shelly, do you think you could wait until tomorrow and make your decision? That way you could talk it over with Brian and the kids and think more about it.

Shelly: I guess I could, but what if it's full by then?

Beth: Shelly, what if it is? Will you still be able to graduate and could you take it later?

Shelly: You've got a point. I'll think about it and talk it over with Brian.

	Positive consequences (+)	Negative consequences (–)
Social and family relationships		
Academic responsibilities		
Job and career responsibilities		
Leisure time pursuits		
Church/community obligations		

FIGURE 3.19   Decision balance matrix—Personal time commitment for self and others.

Skill to be practiced: Learning to say "no" and establishing healthy boundaries.

- "I will use this skill with _____."
- "I will use it when _____ and where _____."

The steps are as follows:

1.
2.
3.
4.
5.

On a scale from 1 to 10 (1 = lowest; 10 = highest), rate yourself on how well you did.

FIGURE 3.20   Ownwork assignment.

Feedback

Elicit feedback from group members regarding the role-playing dialogue.

Ownwork Assignment

Have Shelly complete a decision balance matrix (Figure 3.19). Instruct her to look at the aspects of her life listed in Figure 3.19 and how her decision to take on more coursework would affect her.

Next, ask Shelly to analyze her time commitments for all her courses—that is, how much research per class, readings per class, and special projects—and merge those commitments with family and job responsibilities. Bottom line: Are there enough hours in the week to do all she has obligated herself to do? Ownwork assignments (Figure 3.20) serve to strengthen behavior rehearsal of skills between sessions.

Examples of Homework in Nucleus Psychotherapy: Poetry, Painting, and Touching

Therapist: Eileen Walkenstein, MD

Affiliation: Board Certified Psychiatrist, Private Practice, Wyncote, Pennsylvania

Major works:

Walkenstein, E. (1972). *Beyond the couch.* New York: Crown.

Walkenstein, E. (1982). *Fat chance.* New York: Pilgrim Press.

Walkenstein, E. (1983). *Your inner therapist.* Philadelphia: Westminster Press.

Author of numerous articles, television appearances (e.g., Sally Jessy Raphael Show), and conductor of workshops in the United States and Europe (e.g., London, Paris, Rome, Florence, and Naples)

Population for whom the technique is appropriate: Young and old, individual and group, addicted or food obsessed

Cautionary notes: At the outset it should be made clear that the homework assignments are not presented as dictates or commands but rather as suggestions or even strong recommendations; and, finally, it is the patient's choice whether or not to accept them.

Early in my psychiatric practice it became clear to me that although many dramatic and revelatory moments occurred during the therapy sessions, the most important therapy work was done by patients in their lives outside of my office. Thus, almost from the beginning, I gave homework assignments: things to do, things to write, things to read. And sometimes the results of their homework were as startling to me as to them.

For example, a middle-aged woman had multiple allergies so crippling that she had to carry food packets with her when dining at friends' houses or at restaurants. Her symptoms defied the efforts of allergists and other specialists. In desperation she decided to see a psychiatrist.

In doing my nucleus therapy work with her (a brief sketch of this appears in Rosenthal, 2011), we arrived quickly at her "mother problem." At the end of that particular session I said, "For your homework assignment I'd like you to write a poem about your mother." Immediately she remonstrated: "Oh, I can't do that! I've never written a poem in my life."

Undaunted, I smiled: "This one you'll write. It doesn't have to be a great poem or a work of art. It just has to be about your mother."

When I next saw her she proudly produced the poem, a no-holds-barred outpouring of mother's hateful characteristics and her own hate and fury toward her mother beneath years of encrusted politeness and cool respectfulness. She was stunned not only that she had been able to write a poem but by all those unac-knowledged feelings she had been harboring. I laughed: "Poetry unlocks gates—it's dangerous stuff!"

Shortly afterward, *all* of her allergic symptoms disappeared. With impunity she was able to eat outrageous things such as chocolate cake and even fish, which previously would have sent her to the hospital. But the most important fringe benefit was that her relationship with her aged mother changed dramatically and became more real. For the first time in her life she began to feel a flow of warm feelings and love toward her mother.

* * *

For some years I conducted a work-study program for therapists in Italy (where I began to develop and test my "nucleus concept"), and I noticed how divorced these intellectuals were from their bodies and their emotions. How they loved to talk about and intellectualize everything! As a way of introducing touch and feelings to our educational-experiential process, I suggested that they touch their bodies. Also that they read the book *Touching*, by Ashley Montagu (1996), which fortunately was available in Italian under the title of *Tatto* (Touch). Confrontationally, I exhorted: "How can you expect your patients and clients to be integrated if they can't accept their own bodies?" I subsequently have continued to recommend *Touching* to everyone: parents, couples, even to people who I am not treating.

On this theme, a patient in a distant state was very upset during one of our recent telephone sessions. She was distressed by the condition of her body, especially her protruding soft round belly. Previously she had always prided herself on her lithe body with its dancer's super flat abdomen. I listened to her contempt of her belly and then interrupted her condemnatory tirade: "Right now I'd like you to touch your belly with a full, open palm and touch it not in judgment, which leads to your contempt. No judgment. Just the pure feel. Feel the touch, touch the feel of it. I don't want to hear anything about its size or shape. Just its *feel*."

When she finally allowed herself to feel her belly without criticizing it, she admitted it felt warm. "Good! That's your homework. Feel your belly for the warmth and softness of it, no judgment, just touch and feel. Repeat this a minimum of 4 times a day. This prescription is better than any pill I could give you and has no adverse side effects."

By the end of the session we were laughing. I added that if she wished, she might enlist her husband's help in carrying out her assignment. By her next session, she had already made peace with her belly's bulge and actually began to take pleasure in its round softness.

Another example of an assignment that brought instant symptomatic results: A 35-year-old artist had become so self-denunciatory that he put his art supplies out of sight and stopped painting. He became increasingly miserable. After a couple of gloomy years, he decided to seek help. In one of our early sessions it became clear that his perfectionism didn't allow him to enjoy his creating. Nothing he did was good enough. "I probably just don't have enough talent after all," he said.

"Okay, I have your homework assignment," I told him. "Take out your supplies and start painting, but not real painting. Just play with the paints. Play around. Don't do anything good. If you paint a good painting, you've failed your assignment. And if it's perfect, you flunk out altogether. This assignment is not serious artwork, it's just play. If you don't play and you get too serious, you also fail your assignment." He began to laugh. The bars keeping him from his creative work were melting down even before starting his assignment. Fearful and resistant to picking up his paint brushes for the past 2 years, the mere thought of doing the homework assignment to play with paints was already bringing him joy.

References

Montagu, A. (1996). *Touching.* New York: HarperCollins.
Rosenthal, H. G. (Ed.). (2011). *Favorite counseling and therapy techniques* (2nd ed.). New York: Routledge.

Bibliotherapy Homework for Persons of Mixed-Race Heritage

Therapist: Bea Wehrly, PhD

Affiliation: Counselor Educator Emeritus and Multicultural Consultant, Western Illinois University, Macomb

Major works:

Wehrly, B. (1995). *Pathways to multicultural counseling competence: A developmental journey.* Pacific Grove, CA: Brooks/Cole.

Wehrly, B. (1996). *Counseling interracial individuals and families.* Alexandria, VA: American Counseling Association.

Wehrly, B., Kenney, K., & Kelley, M. (1999). *Counseling multiracial families.* Thousand Oaks, CA: Sage.

Population for whom the technique is appropriate: People with mixed-race heritage in individual or group work; especially men of multiracial heritage who are having difficulty dealing with negative feelings related to experiences of rejection by people of either their maternal or paternal heritage

Cautionary notes: This technique is limited to people who have average or high average reading ability. It is not appropriate for use with people who have developmentally delayed cognitive development or with individuals who are sight or hearing impaired.

Description of Homework Assignment

I have been working with a small group of mixed-race men of African American and Caucasian heritages. The three men (Robert, John, and Andrew) are professionals of middle-class socioeconomic status. A strong level of trust and rapport has been developed within the group, and the men are able to express their feelings with ease. A recurring theme of the weekly group sessions has been that the men feel that no one really understands them, especially what it is like to grow up in an interracial family and to be rejected by relatives.

I asked the group if they might like to read about others who have faced some of the same challenges that they are facing. The men said they had heard that there are stories out there about people of mixed-race heritage, and they expressed a desire to see what was available. I promised to bring two autobiographies of mixed-race men to our next group meeting and asked them to bring in any books that they could find that might be appropriate to read and discuss.

At next week's group, we looked at three books: *The Color of Water: A Black Man's Tribute to His White Mother* (McBride, 1996); *Life on the Color Line: The True Story of a White Boy Who Discovered He Was Black* (Williams, 1995); and *Divided to the Vein: A Journey Into Race and Family* (Minerbrook, 1996). The men passed the three books around, read the descriptors on the book jackets, perused the tables of contents, and decided that they preferred to read *Divided to the Vein: A Journey Into Race and Family* (Minerbrook, 1996). Arrangements were made so that each group member would purchase or borrow a copy of Minerbrook's book and would read the first two chapters by the time we met again.

I gave out a sheet with these two guidelines to reading and thinking about the contents of Chapters 1 and 2 of Minerbrook's book:

1. Select at least one passage (a few sentences or a paragraph) from each chapter to which you can relate. Be prepared to read this passage to the group at our next meeting and to tell why this passage has special significance for you.
2. Note how you feel as Minerbrook shares his deep feelings and self-understandings during his first attempt to make contact with his maternal White family that has rejected him. Be prepared to share these feelings with us at next week's group counseling session.

At the next session, the men were eager to share their reactions to reading Chapters 1 and 2 of Minerbrook's book. John shared a passage from page 3 and talked about how he, too, had been haunted by the feeling of loss of family and how he had built up a wall of anger to protect himself. Robert and Andrew told how feelings of anger about being rejected by some of their relatives surfaced now and then in their daily lives. After they discussed some recent examples of feeling angry, the men wondered if they were using the anger as a protective wall. They realized that these feelings surfaced again as they read the two chapters.

Andrew and Robert reported on sections of the second chapter that they found enlightening. Personal insights were gained about their mothers being outsiders in their local rural communities because they left these communities and married across racial boundaries. This led to considerable discussion of how people from some communities decide who is an insider and who is an outsider.

Additional self-disclosure followed on whether the men realized they may have developed feelings of superiority because they took more advantage of educational opportunities than some of their cousins. Andrew wondered if he used an attitude of superiority as a wall or barrier to accepting cousins and grandparents who have rejected him. Andrew wondered aloud: "Do I consider them 'poor White trash'?" The content of the second chapter of Minerbrook's book also evoked discussion of letting go of anger and learning to understand and to empathize.

Homework assignments for the succeeding sessions followed a similar format. Group members could choose to concentrate on one chapter at a time or continue with reading and reflecting on two chapters per session. This decision was made by members of the small group based on their willingness and ability to commit time to participation in homework assignments and group sharing.

As the group continued to relate to Minerbrook's odyssey, more "Aha" reactions surfaced as the men continued to identify with the author's experiences. They experienced catharsis and came to realize that they were not alone in facing problems of rejection and alienation. Together they explored alternatives to dealing with their negative feelings and felt empowered when they were able to let go of dependence on the use of negative feelings as barriers or as walls.

References

McBride, J. (1996). *The color of water: A Black man's tribute to his White mother.* New York: Riverhead.

Minerbrook, S. (1996). *Divided to the vein: A journey into race and family.* New York: Harcourt Brace.

Williams, G. H. (1995). *Life on the color line: The true story of a White boy who discovered he was Black.* New York: Dutton.

The Ice Station Zebra

Therapist: William J. Weikel, PhD

Affiliation: National Certified Counselor; Certified Clinical Mental Health Counselor; Diplomate, American Board of Vocational Experts; Professor and Chair, Morehead State University, Morehead, Kentucky; Owner, Eastern Kentucky Counseling and Rehabilitation Services

Major works:

Hughes, P. R., & Weikel, W. J. (1993). *The counselor as expert witness.* Laurel, MD: American Correctional Association.

Palmo, A. J., Weikel, W. J., & Borsos, D. P. (2006). *Foundations of mental health counseling* (3rd ed.). Springfield, IL: Charles C Thomas.

Author or coauthor of 35 refereed journal articles, past president of the American Mental Health Counselors Association (AMHCA), and founding editor of *AMCA Journal,* now the *Journal of Mental Health Counseling*

Population for whom the technique is appropriate: Adolescents and adults

Cautionary notes: This approach works best with clients able to develop clear mental images.

I frequently work with clients who, as a result of problems with chronic pain, depression, anxiety, or a combination of these conditions, are experiencing chronic sleep disturbance. Many of these individuals report that the most serious problem is initially falling asleep. They often lie or toss or turn, ruminating on their pain or other problems.

Recently I have begun recommending a homework assignment that I (a frequent insomniac) personally have used for many years. It is a cognitive/imagery task similar to approaches used by the Stoics and not unlike the "Memory Palace" constructed by the fictional Dr. Hannibal "The Cannibal" Lecter, in Thomas Harris's (1999) best seller *Hannibal.* I call this assignment/task "Ice Station Zebra," after the movie of the same name.

Clients are instructed to lie in bed, as comfortably as possible, and to imagine that they have been assigned as solo operator of a polar research station for one year. They are to imagine a large helicopter such as a Huey delivering a dome-shaped structure to a polar region where they are to live and work alone for the next 12 months in isolation. The structure is merely an insulated shell. They must sectionalize, furnish, and equip the habitat, inside and out, not only to survive in this hostile environment but also to live comfortably and avoid extreme boredom. The clients are instructed to "pack" what personal items they desire to help them to fill their "off-duty" hours, such as their favorite books, compact disks, hobby items, or videos. There is no telephone or radio communication and no other human contact, so careful planning is necessary. Food, snacks, drinks, and food preparation items also are needed in quantities to last one year, since they will use commercial rather than military-type food.

With practice, a client can develop a vivid image of their personal "ice station." None, including me, has ever completely equipped, furnished, and provisioned the station in one session, or even come close before falling asleep. Therefore, this can be an ongoing assignment. For example, tonight I'll lay out the floor plan; tomorrow I'll work on foodstuff, then personal effects, and so forth. The more the exercise is used, the easier it becomes to escape your current discomforts and work your way to sleep. Clients are instructed that if they reawaken in the night, they should continue where they left off.

There are of course many variations on this theme. One could design, build, and furnish a dream house; reenact Robinson Crusoe; or voyage alone into outer space. The idea remains simply to distract the mind from its troubles, woes, aches, and pains and to pave the way for restful and restorative sleep. It is an approach that is easy to implement, safe, and effective and that may help clients to avoid the negative side effects of many sleep-inducing medications. Try it tonight … and, oh yes, sleep tight!

Reference

Harris, T. (1999). *Hannibal*. New York: Dell.

Lifeline

Therapist: Ira David Welch, EdD, ABPP

Affiliation: Licensed Psychologist, Colorado

Major works:

Welch, I. D. (1998). *The path of psychotherapy: Matters of the heart.* Pacific Grove, CA: Brooks/Cole.

Welch, I. D., & Gonzalez, D. M. (1999). *The process of counseling and psychotherapy: Matters of skill.* Pacific Grove, CA: Brooks/Cole.

Population for whom the technique is appropriate: Adolescents and adults, as a method of collecting a psychosocial history; especially helpful with adolescents who have difficulty verbalizing

Cautionary notes: This technique may be used as homework or done in the session with the client. If the therapist believes that material might emerge that is highly sensitive or will provoke strong emotions, then it might be more useful to do the lifeline in session.

Technique

This is a method of collecting personal history that can be creative and stimulating. It has the promise of bringing material into the sessions that may not otherwise emerge. It may be used as homework. The therapist says, "I want you to draw a long line on this piece of paper" (8½ × 11 inches, used horizontally). (Use the middle of the paper to allow for variations in how far from average an experience is judged to be. Use a plus sign (+) on the top half of the page for positive experiences and a minus sign (–) on the bottom half of the page to designate negative experiences.) See Figure 3.21.

Then say, "The right end of the line is the present. The other end is as far back as you wish to go. Place everything you think is important in your life and development on the line: positive above and negative below. The line represents neutral experience—one that is neither positive nor negative."

+	+	+	+	+
1975				Present
–	–	–	–	–

FIGURE 3.21   Pictoral representation of a sample blank lifeline.

To assign the homework say, "I want you to take this home with you and take as much time as you want to finish it. Then bring it back next week and we will talk about your experiences."

Variation: You may want to limit the lifeline to some specific experience that is important to the therapy (e.g., divorce or a death). In that case you would say, "On the left side of the page I want you to begin this lifeline with your divorce. Then go forward to the present and list the positive and negative experiences along the lifeline."

Usefulness

This technique provides the therapist with a quick way of obtaining a developmental history that is meaningful to the client that may not have emerged in the initial interview(s) session(s). It is useful also with nonverbal clients as a way to generate material for discussion in therapy.

Processing

As a method of processing the information from the lifeline ask, "What did you learn from doing this lifeline?" Have the lifeline present for each subsequent session as a stimulus and reminder of important material that could be covered in therapy.

The Jabberwocky Approach to Anger Management with Families

Therapist: Jerry Wilde, PhD

Affiliation: Psychologist and Associate Professor of Educational Psychology, Indiana University East

Major works:

Wilde, J. (1992). *Rational counseling with school aged populations: A practical guide.* Muncie, IN: Accelerated Development.

Wilde, J. (1995). *Why kids struggle in school: A guide to overcoming under achievement.* Salt Lake City, UT: Northwest Publishing.

Wilde, J. (2002). *Anger management in schools: Alternatives to student violence.* Lanham, MD: Scarecrow Education.

Population for whom the technique is appropriate: Families with anger problems

Cautionary notes: To be successful, all family members must agree to participate.

Families can be breeding grounds for anger and hostility. Many households are under a great deal of stress both financially and emotionally. Add to the mix the intimate knowledge of each family member's vulnerabilities and you have a potentially volatile situation.

The Jabberwocky technique is a homework assignment designed to help families learn a strategy to interrupt anger chains that can quickly spiral out of control. It is to be used when a disagreement is getting out of hand and family members are concerned that the situation may turn violent.

The exercise proceeds as follows: Anytime a member of the family is feeling unsafe he or she can call out the signal word, in this case, "Jabberwocky." It's important that every family member (adults and children alike) has the opportunity to call the signal word when he or she feels unsafe. All family members are treated equally in this exercise and this parity can give a sense of empowerment, especially to children.

When the signal word is called, the individuals in the disagreement are to stop the arguing and separate for a prearranged amount of time. Each family is different with regard to separation time, so it's important to let them choose the amount of "cool-down" time needed. Sometimes it's helpful to have the family think of the signal word as a verbal "cease and desist" order.

After the prearranged time has passed, the individuals involved in the disagreement must revisit the issue. By giving the members a chance to cool off, it is hoped a reasonable solution can be reached. As I always point out, it's very uncommon for people to make good decisions in the middle of a shouting match.

Most families with a history of anger problems will have an anger-inducing situation naturally arise in the week or two between sessions. When this occurs, the family should try to use the Jabberwocky technique. It is also possible to dredge up some anger by asking the family to discuss an issue they previously argued about as a means of practicing this homework exercise.

One final note to keep in mind as you explain this homework assignment: The Jabberwocky exercise can be sabotaged by family members who (a) use it to shut down discussion on a certain topic and (b) refuse to follow the agreed-upon rules (i.e., keep arguing after the signal word has been called). Do some preventative work as you explain this exercise by examining these two ways families can undermine this exercise. My experience has been that if the therapist openly discusses these issues prior to the exercise, they are much less likely to occur.

Quality Time for Improving Family Relationships

Therapist: Robert E. Wubbolding, EdD

Affiliation: Licensed Counselor; Psychologist; Professor Emeritus, Counseling at Xavier University; Director of the Center for Reality Therapy, Cincinnati, Ohio

Major works:

Wubbolding, R. (1988). *Using reality therapy.* New York: HarperCollins.
Wubbolding, R. (1991). *Understanding reality therapy.* New York: HarperCollins.
Wubbolding, R. (2000). *Reality therapy for the 21st century.* New York: Routledge.

Author of 10 books and over 125 essays and chapters in textbooks

Population for whom the technique is appropriate: Family members who are experiencing tension in their relationships

Cautionary notes: It is important that the therapist first assist clients to decide that they *want* to improve the relationship and that they are committed to following through on the activity.

Couples and families often enter counseling with the presenting issue of an inability to communicate, unwillingness to accept each other without harsh condemnation, unwillingness to compromise, or failure to solve problems. These issues have more specific content, such as substance abuse, arguing, blaming, criticizing, domestic violence, unfaithfulness, psychological distancing, school problems, finances, and many others.

Therapists frequently approach the issue by teaching clients how to talk to each other or even how to verbally "fight fairly." Compromise techniques and communication skills can be the focus of such therapy. The technique of quality time provides a solid footing for therapeutic interventions focusing on communication and problem solving and ensures their more likely success.

Prior to suggesting the homework, the counselor helps the clients discuss how they have talked to each other and whether they have tried to solve the problem. The answer is often that they have repeatedly made such attempts. They are asked to evaluate the effectiveness of such efforts. Invariably the answer is many hours of talking have not resolved the issue. Consequently they are now seeking the help of the therapist. The therapist asks them to limit their discussion of the painful issue and to substitute time together, which is called "quality time." During this time they agree to the following:

1. Do an activity which is agreeable to each party. The clients decide what is at least tolerable to them. If it is painful, it will be discontinued quickly. Clients can be taught that the more internally satisfying their time is together, the higher the likelihood that they will resolve the problem.

2. Do an activity that requires effort. Thus watching television or eating together is not quality time. Often parents or couples take brisk walks with children or each other. The Danish philosopher, Kierkegaard, once remarked that there is no problem too great that it cannot be solved by walking. Such activity requires the expenditure of energy.

3. Do an activity for a limited amount of time. If parent and adolescent have been argumentative, cold, or confrontive with each other, the time should be limited to minutes. The quality time is thus realistically doable. Depending on the stress in the relationship, the activity might be measured in minutes and gradually increased.

4. Do an activity that is mutually enjoyable. No one should experience pain. The activity might involve some discomfort at first, but it should not be agonizing. The goal is to uncover or develop common ground for enhancing the relationship. Once again, walking together for a short time often is agreed upon because of its many individual as well as relationship-building consequences.

5. Do the activity repetitively. Walking around the neighborhood *once* for 10 minutes will not fix the relationship.

Just as physical fitness is not the result of one day's exercise, a wounded relationship is not healed by a quick-fix choice.

6. Do the activity while discussing safe topics. Topics for conversation are selected on the basis of whether they bring the parties together or divide them, whether the relationship is strengthened or weakened. Controversial topics can be dealt with later. Therefore, the ABC's of toxic relationships are out of bounds:

   a. Arguing, antagonizing. Even intellectual arguments and debates should be shunned.

   b. Blaming, bossing, belittling.

   c. Criticizing. If criticism could be eliminated from the entire relationship, the relationship would improve rapidly and significantly. The therapist emphasizes that especially during the quality time, the absolute agreement is made to discuss mutually satisfying topics, not ones where criticism is involved.

   Condemning is an advanced form of criticism and also is out of bounds, as is complaining about each other, the family, the neighbors, or the state of world affairs.

   d. Demeaning. Demeaning is similar to criticizing but implies putting people down in some way.

   e. Excusing one's own behavior. Making excuses on occasion is not seriously damaging. But to avoid responsibility, habitual attempts serve to erect a barrier between family members.

   f. Instilling fear. During this time, dialogue about merited and unmerited consequences and punishment are avoided.

Clearly, the therapist helps clients decide what are the safe topics for them and what to avoid. Implicit in the therapy is a trust in the creativity of the clients to find relationship-building activities and topics for discussion.

This assignment is based on the principle that clients often confuse cause and effect. They relate that they do not spend time together because they do not get along. The therapist sees this differently. The disconnect in the relationship is based on the choice to avoid relationship-enhancing activities.

It is important to note that throughout the therapy the clients are, in fact, negotiating. They are learning to direct their dialogues toward mutually agreed upon activities. Moreover, when they repeatedly spend time together they are building a storehouse of pleasant memories about each other. These serve to replace or at least balance the painful ones. Thus when there are painful problems to be dealt with, as there are in any relationship, there exists a solid basis for facing them in an equitable and mutually satisfying way.

Chapter **4**

Homework in Counseling*

Christopher E. Hay and Richard T. Kinnier

Abstract

Using homework as an adjunct to the work that occurs within the counseling session has been shown to be an effective way to promote therapeutic change in a brief period of time. Increasing the relevance of homework assignments increases the likelihood of compliance and the effectiveness of the between-session tasks. In this article the literature on homework in counseling is reviewed and a guide for helping counselors determine relevant assignments in a systematic manner is presented.

Homework in Counseling

Given the changes in mental health care today, it is becoming almost essential for counselors to use homework with their clients (C. Black, panel, December 16, 1995). As brief therapy becomes

---

* *Editor's Note:* This article is reprinted via permission of the American Mental Health Counselors Association and appeared in Volume 20, Issue 2 of the April 1998 *Journal of Mental Health Counseling.*

the most common modality of mental health counseling, counselors will need to create new ways of amplifying the impact of counseling within a limited period of time. Homework can fulfill this need.

Homework has many different roles in the counseling process. According to Suinn (1990), homework has now become recognized as a means of insuring compliance, as a mechanism for assuring continuity between treatment sessions, as a procedure for developing generalization of gains outside of the therapy session, as a means of obtaining information about progress for therapy planning, as a method for integrating the therapy into daily routines, and to provide personal meaning to the therapy process (p. 123).

In this article we review the literature on the use of homework in counseling. We present an array of the types of homework commonly used and discuss the issues of compliance and effectiveness. A model, derived from the literature and designed to help counselors conceptualize and implement homework assignments, is offered. The model may provide a useful framework for the creation or selection and implementation of relevant homework in a systematic manner.

Defining Homework

Homework has been defined by Shelton and Ackerman (1974) simply as "assignments given to the client which are carried on outside the therapy hour" (p. 3). Shelton and Ackerman suggested that the counselor and client should jointly plan homework assignments. They believed that homework assignments could serve to teach clients how to continue the self-change process after counseling is terminated. Engle, Beutler, and Daldrup (1991) recommended three possible uses for homework: (a) for enhancing the work of the session, (b) for keeping the client aware of incomplete work, or (c) for celebrating a breakthrough achieved in counseling.

Lazarus (panel, December 16, 1995) said that he never uses the word *homework* because it conjures associations with required school homework, which may create resistance within clients. Instead, he suggested the phrase "empowering assignment." For similar reasons, Whisman and Jacobson (1990) suggest the term *between-session task* as an alternative to homework. Although we agree with that concern, the term *homework* was selected for use in this article because a review of literature revealed it to be the more commonly used and recognized term.

Compatibility With Theoretical Orientation

Though the use of homework is not explicitly banned from any of the major theoretical approaches to counseling, it is more commonly associated with some than others. With the increase of technical eclecticism and integration of theory, few counselors are likely to find themselves consistently opposed to utilizing homework with clients. Nevertheless, counselors' theoretical conception of change and healing is likely to influence the degree to which they choose to emphasize homework and how they use it in their approach.

Homework is often used in cognitive-behavioral counseling and in most of the systemic-based marital and family therapies (Woody, 1990). In contrast, homework is rarely used in psychodynamic or client-centered counseling. The psychoanalyst's role is to interpret unconscious conflict with a focus on the transference between client and analyst (Summers, 1994). This reliance upon the relationship necessitates the analyst's presence, which is not compatible with homework assignments. Similarly, client-centered counseling emphasizes the relationship as the primary focus of therapeutic change. Rogers (1980) believed that client growth is facilitated in a caring environment. Therefore, in their purest forms, psychoanalytic and client-centered approaches are not compatible with assigning homework due to their dependence upon the interaction that occurs during the counseling session.

Homework is not emphasized in the literature as the primary force of change in any major theoretical approach, but as a supplement to or reinforcement of what occurs during sessions. As Shelton and Ackerman (1974) stated, homework does "not oppose treatment designs which rely on the therapy hour as the major vehicle for change, but can provide these therapies with extended reach" (p. 3).

Advantages of Assigning Homework

There are many benefits of between-session homework assignments. Shelton and Ackerman (1974) noted that homework provides a valuable opportunity for the client to practice new behaviors in a variety of natural settings. Woods (1991) pointed out that the outcomes of homework can be discussed in session, providing a chance to modify the direction of the counseling.

One of the beneficial aspects of homework is that it places the locus of responsibility for change upon the client in the absence of the counselor. Self-efficacy increases as the client sees that he or she is capable of making changes outside of the session. As stated by Cummings (1991), "Giving homework in the first session and thereafter will make the patient realize that he or she is expected to be responsible for his or her own therapy" (p. 41). Though responsibility for oneself is not always welcomed by the client in crisis, empowerment and self-esteem are likely to increase, as he or she is able to observe changes in daily life.

Kornblith, Rehm, O'Hara, and Lamparski (1983) emphasized the importance of the client's ability to engage in self-monitoring, self-evaluation, and self-reinforcement. Their research showed that clients with these abilities were able to improve more quickly than those who lack those abilities. Homework can foster those abilities.

Hare-Mustin and Tushup (1977) have written about the problems that often arise when a counselor is absent for a period of time due to illness, vacation, or other career-related responsibilities. They recommended that homework be utilized during such times. The benefits of assigning homework during absences are that clients can still feel a connection to the counseling process and they often learn that they can function independently of their counselor.

The majority of research on homework emphasizes that homework increases the effectiveness of counseling, but only if the client complies with the assigned tasks. Therefore, homework must be appropriate to the client's problem and the client must be motivated to follow through on assignments. If homework is irrelevant or the client chooses to not follow through, no benefit will occur.

Research indicates that clients who complete their counseling homework assignments improve more than those who do not complete their assignments (Burns & Nolen-Hoeksema, 1991). Consistent completion of homework has improved counseling outcomes for the problems of depression (Burns & Auerbach, 1992; Neimeyer & Feixas, 1990; Startup & Edmonds, 1994), phobias (Al-Kubaisy et al., 1992), and anxiety disorders (Edelman & Chambless, 1993).

Reasons and Remedies for Noncompliance

Getting clients to do their homework assignments can be a problem. In order to avoid or overcome the problem of noncompliance, counselors should be aware of the common reasons for noncompliance.

Several reasons for client noncompliance have been described in the literature (Burns & Auerbach, 1992; McCarthy, 1985; Shelton & Ackerman, 1974). They can be summarized as follows:

1. The client primarily wants to use counseling to ventilate emotions or to rent a sympathetic ear or friend, not to make difficult changes.
2. The client does not want to take responsibility or to do the work needed to make a change, preferring instead to be the passive recipient of the counselor's magical cure.
3. The client is being forced to attend counseling and is therefore resentful or rebellious. This is common among adolescents.
4. The client feels that he or she does not have the time or energy to complete homework tasks.
5. The homework instructions are unclear or not specific enough, or the counselor is negligent or inconsistent in following up on the completion of assignments.

There are many ways that the counselor can contribute to the client's compliance with homework assignments. Conoley, Padula, Payton, and Daniels (1994) and Cummings (1991) recommended that counselors assign homework tasks that are closely matched to the client's stated problem or goals. McCarthy (1985) emphasized that assignments should be specific and instructions must be clear.

Cox, Tisdelle, and Culbert (1988) found that written assignments were more often completed than verbal assignments. Worthington (1986) identified three factors that increased the completion of assignments. Assignments given early in counseling are more likely to be completed, possibly suggesting that clients lose enthusiasm for homework over time. Talking to clients about their attitude toward homework also increases compliance. Finally, clients are more likely to resist the suggestions of the counselor who tries to emphasize his or her qualifications and knowledge about counseling. Shelton and Ackerman (1974) recommended that counselors present several alternatives or options from which clients are able to choose and that clients be encouraged to participate in the planning of homework.

Kirk (1989) suggested a number of questions to consider when assessing a client's noncompliance with homework. They include: Was the homework specifically planned or merely suggested? Was it too vague? Did the client recall it accurately? Had the counselor routinely reviewed previously completed homework? Did the client understand the rationale for the homework? Did practical difficulties interfere with the client's ability to complete the assignment? Did the client fear the outcome of the homework? Is noncompliance reflective of the client's self-perception?

Wells (1994) and others have suggested that it is helpful to offer clear explanations of the purpose of homework assignments. A possible exception might be paradoxical tasks (such as the instruction to not become sexually aroused for the couple experiencing sexual difficulties). Obviously counselors cannot explain paradoxical tasks, as such explanations obviously will undermine the therapeutic effect of paradox. Of course, counselors must consider ethical guidelines relating to the client's rights as an informed consumer when determining how assignments will be presented.

Types of Homework Assignments

In completing homework assignments, clients can be active, passive, or both (Wells, 1994). For example, a passive assignment could involve listening to an audiotape; an active assignment could involve the client purposively initiating conversations with strangers.

The kinds of homework that can be assigned are limited only by the creativity of the counselor and client. The following types of assignments have been described in the literature and might be used as a resource for counselors. They are: paradoxical; experiential/behavioral; risk-taking and shame-attacking; interpersonal; thinking; writing; reading, listening, and watching videotape; solution-focused; and "don't do anything" assignments.

Paradoxical Assignments

Paradoxical assignments are commonly used with sleeping disorders or sexual dysfunction problems. The purpose often is to create the opposite outcome by taking the pressure off the individual who is trying to force an outcome that must occur spontaneously. Salkovskis (1989) emphasized the usefulness of paradoxical assignments such as telling a client with insomnia to attempt to stay awake as late as possible. However, Woody (1990) cautions that the "use of paradoxical tasks can be very risky in client situations where dangerousness or other ethical issues are present" (p. 292). Prescribing the symptom may result in serious consequences if an individual poses a threat to self or others.

Experiential/Behavioral Assignments

Experiential/behavioral assignments involve taking specific actions between sessions by the client. Walen, DiGiuseppe, and Dryden (1992) emphasized the importance of behavioral change in counseling. The best time to try out and practice new behaviors is between sessions. Wells (1994) especially recommended experiential assignments for the problems of depression and anxiety. For example, a behavioral assignment for depression is for the client to engage in specified pleasurable activities during the week regardless of whether the client feels like it or not.

Risk-Taking and Shame-Attacking Assignments

Encouraging clients to take risks is a specialized form of an experiential assignment for clients who are having difficulty overcoming their fears. For example, Wells (1994) suggested that the client who is afraid to ask others out on a date go out and solicit three rejections. Wells described the assignment of riding on a subway and loudly shouting out each stop as it approaches as an example of a shame-attacking assignment. The point of such an assignment is to help clients become less terrified of perceived consequences such as rejection or standing out in public.

Interpersonal Assignments

Interpersonal assignments are especially applicable to individuals, couples, and families who are experiencing communication difficulties. Burns and Auerbach (1992) suggested that such clients write down excerpts from unpleasant dialogues with others, which can be reviewed during the session. Counselors can then show clients "how they may inadvertently trigger rejection, criticism, and hostility in others" (p. 466).

Thinking Assignments

Walen et al. (1992) suggested that the client make a list of things that are helpful to think about and to practice thinking these new thoughts throughout the day. For example, a person with low self-esteem can be instructed to spend time thinking about his or her proudest accomplishments.

Writing Assignments

Writing in a journal or diary can help clients develop an outlet for their feelings while away from the session. Additionally, written assignments can be brought to the session for further discussion.

Wolberg (1977) suggested that clients keep a diary that lists for each day the frequency of new behaviors that he or she practiced. Lange (1994) encouraged the utilization of written assignments as homework, yet recognized that some clients may have difficulty in writing. For such clients he suggested speaking into an audio tape recorder.

Reading, Listening, and Watching Assignments

Bibliotherapy has increased in popularity due in part to the low cost and accessibility of self-help literature. Shelton and Ackerman (1974) suggested that the advantages of bibliotherapy are that clients can "read at their own pace and can mull over ideas presented in the book" (p. 20). They caution, however, that some clients may find reading difficult or unpleasant. Counselors should inquire about how their clients feel about reading before assigning or suggesting books to read.

Walen et al. (1992) recommended that clients listen to audio tapes of their own counseling sessions. One advantage of such an assignment for busy clients is that they are able to listen to audio tapes while driving in their car or doing chores around the home. Another type of listening assignment is taking the time to listen to professional relaxation or stress reduction tapes. Many clients find that such tapes reduce anxiety and provide a calming break in their day.

Related to listening assignments is homework that involves watching videotapes of recorded counseling sessions. Though this requires specialized equipment that is not available to all counselors or clients, a study by Gasman (1992) showed that watching sessions on videotape was highly beneficial to the therapeutic process. Clients reported "increased objectivity, insight, and self-esteem" (p. 91) as a result of the experience.

Solution-Focused Assignments

Nunnally (1993) recommended assignments that are solution-focused. With solution-focused assignments, clients are encouraged to actively seek solutions to problems identified in the sessions. For example, a client may be instructed to seek a resolution to an interpersonal problem by negotiating with that person.

"Don't Do Anything" Assignments

Claudia Black (panel, December 16, 1995) recommended that clients who are obsessive about remedying their situation will most likely benefit from occasionally taking a break from that quest. The assignment for such a person can be something like not reading anything that relates to the problem for two weeks.

A Guide for Assigning Homework in Counseling

The following guide was adapted from a model developed by Brown-Standridge (1989) and is based on our reading of the literature on homework. In considering the use of homework, counselors might consider the following points and questions.

1. **Determine the Appropriateness of Assigning Homework.** The first step in determining a homework assignment is to consider whether or not homework is even appropriate. Is the client someone who would benefit from homework? Is he or she simply looking to ventilate? Do any factors inhibit the client's ability to complete homework? What is the client's attitude toward homework? The counselor and client can consider these questions together and jointly decide if homework is appropriate.
2. **Determine the Goals for Homework.** Once it has been determined that the client might benefit from homework, it is then important to determine which homework goals are most relevant to the counseling process. What is the client's stated goal? The goals of homework should be consistent with the reason the client is seeking counseling.
3. **Determine the Type of Assignment.** After reviewing the types of homework, which ones seem most related to the

client's goals? Is the client's problem interpersonal? Should the assignment involve other people? Does the client enjoy reading? Does he or she have access to an audio or video-tape player? Is the client attempting to achieve new behaviors, affect, or cognitions?

4. **Determine the Length of an Assignment.** Counselors may need to modify the assignment depending upon the free time the client has available. The counselor's perceptions of an appropriate length of time may not necessarily reflect the client's perception. How much time is the client willing to take to do homework? What else will be going on in the client's life during the upcoming week? A brief, completed assignment is likely to have more benefit than a lengthy, involved assignment that is not completed.

5. **Determine the Complexity of the Assignment.** It is particularly appropriate to consider the education level and cognitive capabilities of the client. One client may benefit from reading a technical article about research on depression while another client may find such material too difficult or uninteresting to read. It is particularly important when working with children or adolescents to assess the cognitive level of the client. Additionally, the counselor will need to assess for any learning disabilities which might interfere with skills necessary for successful completion of the assignment.

6. **Determine Disclosure of Homework's Goals.** After determining appropriate goals and the homework assignment most likely to help the client reach those goals, the counselor must decide whether or not to share the goals of the assignment with the client. In most cases, the client will benefit from this knowledge and compliance will be increased. However, the goals of a paradoxical assignment are less likely to be achieved if, for example, the client with a sleeping disorder knows that the goal behind trying to stay up late is to reduce the pressure of trying to fall asleep and thus fall asleep sooner. Counselors must proceed with great care and cognizance of ethical considerations when using paradoxical assignments. It must be

remembered that a client who does not see the relevance of a homework assignment will be less likely to follow through.

7. **Discuss the Assignment With the Client.** Once the counselor has initially conceptualized an appropriate assignment for a client, it is important to approach it as a suggestion that can be modified based upon the client's feedback. It is crucial to respect the client's feelings about the assignment and take feedback as information as opposed to resistance. Though the client may indeed be resisting, the counselor must first listen and empathize with the client's feedback to determine the ways in which the assignment can be subtly or fundamentally altered to increase compliance.

8. **Write Down the Assignment.** Research has shown that writing down the assignment will improve the likelihood of compliance. Despite a client's claims of a good memory or the apparent simplicity of an assignment, it is best to make sure the assignment is written before the client leaves the session. In addition, writing down the assignment gives the client and the counselor another chance to clarify any ambiguities which still exist about the specifics of the task. If the client is unable to read, then the counselor is encouraged to write down the assignment for a parent or guardian who may later relay the information to the client.

9. **Review the Results of the Homework Assignment With the Client.** When the client returns, he or she may have other concerns that need to be addressed immediately. If, for example, a crisis has taken place since the last session, then it would be inappropriate to neglect the crisis to discuss the results of the homework assignment. Nevertheless, it is important to make sure that the results of the assignment are discussed at some point in the session. Compliance is most likely to decrease if assignments are suggested but then never referred to again. The results of completed homework assignments can often serve as a springboard for relevant discussion within the session.

Summary

As brief counseling becomes a more common necessity, counselors will need to find ways to increase the impact of counseling in a shorter period of time. Utilizing homework as an adjunct to the work that occurs in the session can be an effective way to create therapeutic change in a brief period of time. Homework can serve many functions including creating continuity between the session and the client's life, and as a method of extending therapeutic change beyond the typical hour-per-week session. Increasing the relevance of homework assignments reduces the likelihood of noncompliance, thus enhancing the effectiveness of between-session tasks. The guide presented provides a framework for helping counselors plan and implement homework in a systematic manner.

References

Al-Kubaisy, T., Marks, I. M., Logsdail, S., Marks, M. P., Lovell, K., Sungur, M., & Araya, R. (1992). Role of exposure homework in phobia reduction: A controlled study. *Behavior Therapy, 23,* 599–621.

Brown-Standridge, M. D. (1989). A paradigm for construction of family therapy tasks. *Family Process, 28,* 471–489.

Burns, D. D., & Auerbach, A. H. (1992). Does homework compliance enhance recovery from depression? *Psychiatric Annals, 22,* 464–469.

Burns, D. D., & Nolen-Hoeksema, S. (1991). Coping styles, homework compliance, and the effectiveness of cognitive-behavioral therapy. *Journal of Consulting and Clinical Psychology, 59,* 305–311.

Conoley, C. W., Padula, M. A., Payton, D. S., & Daniels, J. A. (1994). Predictors of client implementation of counselor recommendations: Match with problem, difficulty level, and building on client strengths. *Journal of Counseling Psychology, 41,* 3–7.

Cox, D. J., Tisdelle, D. A., & Culbert, J. P. (1988). Increasing adherence to behavioral homework assignments. *Journal of Behavioral Medicine, 11,* 519–522.

Cummings, N. A. (1991). Assigning homework. In C. S. Austad & W. H. Berman (Eds.), *Psychotherapy in managed health care: The optimal use of time and resources* (pp. 40–62). Washington, DC: American Psychological Association.

Edelman, R. E., & Chambless, D. L. (1993). Compliance during sessions and homework in exposure-based treatment of agoraphobia. *Behavior Research Therapy, 31,* 767–773.

Engle, D., Beutler, L. E., & Daldrup, R. J. (1991). Focused expressive psychotherapy: Treating blocked emotions. In J. D. Safran & L. S. Greenberg (Eds.), *Emotion, psychotherapy, and change* (pp. 169–196). New York: Guilford Press.

Gasman, D. H. (1992). Double-exposure therapy: Videotape homework as a psychotherapeutic adjunct. *American Journal of Psychotherapy, 46,* 91–101.

Hare-Mustin, R. T., & Tushup, R. (1977). Maintaining a sense of contact with the patient during therapist absences. *Journal of Clinical Psychology, 33,* 531–534.

Kirk, J. (1989). Cognitive-behavioural assessment. In K. Hawton, P. M. Salkovskis, J. Kirk, & D. M. Clark (Eds.), *Cognitive behaviour therapy for psychiatric problems* (pp. 13–51). New York: Oxford University Press.

Kornblith, S. J., Rehm, L. P., O'Hara, M. W., & Lamparski, D. M. (1983). The contribution of self-reinforcement training and behavioral assignments to the efficacy of self-control therapy for depression. *Cognitive Therapy and Research, 7,* 499–528.

Lange, A. (1994). Writing assignments in the treatment of grief and traumas from the past. In J. K. Zeig (Ed.), *Ericksonian methods: The essence of the story* (pp. 377–392). New York: Brunner/Mazel.

McCarthy, B. W. (1985). Use and misuse of behavioral homework exercises in sex therapy. *Journal of Sex and Marital Therapy, 11,* 185–191.

Neimeyer, R. A., & Feixas, G. (1990). The role of homework and skill acquisition in the outcome of group cognitive therapy for depression. *Behavior Therapy, 21,* 281–292.

Nunnally, E. (1993). Solution-focused therapy. In R. A. Wells & V. J. Giannetti (Eds.), *Casebook of the brief psychotherapies* (pp. 119–145). New York: Plenum Press.

Rogers, C. R. (1980). *A way of being.* Boston: Houghton Mifflin.

Salkovskis, P. M. (1989). Somatic problems. In K. Hawton, P. M. Salkovskis, J. Kirk, & D. M. Clark (Eds.), *Cognitive behaviour therapy for psychiatric problems* (pp. 235–276). New York: Oxford University Press.

Shelton, J. L., & Ackerman, J. M. (1974). *Homework in counseling and psychotherapy: Examples of systematic assignments for therapeutic use by mental health professionals.* Springfield, IL: Thomas.

Startup, M., & Edmonds, J. (1994). Compliance with homework assignments in cognitive-behavioral psychotherapy for depression: Relation to outcome and methods of enhancement. *Cognitive Therapy and Research, 18,* 567–579.

Suinn, R. M. (1990). *Anxiety management training: A behavior therapy.* New York: Plenum Press.

Summers, F. (1994). *Object relations theories and psychopathology.* Hillsdale, NJ: Analytic Press.

Walen, S. R., DiGiuseppe, R., & Dryden, W. (1992). *A practitioner's guide to rational-emotive therapy* (2nd ed.). New York: Oxford University Press.

Wells, R. A. (1994). *Planned short-term treatment* (2nd ed.). New York: Free Press.

Whisman, J., & Jacobson, T. (1990). Behavioral marital therapy. In R. A. Wells & V. J. Giannetti (Eds.), *Handbook of the brief psychotherapies* (pp. 325–349). New York: Plenum Press.

Wolberg, L. R. (1977). *The technique of psychotherapy* (3rd ed.). New York: Grune & Stratton.

Woods, P. J. (1991). Orthodox RET taught effectively. In M. E. Bernard (Ed.), *Using rational-emotive therapy effectively: A practitioner's guide* (pp. 85–96). New York: Plenum Press.

Woody, J. D. (1990). Clinical strategies to promote compliance. *American Journal of Family Therapy, 18,* 285–294.

Worthington, E. L., Jr. (1986). Client compliance with homework directives during counseling. *Journal of Counseling Psychology, 33,* 124–130.

Chapter 5

Fifteen Recommendations for Implementing Counseling and Therapy Homework Assignments

Howard G. Rosenthal

1. Use only assignments with which you feel comfortable.
2. Carry out the strategy with a spirit of empathy and optimism.
3. Always check ethical guidelines prior to implementing any technique.
4. Use caution to ensure that clients are not embarrassed or physically harmed by the homework assignment.
5. If you are a student or are undergoing supervision for licensing or certification, check with your supervisor before you actually prescribe the homework assignment for the first time.
6. Consider role-playing the act of prescribing the homework assignment with a trained colleague or supervisor before you actually attempt it for the first time with a client.
7. Never attempt a technique for which you have no training.

8. Do not assume that even an effective homework assignment will work in every case.
9. Do not assume that a homework assignment that worked well with a client will work effectively with the same client at a later date.
10. Always take multicultural and diversity considerations into account.
11. Use only verbiage the client can understand and be as specific as possible.
12. Bend, fold, and mutilate existing strategies to increase your comfort level and to meet the needs of your clients.
13. Realize that certain homework assignments need to be used repeatedly to be effective.
14. Realize that therapeutic timing can make or break a technique.
15. Process the impact of the technique with the client when appropriate.